# We Who Work the West

# We Who Work the West

## Class, Labor, and Space in Western American Literature

*Kiara Kharpertian*

Edited by Carlo Rotella and
Christopher P. Wilson

University of Nebraska Press | *Lincoln*

Chapter 1 originally appeared as "Naturalism's Handiwork: Labor, Class, and Space in *McTeague: A Story of San Francisco*," *Studies in American Naturalism* 9, no. 2 (2014): 147–72.

Publication of this volume was assisted by the Virginia Faulkner Fund, established in memory of Virginia Faulkner, editor in chief of the University of Nebraska Press.

Library of Congress Control Number: 2019044425

Set in Lyon Text by Laura Buis.

# Contents

# Editors' Note

*Carlo Rotella and Christopher P. Wilson*

We first met Kiara Kharpertian when she enrolled in the doctoral program in English at Boston College in 2009. Having already completed her MA degree at New York University, Kiara embarked on an ambitious and active doctoral career at BC. Along with completing her coursework and exams with distinction, she presented papers at the conferences of the Western Literature Association and the Association for the Study of Literature and Environment, published her first scholarly article, was a graduate fellow two years running at BC's Clough Center for the Study of Constitutional Democracy, and received the university's graduate teaching award in 2013. She was diagnosed with breast cancer in 2010 and declared in remission in 2011, but in 2013 the cancer returned and metastasized throughout her body. Despite years of terrible struggle against her illness, she completed her dissertation and then a full draft of this book before her death in 2016.

When Kiara first started writing her dissertation, she'd send us wildly ambitious work schedules on the order of "Chapter 1 deadline: October 1st . . . Chapter 2 deadline: November 1st . . . Chapter 3: December 1st." After her cancer returned, the messages typically took the form of a cascade of dire news items followed by a schedule update, something like this: "Hey, so it turns out that the cancer has spread to several other vital organs, and I'm on a treatment program that involves a series of surgeries and highly toxic chemical interventions that will have the side effect of inducing a hallucinatory fugue state, which means that I don't think I can have this chapter done by October 1st. But I'm pretty sure I can get it to you by October 5th."

You can't be around that kind of heart, that kind of gameness, without being changed by it. The absurd levels of courage and purpose Kiara routinely displayed day after day, year after year, have raised the bar for everyone else. When a colleague complains about a deadline or when we're tempted to complain about our own workloads, we find it useful to remember that in the last few months of Kiara's life, after she lost so much motor function that she couldn't keep her head upright on her own, her husband and parents had to take turns holding up her head for her as she raced to finish revising her manuscript. And she won that race.

When her doctors told her—each of the several times they told her—that she didn't have much time left, we had thought Kiara might let research and teaching go by the wayside and do something else, perhaps something bucket list-y. Instead, she took all that heart, all that gameness, and poured it into finishing what she'd started—like this book, her final revision of which she delivered to us at almost the very last moment.

Having promised her that we'd see the book through to publication, we agreed between us on a basic ground rule for that work. We cut, tightened, and occasionally rephrased to sharpen her language, but we made a priority of preserving her voice, and we didn't attempt to substantively change or add to her arguments. It's Kiara's book; we and the press just gave it the polishing up that any manuscript gets on its way to publication.

Volunteers and willing draftees from the wide circle of Kiara's family, friends, and colleagues have stepped forward to give vital help and encouragement. They include her husband, Kai; her parents, Zoe and Ted; and her brother, Devin; Katie Daily, who helped prepare the final version of the dissertation; Deanna Malvesti Danforth, Nic Witschi, and Ashley Reis, who all assisted in placing the book with just the right publisher; Carolyn Ownbey, who proofed the manuscript and compiled the index; and Candace Hetzner, associate dean for academic affairs of the Graduate School at BC's Morrissey College of Arts and Sciences, whose long record of steadfast material and moral support for Kiara extended to her book. William Handley, editor of the University of Nebraska Press's Postwestern Horizons series, welcomed an unusual submission with open-minded graciousness. For the press, Alicia Christensen, Joeth Zucco, contract copyeditor Maureen Bemko, and two conscientious and thorough anonymous readers, among others, polished up the book to a high shine and guided it to publication with a sure collective hand.

A lot of people miss Kiara, a lot of fellow scholars and students were cheated out of the chance to work with her, and readers won't ever get to see the books she was planning to write after finishing this one. But at least she left us this book, as an enduring legacy of her impassioned mind, her heroic work ethic, and her determined courage.

The family of Kiara Kharpertian would like to express their deep gratitude to Drs. Carlo Rotella and Chris Wilson of Boston College, who shepherded Kiara though the creation of this work and took up the gauntlet following her death in order to bring her final wish for publication to fruition. She, and we, could not have asked for more dedicated and compassionate mentors. We are truly grateful for their long-standing support.

Our thanks go also to the University of Nebraska Press, Kiara's first choice, for its decision to publish the work and make it available to the community of western American scholars that she so cherished and to which she strove to contribute.

# Acknowledgments

For my parents, Ted and Zoe, who raised me unconventionally, with one eye always turned to what could be—you convinced me that going after my dreams didn't sound too crazy after all.

For my academic advisors—Carlo Rotella, Christopher Wilson, Min Song—though you each operate in different official capacities, your ongoing friendship and support of my work can never be repaid, and your continued high praise and encouragement kept me going in the most uncertain of moments. To Carlo and Chris specifically, as my academic lighthouses and inspirations, I am forever in your debt for the intellectual space you helped me carve for myself and for the realization that I could fill that space. Without your always generous guidance and insight, I would not be the scholar I am, and for that I will always be grateful.

For the even broader network of support I found at Boston College, including the tremendous academic and personal support of Vlad Perju, Suzanne Matson, Candace Hetzner, Paula Mathieu, Robert Stanton, Robin Lydenberg, Jim Smith, Joe Nugent, Linda Michel, and Tracy Downing, your praise, care, and friendship will always be held closely in my heart. For the institutional arms of that support that funded this project through its completion—the Dissertation Fellowship and the Dean of Summer Session Teaching Fellowship—I am truly grateful. To the institutional support of the Western Literature Association as well, for its giving support to graduate students and welcoming atmosphere, where I always felt at home. And for the Dana Farber Cancer Institute and its excellent community of health practitioners—for saving not just my body but the life that came along with it, for always treating me like a person, for never letting me give up.

For the many, many dear friends I have found at Boston College and beyond who aided this project along the way, as it limped and bounded through various stages, pitfalls, and twists—for Kate Gross and her uncanny prescience and intellectual depth, for Emma Atwood and her late-night sparks of brilliance, for Katie Daily and her resolute, always on-point insights, for Sarah Berry and her gentle and poignant wit, for Ashley Reis and her unfailing enthusiasm, for Josh Anderson and his quiet, profound ideas, for Alison Cotti-Lowell and her unwavering confidence in my work, for Andrew Kuhn and his steadfast encouragement and friendship, for Sean Case and his unwillingness to ever give up on me, for Gary Winslett and his ever-grounding presence—friends, I salute you.

For my brother, who reminded me never to take life too seriously, to write from the base of your heart, and to always have swag. Devin, you're still the better writer, but I'm learning.

Finally, for my husband, Kai, the joy and meaning of my life: your constant love, encouragement, determination, steadfastness, patience, and ever-listening ear brought me and this project to a place of sanctuary only you could. Thank you for always celebrating my successes, consoling my losses, and constantly inspiring me to come back and work the next day.

# Introduction

## How to Tell a Western Story

I'm going to tell you two stories.

My father is a union man. But he's not a typical union man; he's an academic union man—a role that, as I found out during my time as a graduate student, was rare, if it existed at all. In 1985, PhD and energetic new baby in hand (there exists a photograph of him holding me on the day of his graduation), my father returned to his near-native Jersey City (North Bergen was home) and, along with a handful of other recent doctoral graduates, laid the foundation for Hudson County Community College, a school that aimed to bring education to one of the most politically corrupt, economically downtrodden, and socially disenfranchised cities in the state. What this return signified was that, despite an Ivy League undergraduate degree and a pedigreed PhD, he still belonged to the two-family house at the end of Seventy-Eighth Street my brother and I had visited every Sunday as we grew up. On the second floor of that house, his parents—his mother a legal secretary, his father a welder, neither in possession of a high school diploma, but both deeply committed to his education—raised him. My father grew up watching the world from a unique, multidimensional perspective shaped by working-class northern Jersey, the city looming on the near horizon, through the quietly tumultuous 1950s and the loudly rebellious 1960s. He developed an insatiable respect for and pursuit of knowledge that guides him to this day.

In addition to designing curricula, departments, and administrative strategies, my father was union president for a significant chunk of my childhood. I grew up learning that unions were good, and necessary—that they offered those who wielded them properly the protection of their *work*. I learned that my father's greatest challenges were often not the students who alternated class with jail, or had three children by age eighteen, or spent sixty hours a week making minimum wage so they could bring the rest of their family to a new home only slightly less dangerous than their old. His greatest challenge was often higher administration—those my father and his colleagues had to fight for a living wage (his starting salary in 1985 was $13,000), for reasonable class sizes to best teach their students, and for working schedules that left time for family. The union made those fights not only possible but also winnable. The union was our friend.

So you can imagine my shock when, as a second-year master's student at New York University, I received looks of bewildered disgust from my fellow students and professors when I suggested that the union step in as the undergraduates and adjuncts battled the administration for fairer wages. It was the first time I realized that academia was divided by a line of thin, deadly razor wire, even if I couldn't (and still can't) quite identify who stands on what side. And it was the first time I recognized that razor wire as part of the insidious, dangerous, and complicated class warfare that haunts the ivory tower. And suddenly it struck me that growing up in a family balanced between the working and middle class had given me a fairly unique perspective on how important class identity is in everyday life. And so, albeit slowly, this work's focus began to emerge: how class is a function of labor in space and how these three elements can create unique individual identities that nonetheless find common ground in broader, shared communities.

The second story doesn't so easily predict or intersect with my academic interests. This second story in fact begins twice: once near midnight on March 26, 2013, when my attending doctor in the ER told me that my cancer had returned and metastasized to my lymph nodes, bones, lungs, and liver, and in early October 2010, when I was first diagnosed as stage three. Back in 2010 I cried in panic. But the second time, in 2013, I felt nothing. The fear, anxiety, panic, depression, grief, irritation, agitation, and everything else would come later, and repeatedly, as treatments failed, as my case got more complicated, as my health and mobility shook and faltered. To this day, the mountain of medications I take cannot fully shield me from those feelings. They come and go no matter what I do.

In the midst of all that chaos, my interests in class, labor, and space took root in a part of America that has fascinated me ever since I stood, at age fifteen, on a campground in Ozona, Texas, at night with my father and he gestured toward the expanse of stars and told me, "So this is what they call the big sky." The feeling I had of being encircled by that expanse comes back to me sometimes— shortly after my first diagnosis, for instance, when I took my minor exam on mobility in contemporary western American literature. Near the end of the exam, I find myself staring at my hands. When I was a baby, I would wake my parents at three, four in the morning to play with my fingers and toes. They tell me I would spend hours intertwining them, studying their movements and the patterns they could make on the walls. When I used to write poetry, hands and toes featured prominently: a sense of touch, an interaction with the world that stood on the gravity of its own existence, set-tled deep in my bones, and refused to move. I imagine how things *feel*—I diagram space with my body, a biogramming that senses pressures, tangible and intangible, that intermingle just below our skin. Even now the West is still tactile to me; through its literature I feel its weight and grain on my hands. I imagine that I'm texture— mapping the regions I read through the imaginative landscapes these authors create, sketching a coarse, interwoven tapestry that tracks the way individual lives grappled with the consequences of space. Literature can show us how seeming abstractions like labor patterns and class stratification become lived experiences that nestle in and create America through the West. A layered West, thick with the skin of history, unfolding through the pages of its literature. I step out of the room.

In four and a half minutes my examiners will pull me in to tell me good news—I've passed with distinction—but now the anticipation of that moment is displaced by my image in the glass of the double doors I stand beside. I run my hand over my head, slick in spots and rough in others. During my exam, I have forgotten I had no hair. I imagined bangs and a ponytail, or chin-length and asymmetrical, before I shaved it in response to an illness that suffocated me. Strands falling in front of my eyes. Words are enough to displace sickness. The West through its literature opens and encircles with its rapid and unexpected representations of strange lands, strange maps, strange lives lived on those lands, in those maps. The West is a gift.

At the heart of this project are three interrelated intuitions: first, that the West is the seat of much of America's cultural identity; second, that historical iterations of class, labor, and space in the West have shaped that identity; and third, that in our reading of western literature we can track and analyze those transformations and their meaning. What these three intuitions point to is the primary role history plays in our national literature. That is, interwoven depictions of bodies at labor, the political and economic contexts that class those bodies, and the classed spaces within which those bodies live—all those things tell intimate, individual stories that then claim to be metonymic for broader, national narratives. Class, labor, and space are particularly good touchstones for national identity because they are inescapable yet flexible; the degree to which one or the other exists in a text often reveals the larger social pressures to which a community is responding. Lack of labor means human suffering, but where did this lack originate, and how does that loss affect those who once did that work? Obsessions with capital gain can seem to dominate other parts of our identities, but how does labor contribute to or interact with the desire for capital, and vice versa? Labor, class, and space may seem abstract concepts, but together they constitute individuals' everyday lives. And literature often manages to reveal the cultural and social imbalances that may be lurking within a self, an order, a region, a nation.

As I have said, I argue that class is a function of labor in a particular time and space. In other words, western class identities and divisions grow out of certain forms of labor that arise on historically specific environmental, political, and socioeconomic landscapes. And literature, I maintain, is especially suited to showcasing these identities and the circumstances that created them because it can simultaneously converse with, mimic, and disengage from that history. This mutable relationship lends literature the creative flexibility to zoom in imaginatively on individual lives, families, and communities that suffered the consequences of historical changes to the spaces in which they lived and to the work they did. If the West has historically been a stage for what William Cronon et al. (1992, 23) call "flux [and] fixity," then western stories must be read against, rather than in support of, historical myths that homogenize western American social history and lived experience, often resulting in a reductive narrative nostalgia that typically accompanies one-dimensional stories of Manifest Destiny, industrial expansion, and regional development. This book instead focuses on those doing the work and suffering its personal costs. For example, what defenses did families and communities craft to bar the anxiety of getting food on the table during the Dust Bowl? What maneuvers did San Francisco's upper class make to protect themselves from outlandish fears of the city's encroaching working class in the Gilded Age?

Because I focus on these and other actions of individuals in western literary spaces, mapping plays a crucial role in this study. Along the way I've constructed rhetorical maps of the West that chart literary episodes and metaphors that have repeatedly emerged across its history. Again, by "biogramming" these coded spaces, I began to realize how conventional ideas of mapping now dovetailed with the concepts from physics passed on to me by my husband, Kai—notions of gearboxes and superlattices in particular informed my theoretical approach to literature. As best I can represent them, gearboxes and superlattices both represent ways scientists combine materials to observe their effect on each other. Gearboxes, that is, test directional forces to produce a specified outcome—for example, grinding a sheet of aluminum or shaping a machine cog—while superlattices are layers of elements that, when tilted, reveal different conditions or charges to their overall structure. My understandings of these concepts, however rudimentary, helped me identify the different yet reciprocal elements of my own literary study. For example, the different socioeconomic patterns and labor practices represented by a given text became like gears that the central (often tilting) mechanism of space shifted and reciprocally altered. Conversely, specific historical, national, political, and environmental landscapes became the layers of superlattices that, when seen with a different historical orientation, changed my perspective on a text's representation of labor. In all, these concepts helped me grapple with the myriad nuanced, often highly individualized dimensions of a given literary narrative. In other words, novels *themselves* became maps that guided me through my primary terms—class, labor, space, culture, nation, identity, and belonging.

Meanwhile, it is no coincidence that almost all the novels I have chosen for this study represent not those people who "won the West" but those who worked it—who struggled with its unique challenges of environment, legality, politics, and history. Those who faltered, fell, failed—those who, in the end, didn't do so well. I mean to ask, in this way, whether belonging does not always *belong* to the winners of history but to those who lose as well. Or to those who *were* lost. If so, it then becomes our responsibility as scholars to find them.

Naturally, some will interpret me as saying that this side of history is more "authentically" western. Western literature of course has long been fascinated with claims to authentic experience. Yet, like other recent scholars, I actually mean to revise what we mean by "authenticity" itself. As William R. Handley and Nathaniel Lewis (2004) remind us in *True West: Authenticity and the American West*, what "authentic" means—its connections to truth, authority, and originality—is often merely a tactic to grant special standing to some groups and not to others. Such an approach complicates not only spatial determinations of the West (Is this part of the West? What makes that region western?) but what constitutes western identity writ large. Here I follow the lead of Handley and Lewis, who note that the authentic is always just out of reach: "approaching but never meeting the limit it nears" (7). Authenticity thus often serves to invest or divest certain kinds of political, national, cultural, socioeconomic, or ethnic power—it is, as Handley and Lewis suggest, a construct that reinforces its own power yet in doing so also reveals its own limits. As I will try to show here, that does not mean its power fades over time. On the contrary, we need to examine the continuing puzzle of the "authentic West" and its appeal.

To start, I argue that claims of western authenticity often reside in claims of belonging. But belonging itself can be hard to claim, coming up as it does against arguments based in ethnic ties to land, national sovereignty, legal status, and histories of genocide and extermination. In recent decades western literary and historical theory has worked especially hard to rescue the stories of those who may have lost or may have been lost. Because of this work, a whole new West emerges—often a conquered West and yet also a pluralistic West that can encompass the atrocities and scars of its past, the cultures and ethnicities that created the spaces of its present, and the new technological directions of its futures. Paradoxically, those future enterprises often hold the most promise for remembering the full range of pasts actively, in ways that grant the endlessly broad array of communities and networks that compose the West a foothold in belonging. No such mosaic can ever be completed, but we can identify corners of the past thus far left undisturbed that might reveal surprising results. This is why I settled on studying the complex of class, labor, and space in American western literature—it seemed to me a corner of literary study that hadn't been looked into in detail for a long time. Especially in *this* West, a region ravaged by the deep scars of repeated and lasting displacements, deterritorializations, and dispossessions, I ask, how does one find or claim belonging? My fierce belief is that belonging can become a force available to all of us and that literature provides a laboratory in which to test its properties and potentialities.

The historiography behind this project demands some unpacking. By the mid-nineteenth century the North American West straddled a material and imaginative divide between, on the one hand, national and industrial expansion and, on the other, what was regarded as untamed and endless wilderness. In public policy, literature, and everyday practice, those inhabiting the West experienced and reflected what Cronon et al. (1992, 23) have aptly termed a frontier flexibly "shift[ing] from relative newness to relative oldness or from flux to fixity." Even when Frederick Jackson Turner (1998, 32) declared at the 1893 Chicago World's Fair that the frontier had closed much earlier, he also remarked that "the frontier is the outer edge of the wave—the meeting point between savagery and civilization." This tension, Cronon and Turner and others have argued, registers not only the national stakes that hinged on the "successful" development of the western frontier but also the impossibility of a clean transition to a vague and messy second stage. Although the West was hardly devoid of social and civic networks prior to the wave of Anglo exploration and settlement spearheaded by Lewis and Clark's 1804–6 expedition, the terms "open" and "closed" were (and still are) used, in alternation, to mark western expansion. What this book intends to prove in part is that the structures of class, labor, and space that developed during the West's modern history disrupt the notion of an open versus a closed frontier. Indeed, the West reflected in the literature I read here is always in the process of opening its multiple (or what Krista Comer [1999] has called "rhizomatic") layers to adapt to new historical conditions.

Recent trends in western American literary and historical studies, especially those in critical regionalism and the "new western history," have firmly shaped this project. I draw heavily on the pathbreaking work of Richard Slotkin (1998); his effort to read the West as a composite, reiterating space of American identity formed the first backdrop of this project. Patricia Nelson Limerick's (1987) *The Legacy of Conquest* also had a strong influence on my early thinking: across her work, Limerick casts the West as a historically fluid zone of cultural contact that refutes earlier notions of a static, empty space. Limerick argues that the West has always been an embattled ground where cultures, ethnicities, civilizations, traditions, and individuals met and fought to claim rights over land and sovereignty. Moreover, she insists that we must pay close attention to the stories of the conquered to weave a fuller narrative of western identity and history. Along with Limerick, the influence of other new western history scholars, such as Donald Worster, Richard White, and William Cronon, can be felt throughout this book, as can that of a significant cohort of historians who have turned more toward the future and the problem of how we can best rescue or remedy the broken bits—the focus in chapters 4 through 6. *Remedies for a New West*, edited by Limerick, Andrew Cowell, and Sharon K. Collinge (2009), best exemplifies this interest in the "new" West.

I have benefited from several case studies on class and labor at the forefront of this book's theoretical discussion. Mark Seltzer's (1992, 3) *Bodies and Machines* first introduced me to the idea that bodies are work "complexes" that challenge strict divisions between "modes of production and modes of reproduction" in biological and technological settings. Seltzer's literary study of the body-machine complex and "statistical persons" allowed me to question (especially in chapters 1 and 4) how literature represents these working bodies as classed objects with labor output and value. Similarly, Michael Denning's (1987) *Mechanic Accents*, Christopher Wilson's (1992) *White Collar Fictions*, and Eric Schocket's (2006) *Vanishing Moments* pressed me to move beyond the uniform category of "proletarianization" (as in chapter 3, on the Great Depression, and chapter 4, on cowboys) and consider directly the work that bodies produce. I have also been interested in how class identities influenced both social and geographic mobility in an ever-changing West. As Timothy Cresswell's (2006, 1) *On the Move* insists, we must study mobility because it is "everywhere.... It plays a central role in discussions of the body and society. It courses through contemporary theorizations of the city. Culture, we are told, no longer sits in places, but is hybrid." Moreover, mobility produces meaning in time and space that attaches to particular bodies and social contexts; its chaos is a binding force in our lives. A city highway, he notes, becomes a blood vessel to the city, yoking health and urban space through a shared lifeline of movement. That metaphor carries with it connotations of classed spaces and the individuals who inhabit them. Schocket (2006, x) likewise calls class "totalizing" but also "unstable," questioning both representations of class in American literature and the historically contingent contexts that created those representations. Carlo Rotella's (2002) *Good with Their Hands* and Janet Zandy's (2004) *Hands* made personal and specific the value of good hand work in particular. As Rotella (2002, 2) argues, being "good with your hands" is far more nuanced than it sounds; it carries with it degrees of "skill, character, way of life" that determine individual, familial, and communal well-being and pride.

A third scholarly scaffolding for my focus on working bodies and their classed movements is the critical literature on space. Three texts in particular helped me understand the stakes of that relationship. The close focus of Neil Smith's (1984) *Uneven Development* on the lived consequences of capital distribution across often-global geopolitical space helped me particularize the political and cultural implications of the western characters and spaces I examined. Alongside Smith's work, Hsuan L. Hsu's (2010) *Geography and the Production of Space in Nineteenth-Century American Literature* and Tom Lutz's (2004) *Cosmopolitan Vistas*, both exemplary of the new critical western regionalism, clarified why space seemed so pivotal to the other two issues (labor and class) on which I had decided to focus. Hsu in particular reveals how different spatial scales create different notions of national, regional, and subregional belonging. And finally, Neil Campbell's (2008) *The Rhizomatic West*, Krista Comer's (1999) *Landscapes of the New West*, and Comer's (2011) "Exceptionalism, Other Wests, Critical Regionalism" all argue convincingly that we should dispense with totalizing narratives of the West and open up discussions of more pluralistic rhizomes, or roots, that contributed to this region's literary history. Comer in particular—by both borrowing from and subverting the postmodern motifs in western regional literatures—displaces the notion of a western or regional center. Such a disruption dovetails with Neil Campbell's (2008, 21) insistence that the West is a place of multiple possibilities, "at once gridded, rooted, and territorialized . . . while simultaneously ungridded, routed, and deterritorializing, with a capacity for 'lines of flight' as well as mythic closure and stasis." Although these postmodern frameworks are central to my approach as a whole, they can be felt especially in my final chapter, on Philipp Meyer's *The Son*.

As my first case study, chapter 1 argues that Frank Norris's *McTeague* depicts class and socioeconomic identity as products of the kinds of labor that evolve in specific western ecological and social spaces in and around San Francisco at the turn of the twentieth century. Inasmuch as McTeague's work responds to a western environment that demanded particular forms of infrastructure, the novel's primary mechanism of the process of constructing space is labor. Thus, McTeague's work as a dentist and a miner determines both his class situation (as a producer and consumer) and his spatial mobility. Norris uses images of the human body, its physical work, and its socioeconomic mobility to populate—and thus create class in—the novel's San Francisco and Death Valley. Depictions of the (largely immigrant) body as grotesque and brutish coincide with discussions of labor and spatial movement, indicating a reciprocally deterministic relationship between what a body can do and where that body can go. Ultimately, Norris's metaphors of the human body and its (in)capabilities articulate the way class and labor mark the self and the novel's regions, especially in the context of the public discourses surrounding class and labor in the late nineteenth and early twentieth centuries.

Chapter 2 explores class dispossession, masked as ethnic dispossession, in María Amparo Ruiz de Burton's *The Squatter and the Don*. I argue that national affiliations that grant capital security held more sway in the late nineteenth-century ranching society of the Californios than did claims of cultural belonging. Overall, the novel's political contradictions, which puzzle many critics, reveal the fragility of what Ruiz de Burton calls "Spano-American" legal identity when it came in contact with the challenges posed by enterprising Anglo squatters who enacted exploitative land laws to unfairly claim land rights. The novel's re-creations of the lived ramifications and politics of California land policies passed at this time are dramatized in the personal losses felt by the novel's central ranching family—blows to its stability and working identity that ultimately usher in a broad loss of culture. I pair Ruiz de Burton's work with Raymond Barrio's *The Plum Plum Pickers*, which takes place in the same region about one hundred years later, to draw attention to the legacy of class politics and manual labor that continue to influence Chicano identity. Reading the two alongside each other allows me to craft an alternate approach to the Chicano ethos that productively works with, rather than shies away from, national belonging.

Chapter 3 focuses on literature that grew out of the twinned national crises of the 1930s: the Great Depression and the Dust Bowl. I focus in particular on literature that largely goes unnoticed, because such works add richness to the literary history of these events. Sanora Babb's *Whose Names Are Unknown*, John Fante's *Wait Until Spring, Bandini* and *Ask the Dust*, and Frank Waters's *Below Grass Roots* each take as their main theme the instability, vulnerability, frustration, and constriction that these watershed historical moments brought to individuals and families. All four novels focus on the highly damaging individual costs of broader national disasters, a focus that offers important contrast to the national story of struggle and perseverance that we generally associate with these crises. Although these novels eschew and even seek to undo the kind of working-class solidarity commonly found in the proletarian literature of the period, they give careful attention to the stabilizing force of community when families routinely encounter and indeed mimic the lasting divisions of environmental and economic upheaval.

In Chapter 4 I take seriously a familiar western icon—the cowboy—and put him under historical and narrative scrutiny. Reading historical accounts of cowboy work alongside Cormac McCarthy's *All the Pretty Horses*, Elmer Kelton's *The Time It Never Rained*, and Larry McMurtry's *Horseman, Pass By*, this chapter examines how depictions of daily cowboy life figure not only types of labor that defined cowboy identity but also class systems that dictated ranch life and an intimate attention to ecological patterns. Moreover, by zooming in on these narratives' simultaneously idealized and naturalistic presentation of details of cowboy life, I bypass the mythos of the

Wild West to take a more careful look at the labor of figures who are usually reduced to cardboard cutouts. All three novels take place in the years after World War II and during the long Texas drought of the 1950s, which reshaped the massive industrialization that had already begun to redefine cowboy labor.

In my fifth chapter I take a close look at a handful of American Indian novels that interrogate the role of labor, class, and space in reservation life in the American West. Linda Hogan's *Mean Spirit* is the central novel of this chapter, while D'Arcy McNickle's *The Surrounded*, Sarah Winnemucca Hopkins's *Life among the Piutes*, Sherman Alexie's *The Lone Ranger and Tonto Fistfight in Heaven*, and Stephen Graham Jones's *The Bird Is Gone* provide supplementary texts. I use these novels to interrogate Gerald Vizenor's "survivance" and Chadwick Allen's "blood/land/memory complex" as conceptual approaches to the relationship between traditional culture and modernization in American Indian life. Trying to work out how to honor remembrance of the horrors of the past without barring productive engagement with and participation in the future, these novels search for a modus vivendi in which tradition and modernization can exist alongside each other in a thriving American Indian culture. This chapter also ruminates on the way stories of failure in the American West—all of which these novels include—help cobble together a more pluralistic West that enriches our common American history.

Finally, I end with an examination of Philipp Meyer's family saga *The Son*, a "generational postwestern" novel that uses the McCullough family's history to narrate the uneven growth of capital, space, and labor in Texas from 1849 to 2012. My primary objective is to understand how the novel models the process in which socioeconomic development in Texas changes what "belonging" means for these individuals and their families. As such, themes like genealogy, family legacy, civic identity and legitimacy, inheritance, and nation-building feature prominently in this chapter. I also use this final chapter to ask bigger questions about who belongs in Texas, and the West more broadly, and which strategies have been used to establish or deny that belonging. What I term the "kaleidoscopic" qualities of *The Son* offer a rich diversity of perspective on Texas during some of its most significant moments of development and expansion.

# We Who Work the West

# 1   Naturalism's Handiwork

Labor, Class, and Space in Frank Norris's
*McTeague: A Story of San Francisco*

When Frank Norris published his third novel in 1899, he didn't call
it *McTeague: A Story of a Dentist*, or *McTeague: A Story of a Brute*—two
titles that would have described the novel perfectly. He instead titled
it *McTeague: A Story of San Francisco*. What does it mean to identify
a novel, largely about a man of Irish heritage and his descent into
destitution, by the western American city in which the story takes
place? If, as the title suggests, McTeague is a gateway to a broader
portrait of San Francisco, then what story is Norris telling about it?
An early insight comes in the first pages of the novel, when Norris
draws on spatial politics to sketch the class structure of the city. He
starts by telling us that Polk Street, the site of his main character's
"Dental Parlor," is "one of those cross streets peculiar to Western
cities, situated in the heart of the residence quarter, but occupied
by small tradespeople who lived in the rooms above their shops"
(Norris 1997a, 7). And then Norris focuses on a larger grid.[1] He
writes, "Polk Street rubbed elbows with the 'avenue' one block
above. There were certain limits which its dwellers could not over-
step; but unfortunately for them, these limits were poorly defined.
They could never be sure of themselves. At an unguarded moment
they might be taken for 'toughs,' so they generally erred in the other
direction, and were absurdly formal. No people have a keener eye for
the amenities than those whose social position is not assured" (55).
This moment calls attention to Norris's construction of *McTeague*'s

social spaces. Neil Campbell (2008, 9) best articulates what many literary critics have argued about similar western scenes: "One cannot think of the West as rural or urban space without visualizing the powerful checkerboard symmetries of the mesh-like grid as it arrests and orders space."[2] Here Campbell refers to the repeated pattern of intersecting perpendicular streets—a horizontal grid—so common in western cities, including San Francisco and in particular *McTeague*'s neighborhood.[3]

The novel's grid is not just spatial, however; Polk Street's "poorly defined" limits are also social boundaries that reflect flows of capital, patterns of inhabitance, and forms of class mobility, all contributing to a vertical socioeconomic grid interlaced with the horizontal spatial one. Specifically, in Norris's tableau, how characters interact, work, and move registers their social class in geographic terms; not only does Polk Street abut a nearby upper-class avenue, but its dwellers recognize this class difference and consequently act "absurdly formal." Norris's geographic and social casting thus serves to frame—materially and imaginatively—how the movements and labors of bodies mark both social identities and the grid they come to occupy. Mapping the novel's working bodies thus unveils a reciprocal relationship between what a body can do and where that body can go, the social lines people can and cannot cross. In other words, because social class in *McTeague* is not just about acquiring money or nice things but about achieving a combination of a work identity, inhabitance, and social habits, class mobility often proves to be a temporary illusion. In *McTeague* superficial class crossing amounts to a momentary transgression that is ultimately punished by spatial and social exile. Class therefore becomes for Norris an inflexible function of embodied, historically contingent labor in a specific space—Gilded Age San Francisco.

Classically of course it is *McTeague*'s portraits of *three* spaces— San Francisco, California's mining regions, and Death Valley—that have been read in a more abstract, naturalist vein, as straightforward representations of a cruel, untamed, brutal nature writ large.[4] Alternatively, in this chapter I mean to read all three locations as socially constructed landscapes defined in part by the human body, its physical work, and its socioeconomic (im)mobility. Even in the brutal regions to which McTeague reverts, nature is not separate from the social landscape but interwoven into it. Nor is the ecological specificity of Death Valley, the site of the book's finale, merely an occasion for naturalist melodrama. On the contrary, because *McTeague*'s historical lens depicts labor as culturally *and* environmentally influenced, all these spaces help construct, paradoxically, the *horizontal* platform for the novel's profile of nineteenth-century *vertical* class stratification. Specifically, Norris's representations of classed spaces and labor done by hand mutually inform each other; work creates class, and space becomes the ever-changing stage on which both are performed. Ultimately, as if reflecting the salt beds of its famous finale, *McTeague*'s representations of physical labor and spatial class calcify each other, as different characters' dreams of class mobility prove false. Although McTeague himself can play at middle-class domesticity for a while, his origin as a working-class miner is to Norris actually inescapable. The patterns of exile and murder that crowd the second half of the novel are the consequences of indulging such illusions; when lower-class characters aspire to upper-class wealth, they lose personal, socioeconomic, and spatial security, and violence ensues.

My goal in landing on those final, grim sequences is therefore not simply to reframe or recuperate some of naturalism's trademark effects. However, seeing *McTeague* through labor and class and space does take us into what Mary Papke (2003, xi) identifies as the naturalist idiom's signature "journey into the liminal, the transgressive, the pornographically violent, and the morally bankrupt." Yoked to Norris's (1997c, 274) thesis that in naturalism "[e]verything is extraordinary, imaginative, grotesque even, with a vague note of terror quivering throughout it," my critical framework likewise points to the novel's treatment of the fear of social decay (and collapse) that lurked behind the social, economic, and spatial conditions of the Gilded Age, or what Norris called the "great, terrible drama" that occurred "among the lower—almost the lowest—classes, those who have been thrust or wrenched from the ranks, who are falling by the roadway" (274).[5] In *McTeague*, Norris stages the dangers posed by those who are stripped of labor and class identity and are thereby reduced to economic depravity and fatal violence.

A Story of a Skilled Hand

As bodies in *McTeague* do various kinds of work, they are granted certain kinds of social mobility while being denied others. For instance, McTeague's apprenticeship with the "charlatan" dentist from the mining camp, coupled with his inheritance from his mother, provides the essentials necessary to "set him up in business . . . cut loose from the charlatan and . . . [open] his 'Dental Parlors' on Polk Street" (Norris 1997a, 6). At first, McTeague's move out of the mining camp and into the city seems a one-dimensional class mobility, evident in his achieved social identity: "Polk Street called him the 'Doctor' *and* spoke of his enormous strength" (6; emphasis added). Here the novel's apparent collapse of nature and culture, a signature naturalist mode, determines how bodies are situated on the social map. McTeague possesses moderate social and financial strength, but he is mostly identified by a physical strength that enables him to "often . . . [dispense] with forceps and [extract] a refractory tooth with his thumb and finger" (6). Being a dentist might mean that McTeague has knowledge of dentistry, but his occupation also means that he has the brute force necessary for rudimentary, physical dental work.

And yet, although that strength enables his work, it is also paired with an inability to understand the broader political and social debates surrounding labor so evident in San Francisco at the time.[6] For instance, when Marcus Schouler raises "the labor question" and gives voice to a host of labor-related contemporary buzzwords, McTeague can neither parse through nor contextualize the conversation: "These rolled off [Marcus's] tongue with incredible emphasis, appearing at every turn of his conversation—'Outraged constituencies,' 'cause of labor,' 'wage earners,' 'opinions biased by personal interests,' 'eyes blinded by party prejudice.' McTeague listened to him, awe-struck" (12).[7] Here and elsewhere it is as if Norris uses McTeague's (and Marcus's) ignorance of the "labor question" to forestall a more nuanced treatment of late nineteenth-century labor politics and to focus instead on the individual working body—that is, on the process of using a body's physical labor as a vehicle for class mobility.

For McTeague and his wife-to-be, Trina, hands are the primary means to that end. Just as McTeague relies on his hands and their handiwork to be a successful dentist, Trina's hands are her physical tools when she carves wooden animals. In *McTeague*, what hands can produce determines a person's social and economic worth; the affection between Norris's two main characters thus literalizes what Mark Seltzer (1992, 13) calls the "radical and intimate *coupling of bodies and machines*" in literary naturalism. In turn, physical labor becomes yoked to a dynamic, socioeconomic traction in the novel. Conversely, when both Trina and McTeague come to lose their ability to do their dexterous handiwork, they are forced to undertake less skilled, grotesquely coded labor that traps them socioeconomically and spatially. Norris writes that Trina "became a scrub-woman"—cleaning up after the mess of others, specifically the children of the bourgeoisie—when she discovers that "[o]ne can hold a scrubbing brush with two good fingers and the stumps of two others even if both joints of the thumb are gone." She subsequently moves into the kindergarten she cleans, "lost in the lowest eddies of the great city's tide" (Norris 1997a, 193). McTeague, for his part, becomes a piano handler and store watchman, regularly fighting with his coworkers and living behind the music store in "a box of a place that reeked with odors of stale tobacco smoke" (201). Both these fates thereby collapse the space of labor and the space of living, each reciprocally marred by the undercurrents of filth and social depravity of the other. Infamously, for example, McTeague cannot curb his physical impulses, for instance, when he had "kissed [Trina], grossly, full on the mouth" (22) after rendering her unconscious to work on her dead tooth.

It's thus easy to see why, in many ways, McTeague became American naturalism's iconic dumb brute.[8] Nevertheless, we should not turn our eyes away from the work Norris's characters do to make those fates. For instance, in the moment immediately following the grotesque scene above, McTeague "threw himself once more into his work with desperate energy. By the time he was fastening the sheet of rubber upon the tooth, he had himself once more in hand" (22). Here, McTeague's labor as a dentist diverts his degenerate sexual impulses. His shift in focus both engages his mind in a new task and recruits his body to do his work rather than to indulge his desire. And consequently his work displaces his body's grotesque "labor" of assault. By challenging the all-encompassing, uncontrollable force that brings the brute to the surface, such a move invites a more nuanced reading of the novel's laboring bodies and the identities they form.

And then there's that tricky phrase "he had himself once more in hand." Inasmuch as McTeague uses his work to get himself "in hand," Norris actually redefines the nature of this labor. His dentistry, especially when compared to his earlier brutish burst of energy, is now cast as a kind of refined labor that demands physical delicacy—a quality the novel comes to associate with focus, precision, and control rather than savagery and force.[9] In these ways McTeague's work helps him focus—get himself "in hand"—on something other than his desire, thus undermining his brutishness. This reminds us that Norris's attention to

McTeague's dental work had even earlier emphasized hand-iwork as a highly agile form of focused, even delicate labor:

> He told himself that he should have to use the "mats" in the filling. He made some dozen of these "mats" from his tape of non-cohesive gold, cutting it transversely into small pieces that could be inserted edgewise between the teeth and consolidated by packing. . . . He worked slowly, mechanically, turning the foil between his fingers with the manual dexterity that one some-times sees in stupid persons. His head was quite empty of all thought, and he did not whistle over his work as another man might have done. (14)

Crucial to this passage is the way McTeague works "slowly [and] mechanically" with "manual dexterity." In Mark Seltzer's (1992, 4) terms, McTeague might be said to exemplify the "double dis-course of the natural and the technological that, in short, makes up the American body-machine complex." That is, Norris evokes the precision of machinery in describing McTeague's hands, inscribing them as the mechanism of his being. Specifically, his fingers com-mand his body's energy and as such identify him as a dentist rather than a brute. His mechanical precision also nurtures a productive career that McTeague's animalistic traits do not. If, as Seltzer sug-gests, "the hand" can serve as a synecdoche for production, then Norris's focus on McTeague's hands as functional tools further removes him from the status of a one-dimensional monster. As Carlo Rotella (2002, 2) puts it, the work one does with one's hands carries surprising force: "Being good with your hands is a deceptively unsimple virtue. It involves technical skill and finesse, craft mated with strength—in handling tools or machinery or raw materials or bodies in motion, in making or fixing or disassembling things, in labor or art or self-defense—but it implies much more." McTeague is, to borrow Rotella's words, "good with his hands": he is a produc-tive worker who makes his own tools; he has a regular "clientele of butcher boys, shop girls, drug clerks, and car conductors"; and his business is "fairly good" (Norris 1997a, 6, 77). His dexterous hands thus produce his successful career.

At the same time, however, Norris describes the mechanics of McTeague's work as devoid of affect. He works as "stupid persons" do and does not even whistle, "as another man might have" (14). Here, Norris suggests that McTeague's labor is virtually robotic and thus replaceable. Like the working-class hands at the center of Janet Zandy's (2004) *Hands: Physical Labor, Class, and Cultural Work*, McTeague's come to stand for the human who wields them. How a body works determines how that body is classified, yet the work of McTeague's hands is so "learned" as to have become instinctual. Labor in the novel is thus a double-edged sword: it requires skill, but it also reduces the identity of those who labor to that of the work itself. Again, we are reminded of McTeague's momentary sexual impasse with Trina and how his manual labor recalls his biological instinct. Handiwork requires a talent that is not a by-product of evolution or a sign of ultimate security; to be "good with his hands" is not, in Norris's world, to be good enough. Pitting the dexterity of labor and excessive, blunt force against each other, Norris thus uses McTeague's slippage between these two abilities to showcase the instability of class identity's reliance on the body.

This is especially so when that identity is lost. When Trina reads the letter that forces McTeague's retirement from dentistry because he lacks the requisite credentials, McTeague cannot even comprehend Trina's basic questions about his educational background, responding to her repeated query, "'[D]*idn't* you ever go to a dental college[?]'" with a repeated "'Huh? What? What?'" (Norris 1997a, 145, 149). Neither a formal education nor professional documentation had been available to him in a lower-class mining town and on the road as a dental apprentice. Norris had even foreshadowed this problem early on, when describing McTeague's beginnings in dentistry: "He had learnt it after a fashion, mostly by watching the charlatan operate. He had read many of the necessary books, but he was too hopelessly stupid to get much benefit from them" (6). When forced to stop his labor by threat of imprisonment, McTeague becomes little more than a propped-up body. He "tidied [his Dental Parlors] with the greatest care," Norris tells us, and "sat in his operating chair, looking stupidly out of the windows, across the roofs opposite, with an unseeing gaze, his red hands lying idly in his lap" (150). Without labor, McTeague loses his purpose; without a purpose, he has no way to turn his skills into a career—as Trina one day snaps when she grows tired of his prolonged unemployment: "Do you know what I'm doing, McTeague? I'm supporting you" (152). Without a career, the McTeagues must move to poorer quarters. The McTeagues rent their new home, "a tiny room at the back of the flat and on its very top floor." Trina explains, "We've looked Polk Street over and this is the only thing we can afford" (151).

Norris fleshes out this manual and financial failure with McTeague's first postdental job. At first he hopes to capitalize on both his ability to work with his hands and his familiarity with dental tools: "he had by the greatest good luck secured a position with a manufacturer of surgical instruments, where his manual dexterity in the making of excavators, pluggers, and other dental contrivances stood him in fairly good stead" (159). Here McTeague's "manual dexterity" becomes a marketable skill: his capacity for basic implement engineering is more important than his now-irrelevant knowledge of dentistry. As his labor becomes less precise, his body loses precision as well; while at his new job, he also "slipped back into the old habits . . . spent the afternoon lying full length upon the bed, crop-full, stupid, warm, smoking his huge pipe, drinking his steam beer, and playing his six mournful tunes upon his concertina, dozing off to sleep towards four o'clock" (159). The self-sufficiency of his earlier work also has changed. He no longer uses the objects he builds but produces them for the use of others, further widening the novel's gap between those who produce and those who consume.

When McTeague is first married to Trina, their class aspirations superficially rise to match their lifestyle. Prior to this, McTeague's own class aspirations are like his labor: uninformed and limited. He doesn't long to be a part of the bourgeoisie and "[b]ut for one thing [was] perfectly contented" to be a member of the working class: "It was his ambition, his dream, to have projecting from that corner window a huge gilded tooth, a molar with enormous prongs, something gorgeous and attractive" (7). Here the tooth does not represent a higher class status but rather a prize of his labor to exhibit. Instead of using money to achieve class mobility, as Trina does when she wins the $5,000 and begins buying fashionable décor for the house, McTeague only wants money for the tooth: "Trina and the five thousand dollars could not make him forget this one unsatisfied longing" (77). Even his jealousy of the affluent Other Dentist— "that poser, that rider of bicycles, that courser of greyhounds"—is satiated when Trina does purchase the tooth: "No doubt [the Other Dentist] would suffer veritable convulsions of envy; would be positively sick with jealousy" (86). Here McTeague doesn't want class status to one-up the Other Dentist; he merely wants a shiny toy to make him envious. Moreover, the prospect of saving and investing their fortune strikes McTeague as odd: "The old-time miner's idea of wealth easily gained and quickly spent persisted in his mind. But when Trina began to talk of investments and interests and percents, he was troubled and not a little disappointed. The lump sum of five thousand dollars was one thing, a miserable little twenty or twenty-five a month was quite another; and then someone else had the money" (77). Linking his "ambition" to spend the money "in some lavish fashion" (77) to the "old-time miner's idea of wealth" does not indicate middle-class aspiration. Instead, McTeague longs to act as lower-class miners did on payday—consume quickly and save nothing.

Of course Trina by way of contrast misuses her money: she uses "their tidy little income" to flirt with middle-class spending hab-

its and ostensibly to position the McTeagues in that class (77).[10]
She buys "[j]ust things and things . . . some dotted veiling . . . and a
box of writing paper, and a roll of crépe [*sic*] paper to make a lamp
shade for the front parlor; and . . . a pair of Nottingham lace curtains"; later the McTeagues adorn their house with another array of
domestic niceties that mark their "charming" class status (90–91).
Enchanted by the excitement of materialism, Trina participates in
what Thorstein Veblen, in his 1899 work *The Theory of the Leisure
Class*, calls "conspicuous consumption": a purchasing of material
goods to display social rank. Accumulating capital gives their life
meaning; Trina only purchases things, literally objectifying her
class aspirations.

However, because this consumption is merely a material gesture
toward membership in the middle class, the McTeagues quickly
return to the lower class when McTeague's labor vanishes and takes
their income along with it. Now moored in the realm of production
without his own consumption, McTeague experiences a decline in
both personal and professional value. As McTeague's work becomes
more reproducible, the breakdown of his domestic life mirrors the
loss of stable class identity. In this context these declines both cause
and reflect McTeague's distance from his self-worth, from Trina,
and from his prior identity as a dentist. These losses reduce him to
what Marx (1990, 24) in 1867 called "the condition of a machine,"
which creates a devastating dependence on labor for both capital
and identity.[11] And indeed, as the McTeagues "sink rapidly lower
and lower," they rely more and more on the meager sums of money
their increasingly dehumanized, hand-oriented labors can bring
them, a reliance that drives both to decay (Norris 1997a, 184).

It is unsurprising, then, that as the narrative progresses Norris
disparages McTeague's labor as increasingly simple-minded. When
McTeague abandons his dental practice and returns to mining, he
finds it easy to meet the qualifications. Now he only has to answer a
couple of simple questions to get a job—"'Know how to hendle pick'n

shov'le?'" and "'How long sence you mine?'"—and "'[s]how [his] hends'" (211). Once again McTeague's hands become his primary source of employment. But now this labor is lower-class, manual labor: dirty, physically challenging, dangerous, and undesirable. In a bit of sardonic humor Norris has him reflect, "Once it even occurred to him that there was a resemblance between his present work and the profession he had been forced to abandon. In the Burly drill he saw a queer counterpart of his old-time dental engine; and what were drills and chucks but enormous hoe excavators, hard bits, and burrs? It was the same work he had so often performed in his 'Parlors,' only magnified, made monstrous, distorted, and grotesqued, the caricature of dentistry" (213).

If mining is here compared to dentistry—an immense yet incomplete imitation of dentistry—then this grotesque caricature only calls attention to the loss of identity that he has suffered in losing his profession.[12] Now chained to mining's hand-oriented labor, McTeague's dental skill in this ironic reversal only looks to be little more than a chance outgrowth of his working-class background. Early in the novel McTeague had recalled the toll that mining had taken on his family: McTeague himself worked "trundling the heavy cars of ore in and out of the tunnel. . . . For thirteen days of each fortnight his father was a steady, hard-working shift-boss of the mine. Every other Sunday he became an irresponsible animal, a beast, a brute, crazy with alcohol . . . his mother, too, who, with the help of the Chinaman, cooked for forty miners. She was an overworked drudge" (5). McTeague's return to mining suggests that his dentistry only borrowed—unsuccessfully—from the social rank of those he serviced. He can fix the teeth of the middle class but never again can he cross into the bourgeoisie.

Trina's handiwork also tethers her to Norris's theme of class immobility. She whittles by hand Noah's ark figurines for the children of the upper class while using a rhetoric that resonates with the language of McTeague's dental work. Like McTeague's dentistry, Trina's whittling not only spotlights her hands as a source of productive labor but also amplifies the small scope of her work. When Trina "turned the little figures in her fingers with a wonderful lightness and deftness," Norris treats the precision of her work as an accomplishment itself, lending her whittling an air of successful professionalization (160). But when that whittling becomes impossible because McTeague's biting of her fingers results in blood poisoning from her "non-poisonous paint," Trina is told by the doctor that she must "'have those fingers amputated, beyond a doubt, or lose the entire hand'"—a fate that makes her cry, "'And my work!'" (193). And lose her work she does, while simultaneously losing her identity and, effectively, her hands. Her next job as "a scrub woman" for a kindergarten thus resembles McTeague's slip from dentist to piano mover. Now Trina can only clean up the excess waste of the consuming class with what remains of her hands—"two good fingers and the stumps of two others"—and move to a street "[l]ike Polk Street . . . but running through a much poorer and more sordid quarter" (193). Like McTeague living in a room behind the piano shop, Trina's "home" complements her disfigured right hand and new work, although it is much worse—financially, physically, and spatially—than it used to be. Her final transformation thus reinforces the novel's common denigration of manual labor and its resulting class fixity.[13] The grotesque details of his loss of a working identity and subsequent descent into poverty thus communicate a deep fear of the Gilded Age. It is, as Norris (1997b, 279) puts it in his "A Plea for Romantic Fiction," a fear of "the rags and wretchedness, the drift and despair."

In these lights, it is especially ironic—and yet deeply appropriate—that McTeague cannot comprehend Marcus's ill-formed postulations about the "cause of labor": McTeague's direct experience of the denigration of labor makes all talk about it seem, as Norris writes, "clamor" and "noise." Indeed, this irony supports Martin Burke's

(1995, 135) argument that a "conceptual confusion" about labor and class in this era alienated workers from both one another *and* their labor, much as Marcus's words alienate McTeague. McTeague in effect suffers a double ignorance: an unawareness of broader politics germane to the labor movement and an unawareness of his own labor's connection to these politics. (When he loses his dental license, McTeague can only ask Trina, repeatedly, "'Ain't I a dentist?'" [Norris 1997a, 146–47]). Without insight into the politics of class and labor, McTeague suffers the consequences of disconnected work—the loss of capital, social order, and financial security mapped onto his working body.

A Story of the Class Grid

As mentioned earlier, Polk Street, the site of McTeague's Dental Parlors, is depicted as "one of those cross streets peculiar to Western cities . . . occupied by small tradespeople who lived in the rooms above their shops" (7).[14] This "cross street" imagery evokes the city's grid, and Norris yokes that grid imagery to those who occupy it. Class defines that inhabitance: Polk Street is "in the heart of the residence quarter, but [is itself] occupied by small tradespeople" (7). The juxtaposition Norris implies here is clear: some people live elsewhere, but others—those "small tradespeople"—live and work in the same space. Norris's description of McTeague's Dental Parlors as his home is thus relegated to one line: "McTeague made it do for a bedroom as well, sleeping on the big bed-lounge against the wall" (6). This description conveys less luxury and more close-quartered bare necessity, especially when compared to his extensive array of dental instruments—"a washstand . . . where he manufactured his moulds . . . his operating chair, his dental engine, and the movable rack on which he laid out his instruments." Moreover, "[t]he whole place exhaled a mingled odor of bedding, creosote, and ether"—a grotesque scent that hardly suggests a comfortable home (7). These descriptions identify the space more as a dental office than as a home and so marginalize McTeague's comfort to make room for his work.

McTeague's one-room Dental Parlors and living quarters thus recall what Herbert Gutman (1976, 35) identifies as the lived continuity of nineteenth-century working-class laboring folk who "surrounded their way of work with a way of life" that made work more accessible. However, that continuity collapsed labor and leisure and often made it nearly impossible for those workers to structure identities outside their work (45). A collapsed space, such as McTeague's, that so closely chains a sense of self to labor was—and still is—often a marker of the working class; McTeague's living situation is not a choice but a result of financial limitation, as "[his mother] had left him some money—not much, but enough to set him up in business" (Norris 1997a, 6). Even though McTeague "felt that his life was a success, that he could hope for nothing better" (6), his simple contentment reflects his dependency on the classed space of his labor.

But while the Dental Parlors space doubles as a working-class home, Polk Street itself exemplifies a more layered class neighborhood that expresses the tension between work and leisure. Those who frequent Polk Street actually span a variety of classes. These distinct classes even have distinct times when they appear on the street, starting early, when those at the bottom of the scale appear at seven in the morning (7–8). Polk Street thus enacts a kind of class parade that suggests that the wealthier you are, the later and more leisurely your commute can be. First on Polk Street are the newsboys (who appear out of necessity—to deliver the newspaper) and the day laborers, who are depicted as "trudging past in a straggling file" and marked by filth: "overalls soiled with yellow clay . . . spotted with lime from head to foot" (7, 8). Next are the "clerks and shop girls," the "cheap smartness" of their attire indicating that they occupy a more refined working class than the day laborers yet are still not well off. When the newsboys and day laborers pass through, they do so on foot, "tramping steadily in one direction"; the shop girls similarly are "always in a hurry." Both these lower classes must transport themselves to work with a haste that is dictated by their unvarying work schedules. In contrast, their more upper-class employers have the means to ride trains, using their downtime to "[read] the morning papers with great gravity." This group has "huge stomachs" and "flowers in their buttonholes," connoting a group of well-fed and well-dressed individuals with decorative accessories. Last, the upper-class ladies "from the great avenue" are "handsome women, beautifully dressed" who stroll with leisure and often stop, as "[m]eetings took place here and there; a conversation was begun; others arrived; groups were formed" (8).[15] Polk Street thus becomes not the residence of class difference but a place where class, coded by attire and time, is performed.

In the passage quoted above, each class's mannerisms are set to a specific tempo that follows the rhythms of work and leisure, responsibility and enjoyment. A speed that manifests physicality identifies the lower classes, while a leisure that leaves time for talking and reading characterizes the upper. The latter activities occupy the mind more than the body, especially when compared to the lower classes' accelerated pace. Different kinds of movement thus indicate the boundaries of class membership; the socioeconomic parade reduces humans to their labor and so uses people as representations of class in space. As an urban center, Polk Street thus exhibits the multiple yet static qualities of class that reciprocally construct the novel's gridded spaces.

Furthermore, although *McTeague*'s San Francisco is a reflection of urban spatial and class patterns, this West is also uneven and still developing. As Neil Smith remarks (1984, 87), "capitalist development was a continual transformation of natural space—inherited absolute space—into a produced relative space." This collapse of culture and nature proceeded fitfully, even spasmodically; Norris's San Francisco both impinges upon and is impinged on by *McTeague*'s open, natural spaces. When Trina and McTeague visit the B Street station by the bay, this reciprocal push and pull of nature and culture is evident:

> B Street station was nothing more than a little shed. There was no ticket office, nothing but a couple of whittled and carven benches. It was built close to the railroad tracks, just across which was the dirty, muddy shore of San Francisco Bay. About a quarter mile back from the station was the edge of the town of Oakland. Between the station and the first houses of the town lay immense salt flats, here and there broken by winding streams of black water. They were covered with a growth of wiry grass, strangely discolored in places by enormous stains of orange-yellow. (Norris 1997a, 48)

B Street station typifies the West's uneven transformation from flux to fixity: Norris depicts a space that is in the process of becoming "defined" relative to the city, by way of the train system.

The pattern continues when McTeague abandons the city and heads to the mining regions. Just as McTeague had "slipped back into the old habits . . . with an ease that was surprising" when he lost his dental practice (159), once he leaves San Francisco his regression into the lower-class world of mining is seamless: "Straight as a homing pigeon, and following a blind and unreasoned instinct, McTeague had returned to the Big Dipper mine. Within a week's time it seemed to him he had never been away. He picked up his life again exactly where he had left it the day when his mother had sent him away with the travelling dentist, the charlatan who had set up his tent by the bunk house" (212). The passage then describes McTeague's monotonous, daily mining work and how this work and the life that accompanies it "pleased the dentist beyond words" (213). Here and elsewhere in the novel, the living patterns and labor habits associated with the lower class are familiar and pleasing to McTeague. His comfortable ease here also contrasts with earlier moments when McTeague had to learn new class habits over time. Trina, through teaching McTeague to "dress a little better" and "[relinquish] his Sunday afternoon's nap and beer," finds that "she could make McTeague rise to [her level]": "Gradually," Norris reflects, "the dentist improved under the influence of his little wife" (107, 108). However, those improvements are temporary. McTeague's effortless reversion indicates that his lower-class identity is embedded in his sense of self, unlike the middle-class posturing he once learned. Not only do his lower-class roots show in his living and working habits, but his last fight with Marcus reveals the persistent greed for money (in this case, for the stolen $5,000) associated with the lower class in the novel.

Of course urban space in *McTeague* is still counterpointed by a seemingly wild, primordial nature. As Norris writes of the mining district, "[t]he entire region was untamed . . . a vast, unconquered brute of the Pliocene epoch, savage, sullen, and magnificently indifferent to man" (208).[16] However, rather than offering an escape from the rigid, gridded class map of San Francisco, this "natural" region actually turns out to reflect the city's socioeconomic demand. As we approach the end of *McTeague*, the "untamed" West is neither the empty space of possibility nor the brute's origin; it is a space of natural danger that evokes the social problems of the city. Norris almost immediately modifies the wild spaces he has just described: "But there were men in these mountains, like lice on mammoths' hides, fighting them stubbornly, now with hydraulic 'monitors,' now with drill and dynamite, boring into the vitals of them, or tearing away great yellow gravelly scars in the flanks of them, sucking their blood, extracting gold" (208–9). Similarly, when McTeague arrives at the headquarters of the district mines, he arrives at a place that was once "the summit of a mountain, but [now has] long since been 'hydraulicked' away." Although the rough country *surrounding* Death Valley may seem, at first, "unconquered," below the surface and in isolated areas men are tearing away at nature's foundations with machines or are building makeshift towns. McTeague is even able to string familiar outposts together to construct a mental map and find his way through the desert: "He knew exactly where to look for these trails" and "[h]e recognized familiar points at once," such as houses, unlicensed liquor "stores," and mine headquarters (210).

These landmarks are similar to the city's structures, as they give McTeague a sense of place and recall his survey of familiar sites on Polk Street: "There were corner drug stores with huge jars of red, yellow, and green liquids in their windows . . . stationers' stores . . . barber shops" (7). Moreover, these "lice on mammoths' hides" are not fighting the desert with Pliocene-era tools. They use "hydraulic 'monitors,'" "drill and dynamite," and "the stamp mill," and they construct mining towns with administrative buildings and head-gears (209). The structures that populate the Death Valley mining regions impose both early mapping and urban systems onto the landscape. In other words, the environment makes mining work possible and profitable, while also influencing the construction of the places those who live and work in the region build.

Moreover, because the products of mining fund commerce in the city, those who take part in that enterprise replicate urban class stratification in the desert. For instance, the shift bosses have houses, while shift workers sleep communally "in the bunk house" (212). As a shift worker, McTeague does not control his own schedule: "At half-past five . . . sounded a prolonged alarm" that called him to supper and then to his shift; "[a]t six in the morning his shift was taken off," and "[e]very other week the shifts were changed" (212–14). McTeague—moving and working in a pattern as part of a larger group—now more closely resembles the day laborers on Polk Street than the dentist who made his own schedule. And his new schedule is a busy one that leaves time only for sleeping and eating: "All day long he slept . . . the dreamless sleep of exhaustion, crushed and overpowered with the work" (214), which chains McTeague the worker to an all-consuming labor pattern that leaves little energy for anything beyond work. Indeed, McTeague does not once play his concertina while mining. Even in the desert, the tempo of labor marks inflexible class lines.

For a time it does seem like there are opportunities for class mobility. Prospectors can strike it rich and use the desert's goods to launch themselves upward socioeconomically. After he leaves the mining camp to hide from the law, McTeague meets Cribbens, and the two prospect for gold. Drawing back the theme of hand-work, Cribbens has McTeague "[take] the horn spoon and [rock] it gently in his huge hands," as his own hands shake too much for the job (224). McTeague's handiwork momentarily pays off when he finds gold—in Cribbens's words, "the richest kind of pay" (225) and the promise of rising up. However, in *McTeague* men can strike it rich in the desert only if they go far off the grid, even beyond the mining camps. Finding gold in the desert is like finding fool's gold, since it cannot provide class mobility in the world of Polk Street. McTeague will always be a miner from the desert.

Thus, when McTeague and Marcus first enter the seemingly desolate region surrounding Death Valley, nature initially does not seem separate from the social landscape but interwoven with it. Much like the novel's cityscapes, *McTeague*'s desert region is not a one-dimensional deterministic space but an environment that encourages particular kinds of labor that redevelop already-existing elements of the city's class system. From this vantage point, whether or not nature is "magnificently indifferent to man" matters less than what happens to man in nature (209). When McTeague and Marcus first encounter each other in Death Valley, the environment is shown merely to reproduce McTeague's working-class identity all over again—and, in this case, very tragically.

A Story of Barren Space

And yet the paradox is that the novel's final meditations on class are possible only because the alkali flats of Death Valley ultimately remove labor from *McTeague* altogether. Once in the desert itself and beyond the regions of mining, McTeague finds himself surrounded by "the terrible valley of alkali that barred the way, a horrible vast sink of white sand and salt below even the sea level, the dry bed, no doubt, of some prehistoric lake" (229). Here nature, rather than fostering productive labor as do the mining spaces of Placer County, offers no materials for miners to extract: the alkali flats are sand and salts. Here then is nature's ultimate threat in the novel: a new kind of excess, discordant with the industriousness of the time and thus feared by those who profited from the wealth of that industriousness—the empty excess of barren, natural space. As he wanders the "white, naked, inhospitable" desert, McTeague must confront a space that denies any labor identity (230). More importantly, he and, correspondingly, the novel must confront how individuals react when their familiar labor, class, and spatial infrastructures are evacuated. If, as I've been arguing, class is a function of labor in space and yet labor is impossible on the alkali flats, then class is revealed as a form of social dominance that can exist only where laboring identities exist. Death Valley thus stages the fear of what an absence of manual work does to the identities of the members of the working class, the structures that normally organize them, and their interactions with others.

What McTeague and Marcus need in Death Valley, and what Death Valley as a space actually offers, reveals the fragility of class identity, class mobility, and the dangers of losing both. When the men meet in Death Valley, they are accustomed to patterns of class, capital, and survival in the city and so act in ways incompatible with the desert. And when the desert responds in ways unlike the city, both men resort to violent survival instincts. At the same time, despite awareness of their dire situation, both still turn to Trina's money as a familiar vessel through which they can direct their anxieties. When stranded in undeveloped space, men resort to violence and an even more destructive obsession with capital to distract themselves from the fear of death or what Norris calls the "the vast, the monstrous, and the tragic"—the grotesque behavior of which the lower class is capable (274). Thus, the novel's "determinism" has less to do with what critics of naturalism generally refer to— eugenics, ethnicity, or race—and more with the perils of labor and the fragility of working-class identity. Marcus and McTeague have always been lower-class citizens; their temporary class transgression was simply masked by the organizing structures of class in the city. Norris thus elicits the fears of Gilded Age bourgeois citizens who feared the social and financial havoc that the lower classes could wreak upon culture. But *McTeague*'s ending goes even further, exiling the members of the lower class, as if to purge them from society and place them at a safe distance.

Ironically, Marcus himself begins the process of this removal when he joins the sheriff from Keeler and his posse to look for McTeague. When the group discovers that McTeague has left Cribbens and headed into the valley, Marcus is the only one who wants to follow him, against the better judgment of the sheriff: "'I don't figure on going into that alkali sink with no eight men and horses. . . . One man can't carry enough water to take him and his mount across let alone *eight*'" (238). The sheriff's refusal to bring law into the desert marks Death Valley as a place outside of society's socioeconomic and legal boundaries, a classification reinforced when we learn that "[i]n the haste of the departure from Keeler the sheriff had neglected to swear [Marcus] in." Moreover, Marcus's journey into the desert proves disastrous early on when the sheriff's warning comes true: two days in, "Marcus's horse gave out," and that evening "Marcus, raging with thirst, had drunk his last mouthful of water" (239). Here Marcus's transgression is twofold: he disregards both the legal advice (from the sheriff) to stay out of the desert and the biological threats represented by the desert's environment. As he tells the sheriff when he wants to pursue McTeague, "There was no possibility of their missing the trail—as distinct in the white alkali as snow. They could make a dash into the valley, secure their man, and return long before their water failed them" (238).

But Marcus's—and indeed McTeague's—decision to journey into Death Valley is not merely a legal and natural transgression but a socioeconomic one as well. In the novel thus far, gold has been the object to covet because it affirms the wealth of its owner, as well its own value as a commodity.[17] Back in the city, both Marcus and McTeague had understood the promise of such wealth; McTeague "had imagined that [he and Trina] would spend [the $5,000] in some lavish fashion; would buy a house, perhaps, or would furnish their new rooms with overwhelming luxury," while Marcus spends his money to "[dress] with great care . . . a new pair of slate blue trousers, a black 'cutaway,' and a white lawn 'tie' (for him the symbol of a height of elegance). He also carried his cane, a thin wand of ebony with a gold head" (77, 127). Here both men think of capital in terms of its purchasing power—it can buy things (a house, furnishings, and clothes) and the illusion of status (the superficial "luxury" and "elegance" that comes with such things).

But in Death Valley the $5,000 loses its value entirely, a fact that leaves McTeague and Marcus dumbfounded. When Marcus first robs McTeague and retrieves the gold, he mutters with "a gleam of satisfaction," "'Got it at last'" (240). But this satisfaction doesn't last long; immediately "[Marcus] was singularly puzzled to know what next to do." Similarly, their final fight is motivated not by a desire for wealth but rather by "[t]he old enmity between the two men, their ancient hate" (243). In these final scenes gold acts more as a placeholder for greed and pride than a thing of value in itself. What this absence of value reveals is that McTeague and Marcus have transgressed boundaries that are spatial (San Francisco to Placer County to Death Valley), organizational (Marcus acts on his own accord and McTeague abandons both the mining camp and Cribbens), and social (the stolen money and the murders as a result of the chase). Gold has no purpose in the desert because its potential to provide class mobility no longer exists. Labor and its familiar handiwork are also absent. Now Norris's imagery of hands in Death Valley is limited to McTeague standing in front of an armed Marcus "with his big hands over his head" and McTeague's ominous realization that "Marcus in that last struggle [before dying] had found strength to handcuff their wrists together" (240, 243). In a fitting moment that connects the novel's hands, the famous scene, rather than depicting the hands as productive, instead suggests the limits on what hands provide. Only the mule and the water remain; indeed, when Marcus and McTeague finally shoot the mule and lose the water, the occasion is marked simply by the words, "There was no water left. . . . There was a pause. . . . There was nothing more" (242). No class, no capital, no labor—only vacant, unproductive space.

The final moments of this episode thus pull back the smoke-screen of the city to offer a glimpse into the dangerous potential of those trapped by the limits of lower-class labor. Like the "half-dead canary" at the end of the novel, trapped and "chittering in its little gilt prison," McTeague is trapped by the class determinism that imprisons him socially in the lower class (243). As June Howard (1985, 95) notes in her discussion of proletarianization, because the Gilded Age middle-class "fear of revolution and chaos, of the mob and the criminal . . . of becoming the outcast through social degradation and psychological disintegration" is a fear yoked to the lower classes, McTeague's actions become all the more frightening. As the final scene of *McTeague* unfolds, bourgeois fears of the lower class's ability to commit these transgressions come true and culminate in murder.

The desert is the perfect stage for this unfolding because it offers a contained area far from civilization where Norris can purge the novel of the lower-class dangers that McTeague represents.[18] McTeague's actions in the desert simultaneously confirm and eliminate these fears: he fights viciously for gold that he has obtained by committing one crime and ultimately kills another person with his bare hands, assuring his own death in the process. Norris's (1997c, 274) finale is indeed one where characters are "flung into the throes of a vast and terrible drama that works itself out in unleashed passions, in blood, and in sudden death." The final episode is indeed chaotic: when the mule ran away, he "squealed, threw up his head, and galloped to a little distance, rolling his eyes and flattening his ears," and Marcus responds by "danc[ing] with rage, shaking his fists, and sweating horribly" (Norris 1997a, 240). Norris remarks of the landscape, "Chaotic desolation stretched from them on either hand, flaming and glaring with the afternoon heat" (242). It is brutal and cruel: when they pursue the mule, the two men run "[m]ile after mile, under the terrible heat of the desert sun, racked with a thirst that grew fiercer every hour," and when they fight, "[c]louds of alkali dust, fine and pungent, enveloped the two fighting men, all but strangling them" (241, 242). And it is of course violent: when the question of who owns the gold comes up, McTeague's hands "knotted themselves into fists, hard as wooden mallets" and "the men grappled, and in another instant were rolling and struggling upon the hot white ground" (243). Now McTeague's hands are merely like "wooden mallets"—a tool, to be sure, but one used for violence and murder, not labor.

By returning to his central motifs of labor, class, and space, Norris reduces the signature element of his protagonist's body to a mute, violent sign of lower-class existence itself. And like Marcus's death in the desert, two earlier, similar scenes of grotesque, excessive violence—when Trina finds Maria's body and when McTeague murders Trina—are spurred by the lower-class desire for wealth and class mobility as well. Trina's discovery of Maria's body reveals "a fearful gash in her throat" and "the front of her dress . . . soaked through and through" (174). Zerkow kills Maria after his lust for her family's legendary gold dinnerware set reaches its climax; shortly before, Maria has told Trina that "'[h]e's gettun regularly sick with it—got a fever every night. . . . Then he'll whale me with his whip, and shout, "*You* know where it is. Tell me, tell me, you swine, or I'll do for you." . . . He's just gone plum crazy'" (172). In a section Norris removed from the novel's original version, McTeague's murder of Trina is "abominable": "She was a repulsive sight. Her great mane of swarthy hair was all down and over her face, her dress was torn to ribbons, and the little stream of blood running from the corner of her mouth stained as with ink the whiteness of her bare shoulder and breast" (206n4). McTeague too is driven by an insane greed for the $5,000; he warns Trina, "'You won't, huh? You won't give me it? For the last time,'" and when she declares, "'No, *no*,'" he "'sent his fist into the middle of her face with the suddenness of a relaxed spring'" (205). In these cases, as well as in McTeague and Marcus's final fight, the need of one for the capital of another ends in chaotic, violent, lower-class murder.

But there is another thing these three scenes have in common. Each takes place in a space of social and economic exclusion. Maria is killed in her home, a "wretched hovel in the alley" that is "dark and damp, and foul with all manner of choking odors," where Zerkow stores his useless junk—"all the detritus that a great city sloughs off"—which represents "every class of society" (134, 28). Trina is killed in her "little room over the kindergarten schoolroom," which runs "through a much poorer and more sordid quarter" than Polk Street, where she "saw no one" and is "lost in the lowest eddies of the great city's tide" (193). And Marcus is killed in the desert, a space of "brazen sky and . . . leagues upon leagues of alkali, leper white," where money has no purpose but greed, for it still spurs violence. Each of these spaces is marked by its separation from bourgeois society, whether urban or rural. *McTeague*'s last scene thus brings us back to my opening question: What does it mean to title the novel *McTeague: A Story of San Francisco*? What *is* this novel about? This novel, it would seem, is about spaces in and around San

Francisco—spaces where, as Norris (1997b, 280) sees it, "You, the aristocrats . . . will not follow." This novel, then, is about deteriorations: socioeconomic exclusion, the decay of identity, the façades of class mobility, the loss of work, and the grotesque transgressions that occur in the spaces left in their wake.

# 2    Civic Identity and the Ethos of Belonging

María Amparo Ruiz de Burton's *The Squatter and the
Don* and Raymond Barrio's *The Plum Plum Pickers*

In 1992 Arte Público Press published Rosaura Sánchez and Beatrice
Pita's edition of María Amparo Ruiz de Burton's 1885 protest novel,
*The Squatter and the Don*, which renarrates the history of the development of the American Southwest. Through the lens of a family
named the Alamars, Ruiz de Burton's novel narrates the story of
the Californios, a class of land-owning gentry who are descendants
of white Spaniards and were originally Mexican citizens, living in
the parts of California that had belonged to Mexico. In the wake of
the U.S. war with Mexico that ended in 1848, however, the Alamars
find themselves both legally dispossessed of their land rights and
confronted by a group of Anglo-American homesteaders, or "squatters," who are in cahoots with a corrupt political system stretching
all the way to the governor of California. In a complex plot involving
interethnic romance and marriage, a failed development strategy
for the region of San Diego, and betrayal by the United States and
especially the California railroad lobby, the Alamars eventually see
their patriarch, or "don," defeated and dead, his children dispersed,
his family's former way of life all but extinguished.

Since the release of Sánchez and Pita's edition, critical work on
Ruiz de Burton's novel has exploded. Most prominent is scholarship arguing over the ethnic identifications in the text, which in
general sympathizes with the novel's wealthy, Spanish-Californio
and Chicano population. Much of this work, including Sánchez

and Pita's introduction, has tackled some version of the question Marcial González (2009, 41) has posed—"Can a novel in which the narrator unabashedly refers to Native Americans and working-class mestizos in a racially derogatory manner be considered politically resistant?"—and answers have varied considerably. Some, like Sánchez and Pita (1992, 5), claim that the novel "create[s] a narrative space for the counter-history of the sub-altern [the Californios]," while others, like José Aranda (1998, 553–54), argue that such a judgment is "premature . . . because Chicano/a studies has yet to conceptualize adequately the inclusion of writers and texts that uphold racial and colonialist discourses that contradict the ethos of the Chicano Movement."[1] Still others, like González (2009, 42) himself, have probed the novel's contradictions and those of Ruiz de Burton's own class privilege yet argue that such limitations "[do] not exhaust the production of meaning in the novel" itself.

What all of these scholars have in common of course is the understandable presumption that places ethnicity, as well as the long history of Chicano dispossession, at the center of the novel's political ethos. However, my approach in this chapter is different in two ways. First, my reading hopes to illuminate the crucial role *labor* plays in the divisions among American policy makers, business leaders, settlers, squatters, and Californios that Ruiz de Burton dramatizes; second, I focus on the relationship between *nationality* and class status, labor, and space in the imaginative terrain of this novel. That is, my assumption is that it is nationality that often confers certain class privileges and restricts others, specifically because those privileges are defined by laws governing labor and the ownership of the land where that labor takes place. Just as McTeague's identity rests on his notions of dentistry as manual labor, so too does the identity of *The Squatter and the Don*'s Spanish patriarch, Don Alamar, rest on traditional visions of ranching. And just as McTeague's struggles with selfhood, empowerment, and control reflect specific historical anxieties of the Gilded Age, so too do the Don's anxieties about family heritage and security reflect early Californio concerns about cultural identity that still, I will show in my epilogue to this chapter, pertain to discussions about Chicano identity.

In fact the relevance of nations and national identification to labor emerges in an early scene that establishes the initial premises of Ruiz de Burton's plot. Here the book's elderly homesteading American couple, William and Mary Darrell, discuss the consequences of having moved to California. The conversation begins with William outlining how their hopes were "backed" by national power—only to be disappointed:

> "I firmly believed then, that with my fine stock and good bank account, and broad government lands, free to all Americans . . . that I would have saved money and would be getting more to make us rich. . . . [But] I am still poor, all I have earned is the name of '*Squatter*.'" . . .
>
> "I am afraid I shall never be able to see the necessity of any one being a squatter in this blessed country of plentiful broad acres, which a most liberal government gives away for the asking."
>
> "That's exactly it. We aren't squatters. We are '*settlers*.' We take up land that belongs to us, American citizens, by paying the government price for it."
>
> "Whenever you take up government land, yes, you are 'settlers,' but not when you locate claims on lands belonging to anyone else. . . . [D]o not go on a Mexican grant unless you buy the land from the owner." (Ruiz de Burton 1992, 56–57)[2]

Here Ruiz de Burton's Anglo couple recognizes that nations have the power to redefine corresponding class divisions, rather than simply recognizing ethnicity as such—and such definitions drive the novel's story of Californio dispossession. Conversely, the Californios of Ruiz de Burton's novel try to shift their national affiliations to maintain landownership, labor practices familiar to them, and their class status. But all three of these elements are effaced when *other* American citizens and political figures pursue profitable local empire-building ventures—other kinds of labor—like homesteading itself, and especially railroad construction. Because this development must occur on land originally owned by Californios, American politicians enforce laws that dispossess Ruiz de Burton's protagonists of their land; these laws also withdraw political sanction from traditional Californio labor and thus challenge the very basis of their landownership and American citizenship. In other words, the Californios are negatively "coded" as not only the rival (and defeated) nationality but as committed to the wrong kind of labor (ranching). The loss of their land and class status follows suit.

Ultimately, then, I mean to ask how national and political movements depicted in the novel—like late nineteenth-century land laws in the United States, new labor patterns, and railroad building—affect the novel's Californios. How do their working, class, and national identities change as those transformations take place? And what interconnected roles do national belonging, labor, and class play in shaping Ruiz de Burton's political ethos? Unlike other critical approaches that read that ethos as rooted in an ethnicity (and often a static one, at that), my foregrounding of these questions aims to bring to light the *process* of Ruiz de Burton's "ethos-in-becoming," a fluid and fragile negotiation of how national and racial identities fashion and refashion political positions in response to a given historical moment. Space and labor become crucial to this literary refashioning of what I call "ethos." As Hsuan Hsu (2010, 16) writes, citing Henri Lefebvre, "representational space can be mediated and transformed through works of imagination because it is 'alive': it speaks. It has an affective kernel or centre . . . it is essentially qualitative, fluid and dynamic." This is the notion of ethos to which I return at the end of this chapter, when I discuss Raymond Barrio's *The Plum Plum Pickers* as a kind of contemporary counterpoint to *The Squatter and the Don*. There I argue that Barrio's novel reveals how a lack of awareness of the history above continues to shape the present. That failure often arrests the process of ethos and chains it to one-dimensional conceptions of nationality and class dispossession.

Nevertheless, while most critics feel uneasy about Ruiz de Burton's multiple affiliations with often contradictory collectives—Mexican, American, capitalist, land-owning gentry, Spaniard, dispossessed Californio—I argue that this range actually nurtures a narrative plasticity that makes room for both the novel's intersecting, multiple-subject positions and the winding route the Chicano ethos has taken. Specifically, Ruiz de Burton uses the Alamars' response to draw fine distinctions between *membership* and *affiliation* in her Californio ethos. Whereas memberships are often dictated by outside forces, affiliations are much more personal, delicate, and contingent. Responding to political and cultural pressure from within and without, they often shift as need arises. While most critics argue that *The Squatter and the Don*'s depiction of class dispossession is virtually equivalent to ethnic dispossession, I argue that class marginalization in the novel responds more immediately to national belonging. Class lines in the novel are drawn along flexible national affiliations that shift with changes in wealth, land-ownership, and labor practices; these transformations in turn call attention to the flexibility of the novel's ethos.[3] In the end Ruiz de Burton's characters are conscious of and outspoken about their ethnic membership and dispossession, but their actions indicate that they are more committed to pursuing national affiliations that benefit them at particular moments.

Turning our attention to labor in particular reveals a crucial component of the novel's "ethos-in-becoming": if Don Mariano and his sons identify as Californio ranchers yet contract the work of raising livestock to those whom they devalue, what can that situation tell us about how labor functions as an empowering, degrading, or imprisoning force?[4] These questions draw attention to the often unstable role labor plays as the ground on which the novel's Chicanos balance their civic and class identities chaotically shifts in response to national-spatial changes.

## On Class

As I have said, the new generation of scholars discussed earlier has already explicated the history of the American Southwest invoked by Ruiz de Burton's novel. At the close of the U.S. war with Mexico in 1848, representatives of both nations signed the Treaty of Guadalupe Hidalgo, which transferred control of large portions of the Southwest from Mexico to the United States. Mexican nationals who remained in these areas were given one year to claim American citizenship or return to Mexico; if they chose the former path, they were assured they would keep their property and gain the right to vote. However, over time two of the primary American expressions of Manifest Destiny—homesteading and railroad construction— encouraged American squatters, policy makers, and railroad tycoons to disregard the prior assurances of the treaty, favor grain planting by American settlers, and make it possible to homestead upon contested haciendas. Land grants for railroads in turn encouraged this cycle of legalized dispossession of the Californios, including the isolation of the Texas-to–San Diego railroad spur that is featured in the novel. Because the novel's central Californio family, the Alamars, live in San Diego, they support the Texas-Pacific spur, explicitly linking its success to sustaining the family's identity and ethos. The class tensions between those who back the "right" railroad or do the "right" labor therefore become issues of national membership and political citizenship.

Ruiz de Burton thus figures national identity as the defining factor of class hierarchy through laws that reward American citizenship with landownership and development. The members of Congress and the monopolists Ruiz de Burton identifies by name are wealthy, powerful Anglo-American citizens who prey on Californio citizens by using their particular brand of political-economic corruption and thereby forge new class alliances:

> The monopolists are essentially the most dangerous citizens in the fullest acceptance of the word. They are dangerous citizens, not only in being guilty of violation of the law, in subverting the fundamental principles of public morality, but they are dangerous citizens because they *lead others* into the commission of the same crimes. Their example is deadly to honorable sentiments; it is poison to Californians because it allures men with the glamour of success; it incites the unwary to imitate the conduct of men who have become immensely rich by such culpable means. (Ruiz de Burton 1992, 366)

> These two men . . . had heard strange rumors about Congressmen being "*bribed with money*" and in other *ways improperly influenced by a "certain railroad man," who was organizing a powerful lobby to defeat the Texas Pacific Railroad.* . . . Mechlin had come across some startling facts regarding the manipulation of railroad bills, especially in the Congressional committees. . . . George . . . felt, also, a reluctance to believe that the Congress of these United States could be packed, bundled, and labeled, by a few of its treacherous members, who would sell themselves for money. (210)

As American politics, railroad building, and Manifest Destiny take center stage in the novel, Don Mariano's complicated class status is articulated through national affiliations with Mexico and the United States. American legislators use various markers of identity to distinguish who could claim American citizenship and who couldn't, thereby calcifying both the "rightful" U.S. ownership of western land and the money to be made through agriculture, business, and travel. One of the easiest and most effective methods was to draw new class lines along existing national lines, which solidified American identity by identifying Others against which it could be compared. Moreover, legislators also gave political power to those who could claim land in the name of American progress. Labor was a crucial component of this claim, as Anglo settlers' cultivation of nature supposedly marked U.S. ownership and control of space. The California Land Act of 1851 in particular declared that all squatters who fenced the land for their own labor then owned that land and were in turn U.S. citizens. Describing this ruse, Ruiz de Burton writes that instead of being "'[a]n Act to ascertain and settle the private land claims in the State of California,' . . . [i]t ought to have been said, 'An Act to *unsettle* land titles, and to upset the rights of the Spanish population of the State of California'" (88). Because these land claims drew legitimacy from particular forms of labor done by those claiming particular national identities, the work of Manifest Destiny literally became the *work* of constructing class—in other words, the work of legally sanctifying one class over another.

However, while these laws certainly dispossessed the Californios of their native land and their ethnic stability, ethnic dispossession was more a secondary effect of such laws, which primarily sought to give labor rights—and so land rights—to U.S. citizens and, as I've said, support certain kinds of agricultural labor and railroad building that would prove financially beneficial to the United States as a nation. In other words, those who enacted these laws sought primarily to secure national space and identity through any means necessary. Hence George Mechlin's answer to his wife's inquiry as to why Congress should "refuse to aid the Texas Pacific": "'They have no earthly *right* to oppose the Texas Pacific, and all their motive is that they *don't want competition* to their Central Pacific Railroad. They have already made millions out of this road, but they want no one else to make a single dollar'" (297; original emphases). In the novel this perspective is also evident in the subtly shifting affiliations that characters choose as laws about landownership and railroad building—and thus nation-building—are enforced. As the Alamars' landownership and class status grow more tenuous because of their legal battles, Ruiz de Burton even distances the patriarch Don Mariano from Mexico as he begins to invest in specific legal and political processes, including railroad development, that he believes will benefit him and his family.

Ruiz de Burton's apparent approval of Don Mariano's strategy of transformation has led many critics to argue that her reciprocally disparaging commentary on working-class mestizos and Indians troubles the ethnic and class sympathy she has for the aristocratic Californios. Her contradictory opinions on socioeconomics are often seen as similarly unresolvable. Thus, while representing the Californios as eager to join the emerging capitalist system, she also attacks the capitalistic monopoly of the Big Four—the wealthy Anglo merchants, politicians, and founders of the Central Pacific Railroad Company (Sen. Leland Stanford, Mark Hopkins, Collis P. Huntington, and Charles Crocker)—and blames them for the loss of Californio class status, labor, land, and way of life. Critical unease about these contradictions has led some interpreters to suggest that the Alamars, as Chicanos, should feel obligated to be in solidarity with the mestizos and Indians and reject the practices of the Anglos.[5] However, Ruiz de Burton's "Indians" are not the only representation of Mexico that comes in for criticism in the novel. Critics have often overlooked how critiques of the Mexican government in *The Squatter and the Don* suggest that, to Ruiz de Burton, class derives from national identity.[6] In her treatment of these land grants, Ruiz de Burton emphasizes the Mexican government's failure to defend the Californios' rights to land under the Treaty of Guadalupe Hidalgo and their consequential national and financial losses. William Darrell's bias against the Californios foreshadows these losses when he expresses anger that the Californios are initially "'better off than the Americans! They should have been put on an equality with other settlers. . . . I always will maintain that the Spanish Californians should not have a right to any more land than Americans'" (222). And those financial repercussions are clear when Don Mariano explains the injustice of U.S. land laws to George Mechlin, a sympathetic settler. In response to Don Mariano's troubles caused by the land acts, Mechlin prods, "'I thought the rights of the Spanish people were protected by our treaty with Mexico,'" which identifies the Mexican government's legal agreement with the United States as the primary, original mechanism of the Alamars' class security. Likewise, Doña Josefa's morose response earlier in the novel links socioeconomic instability to the gulf between national belonging and national inhabitance: "'Mexico did not pay much attention to the future welfare of the children she left to their fate in the hands of a nation which had no sympathies for us,'" she says (66). Don Mariano elaborates on his wife's idea:

> "[W]hen I first read the text of the treaty of Guadalupe Hidalgo, I felt a bitter resentment against my people; against Mexico, the mother country, who abandoned us—her children—with so slight a provision of obligatory stipulations for protection. . . . The treaty said that our rights would be the same as those enjoyed by all other American citizens. But, you see, Congress takes very good care not to enact retroactive laws for Americans; laws to take away from American citizens the property which they hold now, already, with a recognized legal title. No, indeed. But they do so quickly enough with us—with us, the Spano-Americans, who were to enjoy equal rights, mind you, according to the treaty of peace. This is what seems to me a breach of faith, which Mexico could neither presuppose nor prevent." (66–67)

The ethnic markers appearing in this conversation *seem* to flow seamlessly among Spanish, Mexico, and "Spano-American" characters. But the fine lines Darrell, Mechlin, Doña Josefa, and Don Mariano draw among the Alamars as Spanish or Spano-American, their original government as Mexican, and their current government as American, point to Ruiz de Burton's suggestion that class status can be either reinforced or undercut by civic identification. The Alamars are indeed Spano-American citizens (calling on the class power the Spanish once derived from their land grants and the present power the United States holds), yet they have also been legally abandoned and financially ruined by the Mexican *and* U.S. governments. Don Mariano explains to Clarence Darrell, who is William Darrell's son and soon the romantic interest of Don Mariano's daughter, the unjust U.S. laws used against Californio land owners: "'here again come our *legislators* to encourage again wrong-doing—to offer a premium to one class of citizens to go and prey upon another class'" (173; original emphasis). Those in political power want to use this distinction—Spanish or American—for their own class and political power: if they can grant U.S. citizens land rights, they can grant them voting rights as well. And Ruiz de Burton figures Congress's desire to seize this dual national-political and socioeconomic power as beyond control: "the politicians, who make and unmake each other, they are the power. . . . And if these law-givers see fit to *sell themselves* for money, what then? Who has the power to undo what is done?" (207; original emphasis). In other words, Anglo-American lawmakers and railroad tycoons (often, in the novel, one and the same) want to secure California both as U.S. land and as the basis of political power: as Don Mariano explains to Clarence about who would contribute to "'the prosperity of the state,'" "'The motive was that our politicians wanted *votes*. The squatters were in increasing majority; the Spanish natives, in diminishing minority'" (175). Votes constitute political and financial power in the novel because "'the bribes of the Central Pacific monopolists have more power with some Congressmen than the sense of justice or the rights of communities'" (297).

Not coincidentally, that same railroad development would also bring widespread financial benefit to the towns it would run through; as George Mechlin points out to his wife and to Don Mariano's daughter, Elvira, "'Don't you see here in our little town of San Diego how everything is depending on the success of this road? Look at all the business of the town, all the farming of this county, all the industries of Southern California—everything is at a stand-still, waiting for Congress to aid the Texas Pacific'" (297). Even when he wrongly guesses which railway will come to fruition and benefit a burgeoning California city (San Francisco, not San Diego, gets the railroad spur), Mr. Holman correctly pinpoints the importance of the railroad to nation-building, both financial and structural: "'the building of the Texas Pacific was an issue of national importance so manifest that Congress would never have the hardihood to deny it existence'" (231). Clarence arrives at the same conclusion when devising his own plans to gain wealth: his success "'will entirely depend upon the building of the Texas Pacific Railroad; for if San Diego is to not have population, my plan will be impractical'" (163). In each case the railroad's national benefits are socioeconomic benefits, tying nationality to class privilege. Ultimately, however, Congress grants legal status to settlements whose owners vote in favor of the "right" railway, the one controlled by U.S. monopolists. The Californios, as Mexican citizens who live in San Diego and support the Texas Pacific, stand in the way of that goal. And so their land grants, formerly backed by national legal agreements, must be negated.

The links among railroad politics, nation-building, and financial security connect not only to public issues but to private affiliations as well. As George Mechlin tells Elvira,

> "Look at our two families. All the future prosperity of the Ala-mares and the Mechlins is entirely based upon the success of this road. If it is built, we will be well off, we will have comfortable homes and a sure income to live on. But if the Texas Pacific fails, then we will be financially wrecked. That is, my father will, and Don Mariano will be sadly crippled, for he has invested heavily in town property. . . . So my poor father and yours will be the worst sufferers. Many other poor fellows will suffer like them—for almost the entire San Diego is in the same boat with us. It all depends on Congress." (297)

Here class continuity depends on national and urban belonging, as well as on bonds *between* the Mechlins and the Alamars. The Mechlins and Clarence are Americans; therefore Don Mariano comes to recognize that friendship and partnership with the Mechlins depend not on ethnicity but on landownership and nationality. Reciprocally, the affiliations Don Mariano must forge during this time reveal that he recognizes that his identity as a U.S. landowner could hold more political and class sway than his identity as a Californio. Together, in turn, these men "go to see Governor Stanford" to assess his position on the Texas Pacific (306).

During her depiction of that meeting, however, Ruiz de Burton makes clear that Stanford flexes his political muscle by emphasizing his ability to use the power of his government connections to override the popular will: "'The American people mind their business, and know better than to interfere with ours'" (316). The divide between everyday American citizens and their government itself reflects that access to resources and funding is only for the privileged: as Mechlin points out, "'as the Central Pacific was constructed with Government subsidies, and the earnings of the Central Pacific were used to construct the Southern Pacific, it follows that you were helped by the Government to build both'" (317). Nevertheless, although he is the novel's ostensible representative of this political compact, Stanford himself openly flaunts it at the close of their meeting: "'Money commands success, you know'" (319). Moreover, Stanford's political power has granted him legal authority to encourage American settlers to stake their claims on land owned by Mexican nationals in the first place. Holman recognizes the injustice here—"'How confident he is of [the railroad tycoons'] power over Congress! And he certainly means to wield it as if he came by it legitimately'"—and though his acknowledgment distinguishes Congress from the Big Four (a partial fallacy, as Stanford is governor), Holman's despair is poignant (322). Congress now benefits from, and redistributes, the class power Don Mariano once enjoyed.

The fate of Gabriel Alamar and Lizzie Mechlin—whose marriage originally testifies to the bond between their families—demonstrates the consequences of that dispossession. Without the railroad to bring his family prosperity in San Diego, Gabriel must move to San Francisco to find work; however, his continuing responsibilities back at the family ranch draw him away from that work and interrupt the stability of his family's new life. Ultimately, his failure to find a stable, middle-class existence in San Francisco further attests to how being originally bound to space and nationality has now affected his loss of class status. Lizzie, meanwhile, once "moved in what was called San Francisco's *best* society," but her marriage to a Spanish-Mexican national who has lost his family's wealth, as well as his position at the bank in San Francisco, causes her friends' past "cordiality [to] soon vanish. . . . The fact that Gabriel was a *native Spaniard*, she saw plainly, militated against them. If he had been rich, his nationality could have been forgiven, but no one could tolerate a *poor native Californian*" (351; original emphases). Similarly, when Clarence recommends the Alamars come to San Francisco because "'San Diego is dead,'" Doña Josefa recalls the distance between sound, enterprising intentions and the power of class in determining personal worth: "'Business without capital? See where my poor Gabriel is now'" (359). His eventual injuries as a manual laborer, as I will explore subsequently, only amplify the meaning of this dispossession.

Ultimately, therefore, the class fate of the novel's Californios becomes yoked to national status in ways that continually bend and reshape their ethos-in-becoming. Whether Ruiz de Burton refers to the Alamars variously as Spano-American, Californio, native Californians, or Spanish, the irrevocable truth is that their abandonment by the Mexican government—itself impotent, financially bereft—is the source of these characters' dispossession and the antithesis of the power that Stanford, his railroad partners, and the U.S. Congress now embody. The Alamars succumb to a trinity of losses: of status, of law, of ownership. Indeed, the ineffectuality of the Mexican government further splits the affiliations within this novel that many critics have struggled to explain: the fact that working-class mestizos are disguised as "Indians"; the fact that Don Mariano claims membership in Spanish ethnic identity and yet forms affiliations with other American settlers (and the United States as a nation), only to fail at both; and, again, the fact that the text identifies the Alamars as Mexican but binds their loss to the past rulings of the now-defunct Mexican governance of California. In order to account for and adjust to the changes in the Californios' class status, Ruiz de Burton's tragedy depicts the power of nationality as fluid and contingent—indeed, something the Californios themselves must continually refashion and defend. In these lights, the novel's derogatory take on Indians and mestizos merely makes sense: for Ruiz de Burton, they remain tied to Mexico's past, emblems of that nation's failures and losses and, in time, even those of its most elite citizens.

## On Labor

Both Californio and American identity in *The Squatter and the Don* also are contingent on legal and personal definitions of what constitutes good or productive labor. Yet even here, their ethos is fluid and fungible. On the one hand, the Alamars, and specifically Don Mariano and his sons, identify as landed Californio gentry who oversee fruit growing and ranching—labors they see as best suited to San Diego's ecology; when he defends these labors to the settlers and squatters, Mariano claims, "'[Y]ou would not have to wait very long to begin getting a return from your labor and capital'" (92). However, because that labor occurs on land they own under the defunct Treaty of Guadalupe Hidalgo, it loses traction as American squatters use the exploitative land acts to acquire that land for their own style of labor. On the other hand, the Alamars repeatedly refuse to identify as Mexican and make derogatory references to the "Indians" who work on their ranch: though they are Mexican by citizenship, the Alamars avoid a national membership that would link them to lower-working-class Mexicans. Distancing themselves from the working-class mestizos and Indians thus differentiates them from the manual labor of the "Indians," whom the Alamars oversee. The ethos set forth here is thus one that responds not to ecological responsibility but to a dependence on the aristocratic privilege of hiring workers to do the physical labors of working the land. (As I will discuss later, this environmentalism falters in the face of class pressure, again accentuating the role nationality plays in the novel's Chicano ethos.)

It is from that privileged position that Don Mariano demonstrates financial and practical insight into San Diego's ecology. As Priscilla Ybarra (2012, 136) has pointed out, over the course of their long tenure in Southern California, "landholding Mexicans had learned a great deal about how to profitably and sustainably maintain their haciendas." But that knowledge and its benefits suffer when American squatters' rights take legal precedence:

> "By those laws any man can come to my land, for instance, plant ten acres of grain, without any fence, and then catch my cattle which, seeing the green grass without a fence, will go to eat it. Then he puts them into a '*corral*' and makes me pay damages and so much per head for keeping them, and costs of legal proceedings and many other trumped up expenses, until for such little fields of grain I may be obligated to pay thousands of dollars. Or, if the grain fields are large enough to bring enough money by keeping the cattle away, then the settler shoots the cattle at any time without the least hesitation. . . . And so it is all the time. I must pay damages and expenses of litigation, or my cattle get killed almost every day." (Ruiz de Burton 1992, 66)

These practices threaten Don Mariano's labor in two ways: first, they endanger its necessary components by forcing him to pay or lose his cattle; second, they endanger his labor practices because planting grain is, Ruiz de Burton lets us know, an unwise and wasteful agricultural decision: "'[I]t is a mistake,'" Don Mariano says, "'to try to make San Diego a grain-producing county . . . [it is] one of the best counties for cattle-raising on this coast, and the very best for fruit-raising on the face of the earth'" (91). If settlers institute new ways of working the land, they will undermine the legacies of the Alamars' ranch, financial and otherwise.

And because labor plays a large part in shaping identity in the novel, losing work also offends virtually all of its characters. Early in *The Squatter and the Don*, for example, an exchange about the weight of work on identity occurs between William Darrell and his fiancée, Mary:

> "You know, Mr. Darrell, I teach to support myself."
> "Yes, only because you have a notion to do it."
> "A notion! Do you think I am rich?"
> "No, but there is no need of you working."
> "It is a need to me to feel independent. . . . I know how to earn my own living." (59)

This exchange indicates two purposes of work: to provide material *and* immaterial stability. That is, Mary not only supports herself financially with her labor; her work supports her sense of self as well. She has a particular skill—teaching—that fosters her sense of individuality: her need "to feel independent" is satisfied because she knows "how to earn [her] own living," thus yoking financial stability to her independence. Work tells Ruiz de Burton's characters, as individuals, what they do and who they are.

Yet working identity is not only tied to individual skill in the novel; that sense of self is also tied to the place of work. Indeed, the title of the novel itself—*The Squatter and the Don*—references broader social identities that derive from the kind of labor that can be done in the San Diego region under specific legal contexts. As mentioned above,

Don Mariano prefers cultivating cattle and fruit because each is more sustainable in the local environment. His ownership is legitimized through such stewardship. The squatters, conversely, want to fence the land and grow wheat, a crop that would be unsustainable in that environment. Moreover, fencing off farms will prevent cattle from grazing, effectively undermining Don Mariano's business. In one way or another, all the major struggles in the novel occur because the work of the squatters (and their sponsoring legislators) and the work of the dons do not mix. As Don Mariano explains, this ruinous conflict is devastating to a way of life rooted in a specific kind of labor: "'[A]s we, the Spaniards, are the owners of Spanish—or Mexican—land grants and also the owners of the cattle ranchos, our State legislators will not make any law to protect cattle. They make laws *to protect agriculture*" (they say proudly), which means to drive to the wall all owners of cattle ranchos. I am told that at this session of the legislature a law more strict will be passed, which will be ostensibly "to protect agriculture," but in reality to destroy cattle and ruin the native Californians'" (66). Here labor and nation enter a feedback loop whereby legally sanctified work serves to define national power. The legal work done by state legislators trumps the legitimacy and ecological stewardship of a particular kind of labor.

However, a careful look at this matter begs the question I have implicitly raised in my earlier focus on class: does Don Mariano actually *do* ranch work? When Don Mariano and Darrell initially meet, they both *seem* to be working: "Don Mariano, accompanied by his two sons, rode up to the place where [Darrell] was then superintending his workers" to confront him about Darrell's settlement on his land (79). Here Darrell oversees the construction of his new house and "his" plot's cultivation. However, it is unclear whether Don Mariano is at work—actually "superintending"—or merely using his cattle horses for the trip. A similar ambiguity occurs elsewhere in the novel, when, for instance, Don Mariano explains "ranching" to the settlers he befriends: "'You will not have to be a vaquero. I don't go "*busquering*" around *lassoing* unless I wish to do so'" (94). Work here is therefore a choice for Don Mariano, rather than something he must do to claim his land, as Darrell does when he fences his fields to make them productive. In these lights, Darrell is actually more concretely tied to labor than Don Mariano is—a feature of identity that carries political and class significance when we recognize that the squatters are "planters" and the dons merely "owners." Ruiz de Burton thus uses physical labor to underscore an unsettling class and national difference: Darrell must work to eke out a living and claim his space, while Don Mariano already lives in comfort and so does not need to do so. If labor is how one claims land in the novel, then it would seem that Darrell and the other squatters claim land more vigorously in the present, whereas the Californios only claimed it vigorously in the past. And, to further yoke a Chicano ethos to national identity and class privilege, Don Mariano explains why he doesn't have to go "busquering" (searching) around: "'You can hire an Indian boy to do that part'" (94). Thus, although Ruiz de Burton sympathizes with the Californios, she clearly connects the "work" they do merely to upper-class landownership. Following a pattern of American colonization, the Alamars use marginalized populations for physical labor.

In fact Ruiz de Burton rarely portrays prominent Chicano characters doing physical work in the novel. Work is more often described through political debate, which questions the legitimacy of the Californios' ecological know-how and even their identities through the work of ranching. The few moments of actual work that are represented reveal curious differences between the national-class distinctions of the Californios and the American squatters. More often than not, when physical labor is depicted in the novel, Darrell and the other squatters are the ones doing it. In that first conversation, Darrell's work is clearly outlined: "All the crops must be in first, so that Everett and Webster could take care of the dairy, but still, Darrell made his boys give their personal attention to all the work on the farm" (78). And again, "the settlers had harvested their crops of hay and grain, and were hauling them to town" and "[t]he whir of the threshing machines was heard in the valleys of the Alamar rancho, and wagons loaded with hay went from the fields like moving hills" (185, 286). And although Don Mariano disapproves of this labor because it is bad for both ecological and financial health—"'it is a mistake to try to make San Diego county a grain-producing county,'" he explains, "'an orchard of forty acres or a vineyard of twenty will pay better after three years' growth than one hundred sixty acres of wheat or barley in good seasons'" (91, 92)—his rhetoric is not really matched by work on its behalf. Instead, although Ruiz de Burton uses Don Mariano's ecological awareness to amplify his national belonging and class status, that sophisticated knowledge remains abstract, a fact that may foreshadow other reasons for his loss of land, class, and identity. And not unimportantly, that absence also makes his claims to Chicano affiliation less concretely connected to labor. Without work—either to do or, eventually, even to assign to others—Don Mariano loses his sense of self and ultimately dies.

Moreover, in the few scenes in which Don Mariano and his family are depicted doing work, it is not work they want to do or are good at. Visible labor done by the Alamar family often occurs only because of an action Americans take: when Clarence offers to buy and essentially save his cattle from the squatters' culling, Don Mariano and his sons feel they must "ride out every day to superintend personally the collecting of cattle" and assure the safety of the herd (224). Victoriano calls this work a "'*rodeo triste*'" (224), accentuating the uneasy melancholy Ruiz de Burton maps onto images of Californios performing heavy labor. Likewise, at the end of the novel, when Victoriano must take on heavy ranch work, he is unprepared for the task at hand: "he worked very hard, in fact, entirely too hard for one so unused to labor. Work broke him down" (344). Similarly, Gabriel cannot even find work in the city: when he "[tries to] find employment to support [himself and his wife, he] found the task most difficult" (340).

Losing their identity as landowning elites only invites the wrong kind of work into these characters' lives. Late in the narrative, when Don Mariano, Victoriano, and Gabriel are forced to work to provide their livelihood, all three succumb to illness or injury as a result of out-of-the-ordinary labor. Victoriano loses mobility while herding cattle on an unexpectedly inclement ride with his father: "'Father, I cannot stand up. From my knees down I have lost all feeling and have no control of my limbs at all'"; from the same ride Don Mariano "himself [took] a severe cold in his lungs" (302); and Gabriel, when he loses his bank job and finds work (as a stonemason) for which he "had no training" (301), falls while carrying bricks up a ladder (342) and "the bricks fell upon him" (347). Unlike the ethos of ranch ownership, these labors are not tasks the Alamars feel they can be proud of. Instead, their work is demeaning and cripples them physically and psychologically; physical labor becomes a task that marginalizes a sense of self and ruins the body, in turn preventing future work. (Moreover, Don Mariano and Victoriano fall victim to unusually cold weather and heavy snow, which hints that even their ecological know-how cannot adjust to changing climates— environmental or political). On Ruiz de Burton's canvas certain kinds of labor are for certain classes of people, and blurring those distinctions has dire consequences. Even their cattle ultimately die: those that were not shot by squatters "perished in the snow" that has left Victoriano lame and Don Mariano sick (359).

Once Don Mariano dies—when he dramatically proclaims, yoking the work that is killing him to the laws that made that work necessary, that it is "'[t]oo late. The sins of our legislators!'" (329)—the remaining Alamars are left with no resources for ranching, and they agree to sell their ranch to Clarence and move to San Francisco. It is at Don Mariano's suggestion: "'San Diego is dead now, and will remain so for many years, but San Francisco is a good business field. So we can all locate there, and Gabriel and Tano go into business easily'" (359). That the family moves to San Francisco—the city figured as San Diego's nemesis in railroad building—brings into focus the changing patterns of labor and development in the now "American" West. Yet this new infrastructure does not feature the kind of labor with which the Alamar children are familiar, nor is it one they perform well. If, as Lee Edelman (2005, 4) has argued, the child represents "the emblem of futurity's unquestioned value," then the disabling of Don Mariano's children, the loss of the Alamar ranch, and the loss of the family's ability to ranch effectively eliminate, both in the present and for the future, not only the Californio rancher identity but also the national, familial, and financial resources that identity carried into the future.[7] The Californios, Ruiz de Burton suggests, are effectively wiped out. If Don Mariano was not actually a rancher but rather a businessman who hired others to ranch for him, his children can neither ranch nor do the work of the modern business world; it would seem that the Californios lack any working identity at the end of the novel. These losses, which Ruiz de Burton has linked to labor, class, and national dispossession, clearly trouble the futurity of the Chicano ethos itself. Indeed, when we remember the Indians who work the Alamars' ranch, that future seems an unavoidable, cyclical pattern that divorces productive land use from labor for the sake of profit and nationally exploitative work.

Ultimately, then, it is again clear that Ruiz de Burton's relation to a wider Chicano sensibility is itself only tentative, uneven, even messy—an ethos-in-becoming. On the one hand, the fate of the Alamars does portend the widespread exploitation of Chicano workers in the present day. On the other hand, if the Alamars represent Spanish-Mexican nationals, their complicated relationship to work makes it hard to trace such a logical political lineage, much less to the cause of ethnic solidarity (or "proletarian" consciousness). In the end, despite the fact that Clarence's generosity and marriage to Mercedes ultimately saves what is left of the Alamar family, his decision to sell the ranch and move to San Francisco only reinforces this mixed outcome. Although he is the son of a squatter, Clarence is the only character poised to inherit the future at the end of the novel—we learn that, once settled in San Francisco, he is "worth twelve million dollars"—but his work in business represents the only financially feasible future possible, other than the exploitative railroad, another business venture (Ruiz de Burton 1992, 364).[8] Clarence and the railroad owners, all American businessmen, represent the future of California; the Californios as ranchers (and indeed ranching itself) have slipped into the past.[9]

## On the Aftermath: Space, Ethos, and *The Plum Plum Pickers*

Nowhere is the complicated, fluid, and contradictory process of ethnic affiliation more evident than in *The Squatter and the Don*'s depiction of the Alamars' relationship to space, in the way that (as scholars of critical regionalism have shown) even "land" in the material sense can "ground" feelings of belonging, emotional identification, security (see, e.g., Hsu 2010, 7, 173, 177). It is in this vein that many Chicano literary scholars have argued that the novel's apparent eco-consciousness offers an avenue through which to articulate racial persecution and marginalization. In this reading Ruiz de Burton aligns environmental misuse and ethnic disenfranchisement to emphasize how land and ethnicity bear witness to a parallel exploitation; as Raúl Homero Villa (2000, 2) argues, exploiting Chicanos via geographical re-ordering reveals "manifestations of the 'spatial practice' of the new American rulers of the land" that unfairly privilege one ethnicity over another. Because, as Teresa McKenna (1997, 10) argues, "the Mexican is asked to feel not only like an immigrant in his or her own land, but like an alien in society as well," the novel's seeming conflation of space and national identification weighs particularly heavily on the growth of the Chicano ethos.

However, the novel's ostensible "Chicano eco-consciousness" is not quite so one-dimensional in the first place. Ecological awareness and national identities are indeed intertwined in the novel, yet they often cast quite different ripples on characters' lives. That is, Ruiz de Burton braids these two forms of spatial affiliation and consciousness; disentangling them, however, unveils how legally sanctioned labor in specific spaces grants national belonging and power through monetary and capital gain. The latter part of the novel on these legal maneuvers suggests that land is most important for those civic and economic benefits, although the consequences of using land for profit and national identity are again dire. In other words, rather than privileging ethnic or ecological awareness as such, Ruiz de Burton documents a series of losses that can result when individuals rely on national belonging for financial stability and identity. In her novel, nationally coded changes to spatial belonging, such as those affected by land laws, ultimately consume the Chicano ethos and identity. In these ways, she articulates a history very relevant, as I will show, to continuing discussions of that ethos.

For Ruiz de Burton the laws that codify national lines, to begin with, reward not environmental but financial insight. National belonging and political power are key to economic security and so take precedence over ecological health. As Don Mariano explains to Clarence,

> "California was expected to be filled with a population of farmers, of industrious settlers who would have votes and would want their one hundred and sixty acres of each of the best land to be had. And as our legislators thought that we, the Spano-American natives, had the best lands, and but few votes, there was nothing else to be done but to despoil us, to take our lands and give them to the coming population. . . . Then the cry was raised that our land grants were too large; that a few lazy, thriftless, ignorant natives, holding such large tracts of land, would be a hindrance to

the prosperity of the State, because such lazy people would never cultivate their lands, and were even too sluggish to sell them. . . . The settlers want the lands of the lazy, the thriftless Spaniards. Such good-for-nothing, helpless wretches are not fit to own such lordly tracts of land." (Ruiz de Burton 1992, 175)

In this explanation, even though Don Mariano frames land as something to "cultivate" for financial gain, American lawmakers argue that "lazy" and "thriftless" Spaniards would not do so. In their view, American settlers perform the "right" kind of labor, while Spanish citizens seem to perform an outdated, supposedly unprofitable form of labor. Land use, in other words, gives the U.S. government a foundation for the civic marginalization of the Californio population. And as I have shown, railroad expansion likewise displaces them from power and belonging. Ironically, even Clarence's rival plan to have the rail spur run through San Diego effectively sidelines the region's environmental well-being. As George Mechlin says to Stanford, "'We have plenty of national resources, which, if developed, would make plenty of business'" (313). These railroad politics thus trouble any one-dimensional claim to Ruiz de Burton's eco-consciousness.[10]

Calling attention to this shift in perspective between space as ecological and space as nation also troubles the link between class and environmentally sound labor practices that the novel advocates early on. For instance, early in the book even the squatters make their pitch in climatological terms: "'Our perfect climate, the fine sloping ground of our town site, our eucalyptus trees, sea breezes and mountain air, make San Diego a most healthy little city. . . . All we want now is a little stimulus of business prosperity, and the railroad is sure to bring us that. Then San Diego will be the best place on the coast for a residence'" (73). Yet before long the link here between profit and environment bodes poorly for attentive land use in the future. Later in the novel Don Mariano, Mechlin, and

Holman petition Leland Stanford to build a railroad through San Diego, but the Don does so having abandoned his ecological grounding: "'[H]aving lost all my cattle, I have only my land to rely on for a living—nothing else. Hence my great anxiety to have the Texas Pacific. My land will be very valuable if we have a railroad and our county becomes more settled; but if not, my land, like everybody else's land in our county, will be unsaleable, worthless. A railroad soon is our only salvation'" (315-16). Whereas once Don Mariano objected to more settlers on the basis of their impact on his land (and he wanted the settlers already there to practice his kind of labor), now he sees their financial benefit. As such, land becomes an object valued for how financially fungible it is. Preserving class and national stability, and thus space as nationalized capital, outweighs environmental attention. Ultimately, the novel's ethos focuses any Chicano sense of belonging on the financial potential of San Diego and so resituates identity in national and civic terms.[11]

Moreover, throughout her novel Ruiz de Burton reaffirms that the rewriting of spatial boundaries effectively concretizes the nationality of the squatters as Americans and erases the national identity of the Californios. Since land rights now privilege those who enact and benefit from these laws, they conversely become a means of civic dispossession. As I have suggested, the novel's own braided form, which weaves together legal rhetoric with more conventional romantic storytelling, mimics these intersections to underscore that land is most *legally* significant (acquires the most power) when it is sanctioned by a nation. In fact Ruiz de Burton quotes the actual text of the California Land Act of 1872 to call attention to the act's focus on landownership as an avenue to legalized national belonging:

With a date of February 14, 1872, the Honorable Legislature of California passed a law "*To protect agriculture and to prevent the trespassing of animals upon private property in the County of Los Angeles, and the County of San Diego, and parts of Monterey County.*"

In the very first section it recited that "every owner or *occupant* of land, *whether it is enclosed or not*," could take up cattle found in said land, etc., etc. It was not stated to be necessary that the *occupant* should have a good title. All that was required seemed to be that he should *claim to be an occupant* of land, no matter who was the owner. (80; original emphases)

The twofold legislative reason behind this act—to bring in settlers who could claim land under federal law and then become voting U.S. citizens—affirms the intersections between land and citizenry, and spatial boundaries are pivotal: the Californios stand in contrast to those who own "*private property in the County of Los Angeles, and the County of San Diego, and parts of Monterey County*." The law posits that land has power when treated as national space, not ecological space. As Clarence observes, "'it would have been better to pass a law of confiscation . . . [the law targets] the most defenseless, the most powerless of our citizens—the orphaned Spano-Americans'" (103).

Read alongside one another, these legal documents, discussions about the railroad, and discussions about the (legal) use of space not only situate California's political history at the novel's core; they also use that core to comment on the Chicano ethos and national identity. Driven to desperate measures because of these unfair socioeconomic developments, the novel's Californios must construct a relationship to land that leverages it for class and national power. The specific class identity this relationship revolves around suggests that *The Squatter and the Don*'s early incarnation of a Chicano ethos draws from the political issues surrounding space. And because that space is so crowded with issues of national belonging and security, there is no space for ethnic solidarity—nor a strategic need for it. In order to prove that the Californio upper class deserves its rights, Ruiz de Burton feels she must pit that population against its ineffective Mexican homeland, and those who would identify with it. The Californios, in other words, must feel different. Ironically, however, the Alamars end up losing the markers of identity that had made them Californios and thus *do* become the dispossessed children of Mexico, abandoned by their home country and left to falter in a hostile new nation.

As I have suggested, a lack of awareness of the history above continued to shape the Chicano experience, often chaining its ethos to static or one-dimensional conceptions of nationality and even class dispossession. For instance, Raymond Barrio's 1969 novel *The Plum Plum Pickers* looks at the long-term effects that land, viewed as nationalized capital, has on class politics and the Chicano ethos in the Santa Clara Valley of California—a space ecologically similar to Ruiz de Burton's San Diego. In *The Plum Plum Pickers*, the dispossessed Mexican Americans who are now manual laborers in American fruit orchards inherit the dispossession of the Californios, the landed gentry who had once employed such laborers; meanwhile, the Anglo owners of the fields represent the lineage of the Anglo settlers from *The Squatter and the Don*. And doubly ironic, Don Mariano's charge to the squatters—to prosper by planting fruit—is realized in the exploitative employment practices of the California fruit-picking industry, led by Frederick C. Turner, owner of the Western Grande Compound; Morton J. Quill, Turner's manager and warden; and Roberto Morales, the head labor contractor. Together, Turner and Quill represent the now-landowning Anglos who control the fate of Mexican migrant workers, while Morales represents the only (painful) option for Chicano workers who want to better their class status: to exploit those of their own ethnicity. Turner sits at the top of this food chain, and his power rests on control of the land, which he acquires because of the capital and class status his nationality permits. That control also grants him the power to imprison the novel's Mexican workers by forcing them to interact with land only as their work environment, as they are barred from national citizenship and class mobility. However, this novel does more than replicate the familiar story of class dispossession and Chicano belonging. Indeed, reading Barrio's novel alongside Ruiz de Burton's suggests that *The Squatter and the Don*'s earlier ethos-in-becoming took hold on even more infertile soil, a turnabout that further eroded the elements of ethos and ethnic identity.

Barrio does reaffirm familiar, fully understandable claims about the politics of the Chicano laborer's ethnic dispossession—indeed, what little critical work there is on the novel largely concerns the proletarian thrust of *The Plum Plum Pickers* (see Miller 1976). Barrio's Turner recognizes the necessity of controlling space in order to control individuals and their potential for personal and capital gain. To a fellow landowner he says, "'You've got to keep control over every single square inch of soil. You don't let 'em plant one goddem single stalk of corn or boom you're in trouble'" (Barrio 1971, 79). Nevertheless, the narrative's discussion of national belonging, especially in light of its depiction of labor, complicates broad assumptions about the Chicano ethos. In particular, California's long historical connection to a defunct Mexico is reflected in the novel's depiction of unstable futures for adults—who are figured as childlike—and children alike, both of whom are preoccupied by their uncertain national belonging. Alienated from land and nationality, these characters are hindered from navigating a mature and productive relationship within their socioeconomic and environmental surroundings. Potentially that relationship could shape a productive Chicano ethos; instead, it redirects those energies to worries about civic security.

Like Ruiz de Burton, Barrio metaphorically links a defunct Mexican government to childhood and immaturity; he also connects the novel's "children of Mexico" to a damaged Mexican ecology. For instance, Lupe Gutiérrez, one of the book's central characters, recalls her childhood in Mexico as one doubly marked by illness and ignorance: "There had been disease and hunger in her childhood. . . . Two of her little brothers had died as small boys. And ignorance. Here in America she dreamed of a chance of keeping her children in school so they would not suffer from her ignorance. Every family back home had children who had died of some sickness or another" (123). Similarly, Lupe grows an avocado plant that she identifies with, that "originated in her homeland, in southern Mexico": "Like herself. Another child. A child of the earth. An earthling. This treelet would never reach maturity. She knew that. She lost too many others. It would never bear fruit. The odds were too great against it. It would never shade her nor her children" (62, 63). And her children suffer a similar fate; they are consigned to the restrictive labor of their parents, even anticipating their fate in their play: "The children enjoyed digging up the soft friendly brown earth. It was just another day and, like all days, full of wonder and stunted promises and twisted dreams" (68). The young children find happiness in playing with "the soft friendly brown earth," but that happiness is tinged by the limitations that engaging with that ecological space carries. Lupe's children enjoy, in blissful unawareness, mimicking the work she fears will lead to a destructive personal and civic relationship to both Mexico and the United States. And in response, Mexico, at its physical and political distance, can do nothing about this dispossession. The novel's children and child-like adults alike signify that stasis: Roberto Morales, as the representation of Mexico at its most "effective," captures that ineptitude because, although he is "an organization man . . . a built in toll gate . . . [h]ad he not been Mexican, he would have made a fantastic capitalist" (85). Although he has the capacity for leadership, his nationality acts as a socioeconomic tollgate, one he cannot pass through.

Nevertheless, I do feel that Barrio's take on Mexico also offers an opportunity to move beyond this familiar, one-dimensional story of class dispossession and to ask questions about how these layered elements of national belonging might contribute to the Chicano ethos. Manuel Gutiérrez and Margarita Delgado, another two of

Barrio's key characters, articulate the consequences for a personal ethos of identifying with space as nation. After Barrio casts him in terms that highlight his childlikeness—for instance, "Outwardly, physically, Manuel was rough and strong. Inside he was soft and kind and even innocent" (122)—Manuel asks himself "WHAT AM I?":

Am I a rotting weed?
Am I no good?
Am I indeed a proud Mexican?
Am I indecent?
Am I Indian?
Or am I undemocratic?
Am I American citizen?
Am I—ignorant? (158)

Here Manuel runs through a number of identities—linked to ecology, nation, ethnicity, citizenship—that could contribute to a sense of personal ethos. Yet ultimately he lands on a far more uncertain question that betrays his lack of confidence in his own identity: "Am I—ignorant?" Margarita—a young woman, and so another child figure—also reveals her sense of national confusion and her uncertain Chicano ethos:

What was the good of being born a perfectly good, honest, private, legal citizen of the United States of America if everyone was going to snarl Mexican in your face like it was some dirty word? Where did she belong then? Back in her mother's hometown? Her father's? . . . But what if she wasn't from any of those places either? What then? She didn't belong there, in old Mexico, either. She was California born. California . . . which was once Mexico. California . . . which once belonged to her people, for hundreds and thousands of years. And now she didn't belong. In Mexico, on her two brief visits, the native Mexicans there always considered her as an American. (102)

Each of these moments draws attention to how U.S. citizenship only seems to make a Chicano ethos more uncertain. Where do Mexican American citizens of California belong, both seem to ask, and what is Mexico's role in that belonging? Neither Manuel nor Margarita knows how to identify themselves, despite their civic membership in the United States and their cultural affiliations with Mexico. Their uncertainty is rooted in a deeper ignorance of Chicano history and their racial and ethnic heritage. And because every Chicano in the novel suffers from that condition, the novel's dialogue about a Chicano historical ethos and its relationship to space is also diminished. Even Lupe, who, according to Francisco A. Lomelí (1984), develops the most complete Mexican historical memory in the novel, lacks the cultural-historical memory necessary to extract her family from the destructive cycle of working-class migrant labor.

Moreover, when Manuel fails to recognize the historical significance of his work above the Diablo range, that unawareness gestures toward the persisting divide between land as nation and land as ecology: "What Manuel couldn't really know was that he was completing yet another arc in the unending circle that had been started two hundred years before—for even the memory of history was also robbed from him. . . . Both don Gaspar and don Manuel were landlords and landless at precisely the same instant of viewing all this heady beauty" (Barrio 1971, 90–91). As an ecological space, the Diablo range is somewhere Manuel and Don Gaspar belong because of Mexico's historical connection to it. However, the men are "landless" because that space ultimately becomes American. Land in the novel thus exists doubly as an environment in which one can live and work and as a nation to which one belongs. And yet those ignorant of the background of either are fettered to the most marginalized of existences in relation to both.

These moments also point to the same kind of disenfranchisement from nation that the Alamars of *The Squatter and the Don* suffer. Lupe, Manuel, and Margarita all keenly feel the oppositional tugs of a damaging American nationalism, which chains them logistically to poorly paid manual labor on ecological land, and an ineffective Mexican nationalism, which chains them to a national space and government that cannot act on their behalf. Their civic identities are thus locked to the land on which they work. Those forces ultimately prevent any Chicano characters in the novel from being able to enlist national identity to better their class or working situation. Moreover, that twofold pressure limits any significant growth of a Chicano ethos because those who could construct that ethos cannot move beyond the problem of national belonging. Thus, if the abandoned children of Mexico—the conceit that Ruiz de Burton articulates—find historical and contemporary purchase in Barrio's work, it ultimately rehearses a long tradition of national identity overshadowing a more comprehensive Chicano cultural history. In other words, in both Ruiz de Burton's and Barrio's novels, ethnicity becomes a story of those struggling to use U.S. or Mexican citizenship to gain legal entitlement, or what few rights they are afforded in that contested middle ground. And because those limited rights primarily orbit exploitative labor on the land, Chicano and environmental misuse and abuse become linked together. Thus, in Barrio's telling, California—"the richest, the greatest, most productive chunk of rich earth in the world"—is tethered to "agricultural production . . . as the U.S. headed toward its glorious 21st century, combining big land combines with perpetual migrant slavism" (80–81). A large part of California's richness is ecological, yet the benefits of that wealth are national and capital privileges enjoyed by Anglo-American citizens.

Therefore, if, as Villa (2000, 1) argues, the long-term "geographic displacement" of Chicanos from multiple national and cultural grounds has "been an essential element of Chicanos' social identity," then both Ruiz de Burton's and Barrio's novels speak to a broader problem inherent to that ethos. A comprehensive, thoughtful debate over this productive ethos can only proceed from a fuller understanding of the interwoven historical and contemporary elements of ethnicity, rights, environment, culture, nationalism, gender—the list goes on—that literary depictions such as these can detail. And thus I would return to González's initial question—"Can a novel in which the narrator unabashedly refers to Native Americans and working-class mestizos in a racially derogatory manner be considered politically resistant?"—and argue that yes, it can. Through works such as Ruiz de Burton's especially, understanding a mode of resistance, its imperfect consciousness, its alliances and memberships, and its often illogical path can shed light on the uneven, messy development of a political and cultural ethos. In the context of *The Squatter and the Don*, resistance constantly changes with the socioeconomic and spatial demands California labor laws place on native Spanish Chicanos. In contrast, the more single-minded representation of resistance to socioeconomic disenfranchisement—like that in *The Plum Plum Pickers*—can lead to a reductive and one-dimensional understanding. How then can Chicano novels be resistant? Well, such a contrast might suggest that resistance is more personal than public; that consciousness and affiliations develop fluidly, unevenly, and irregularly alongside changing historical contexts; and that such an ethos can be delicately winding and untidily imperfect, responding as it does to changes in class, labor, and national boundaries.

# 3 Watching the West Erode in the 1930s

Sanora Babb's *Whose Names Are Unknown,*
Frank Waters's *Below Grass Roots*, and John Fante's
*Wait Until Spring, Bandini* and *Ask the Dust*

"This is a story about the West," writes Joe Gordon (2002, vii) in his foreword to Frank Waters's *Below Grass Roots*, "the day-to-day reality of the men and women who came to a frontier town to build homes and businesses and to raise families." And it is a story about the lived experiences of a lower-working-class family in the hostile spatial and economic climates of the 1930s—as are the other books discussed in this chapter: John Fante's *Wait Until Spring, Bandini* and *Ask the Dust* and Sanora Babb's *Whose Names Are Unknown*.[1] But Waters's novel (like the others) is also, as Gordon points out, about failure and its consequences: "it is the story, not often told, of those who failed" (ix). Unlike Steinbeck's *The Grapes of Wrath*, the popular narrative that so many readers feel captures the perseverance of the human will to succeed during the Dust Bowl and the Great Depression, these novels instead accentuate the impact of financial and ecological failure on senses of self and family. Perhaps that is part of the reason they have been largely ignored—they are overshadowed by the accessibility, ultimately uplifting message, and sheer popular-literary weight of Steinbeck's novel. As Walter Nugent (1999, 242–43) puts it, individual determination in the face of environmental and economic misery was "made legendary . . . by *The Grapes of Wrath*." That legendary aura pervades current critical scholarship and popular memory of this era in the West: critics

and wider reading publics alike gravitate toward Steinbeck's novel because it memorializes and projects hope for success rather than recognizes failure, a much more common fate during this time.[2] In other words, while the narrative is often bleak, we as readers are seduced by how in the end it celebrates the determined fortitude of the human spirit. Popular memory and critical scholarship are therefore inclined to view labor literature of the 1930s as fertile ground for stories about families and communities who come together to conquer environmental and economic hardships and so thrive as unified collectives.

But the novels of this chapter tell a different story. I want to recover them because they add dimension and depth to the literary history of the West during the Depression and Dust Bowl eras through stories of splintered communities and families—stories that uncover a hidden cross-section of 1930s politics. Read together, these novels, yoked by their depictions of hardship in the 1930s West, provide a counterpoint to Steinbeck's dry Oklahoma and fertile California, pluralize the western landscape with places that experienced this period's hardship in differing ways, and challenge traditional faith in collective labor politics. They use naturalist and realist rhetoric to paint failing conditions in a multifaceted western drylands ecosystem consisting of Oklahoma, Colorado, and the desert regions of Southern California.[3] Communities and families in these spaces break apart as they encounter economic and environmental crises that cut across party lines and trouble Popular Front–style faith that the dignity and cohesiveness of labor can restore order in more stable regions. As these novels bind economic crises to ecological crises, they recast and resituate political identity by imagining it as rooted in and fluidly responsive to spatial challenges native to specific locales. Reading these texts alongside one another thus suggests that the harsh ecological, economic, and political conditions of the drylands West in the 1930s troubled familiar leftist and liberal ideologies that valued

organized labor and New Deal–style government intervention; instead, these authors imagine labor and its structures as always dictated by intertwined and contradictory space and class politics. Representing the period's uncertainty, failure, and loss through episodes that explore daunting and constricting spaces, hard labor, and the limits of class, these novels narrate declines in choice and security that individuals and families faced as the circumstances of the Dust Bowl and the Depression dictated their lives. And, similar to the other texts of this project, these politicized thick depictions of class, labor, and space are crafted from a detailed naturalist and realist rhetorical style that responds to particular western places. That specificity unveils how individual relationships to class as a function of labor in those spaces draw out the subtle, cross-partisan nuances of fluid, kaleidoscopic western identities that played a major role in the shaping of broader national identities during the Depression.

In this moment from *Below Grass Roots*, for instance, Joseph Rogier's obsession with mining Pikes Peak reveals his anxieties about the cost of labor and its spatial challenges:

> Work on the Sylvanite progressed steadily. The shaft was down a hundred feet, commonly assumed the proper depth for a level, but Rogier was insisting on another forty feet before cutting a station. Cross-cutting would then be commenced to tap the vein traversing the property. Overhand stopping, working up on a raise instead of down on a winze, he had figured would be a good thirty percent cheaper; they could take advantage of gravity instead of having to install a small lift. . . . But it cost so much—the dom hard country rock! He had to spend half his time in town, not daring to let his business drop; it was the only source of income to carry the mine. . . . There were no mistakes made at the Sylvanite. He went over every detail a dozen times, spent half the night figuring and brooding over his plans. (Waters 2002, 114–15)

As protagonist and family patriarch, Rogier is the character whose perspectives and demeanor set the tone for both the novel and his family. Here his preoccupation with mining is less choice and more desperation as it continues to sap the family's finances. Despite his intimate knowledge of this labor, which Waters indicates through specialized mining jargon, Rogier is overwhelmed by the "great Peak . . . which destiny has marked for his own" and so dedicates his life to pursuing the wealth that may be hidden within (1). However, this wealth is merely speculative, which renders the success of mining the Peak uncertain. Rogier's certainty about the practice of his labor contrasts with and accentuates the uncertainty inherent in the space in which he labors. Moreover, as the novel progresses, scenes exploring this contrast become more frequent, gesturing toward the increasingly constricting force of Pikes Peak and the hard labor of its mining. Thus, this moment embodies a series of interlocking gears common to all four novels: the environment shapes work that should but usually does not pay off.

That equation and its inevitable feedback loop—that space dictates labor, which dictates class, which in turn determines interactions with and understandings of space—reveal crucial ways this literature weaves landscape and economics together to create fatalistic tapestries. These intersections constitute the kind of literary "superlattice" I proposed in my introduction. If you turn the nanostructure toward leftist community building, one familiar narrative emerges, and it leads to the kind of reading of labor in 1930s Depression and Dust Bowl–era space found in the work of critics like Barbara Foley, whose *Radical Representations* stands as one of the most prominent critiques of the proletarian literature of the 1930s. Foley (1993, 45) traces the national influence of the Communist Party of the United States of America and the international influence of Marxism on leftist fiction of the 1930s, arguing that both "inspire[ed] [these authors] with a sense of revolutionary possibility [while] setting the limits within which they could imag-

ine that possibility." But if you shift the political nanostructure to account for cross-partisan ideologies, a new, denser narrative lattice emerges. Reading the representation of class as a function of labor in the patchwork of spaces of the West allows for a more particularized and complicated literary portrait of the challenges and tolls that unforgiving political, ecological, economic, and working conditions placed upon individual, familial, and collective survival in the West.

Black Tuesday—October 29, 1929—most often marks the Depression's beginning, when the U.S. stock market crashed after falling steadily since September 4 of that year. Unemployment ultimately reached 25 percent as cities and rural communities alike were hit hard by the falling value of agriculture, industry, and labor. Except for New York City, Washington DC, Denver, and Los Angeles, large cities and rural areas saw populations decrease dramatically, while smaller cities and towns absorbed those who had failed in other areas. Herbert Hoover, president at the start of the Depression, pushed a number of "suggested" regulations and a few acts meant to stimulate the economy, but the broad lack of success of these ventures led to Franklin Delano Roosevelt's election in 1932. The Dust Bowl almost immediately followed Roosevelt's inauguration and inspired him to craft the New Deal, which aimed to redesign the national economy through increased government spending on programs that would not only help Americans get out of debt but also install new financial reforms and regulations.[4] Many of these components of the safety net benefited farming and banking, though numerous bills constructed to aid economic reform in agriculture by controlling supply and demand never became law. And while these policy changes encouraged farmers to lobby more aggressively for themselves, aligning government aid with private-sector demands proved arduous. During Roosevelt's first term, unemployment initially fell to between 9 and 11 percent. Although the country started to bounce back in 1934, the roughly year-long recession of June

1937–38 brought a new round of financial strain and high levels of unemployment, as much as 19 percent. Not until the beginning of World War II did the United States truly begin to recover.

The Dust Bowl, one large element of and contributing factor to the Great Depression in the United States, was a widespread drought in the southern Great Plains that enveloped the Oklahoma and Texas Panhandles, about one-fifth of Colorado, half of Kansas, and a slice of eastern New Mexico from roughly 1932 through the late 1930s. In Brad Lookingbill's (2001, 4) words, "Desertification [in the Dust Bowl] represented a sign of failure and would continue to plague a capitalist culture" that crossed party lines. That area was viciously difficult and primed to suffer the worst effects of the Dust Bowl. As Donald Worster (1979) comments,

> The Southern Plains are a vast austerity. They sprawl over more than 100 million acres, including parts of five states—Kansas, Colorado, New Mexico, Oklahoma, and Texas. Nothing that lives finds life easy under their severe skies; the weather has a nasty habit of turning harsh and violent just when things are getting comfortable. Failure to adapt to these rigors has been a common experience for Americans, so that the plains have become our cultural boneyard, where the evidences of bad judgment and misplaced schemes lie strewn about like bleached skulls. Few of us want to live in the region now. There is too much wind, dirt, flatness, space, barbed wire, drought, uncertainty, hard work. Better to fly over it with the shades pulled down. (3)

The legacy of poor wheat-farming practices that contributed to the Dust Bowl had roots in notions of American expansion and one's right to profit from land. In Worster's elegant summary, "Americans blazed their way across a richly endowed continent with a ruthless, devastating efficiency," while paying little attention to the need to work carefully an environment with light topsoil, little rainfall, and strong winds, all of which set up the plains to "unexpectedly

become a prime example of an older America that had failed" (4, 100). Following an increase in the price of grain during World War I, farmers began ripping up natural grasses, which protected the delicate topsoil from high winds and regular drought, on a larger scale to plant more wheat and make more money. The results were disastrous. Massive dust storms became regular occurrences that choked land and livestock, infiltrated houses, and ruined agriculture. Those who lived on farms found their previous work unsustainable and often turned to doing migrant labor, such as picking fruit and cotton in California. And while the government provided housing and camps at these temporary workplaces and encouraged labor unions, such measures were generally ineffective against the exploitative practices of those who owned the workplaces.

All four of the novels discussed in this chapter respond to one or both of these historical moments. Waters's novel is set in the Pikes Peak district of Colorado in about 1937, at the tail end of the Depression; Fante's novels also take place in the late 1930s and are set in the fictional town of Rocklin, Colorado, modeled after Colorado Springs, and in Los Angeles; Babb's novel takes place in Cimarron County, Oklahoma, and in California and begins in the early 1930s. Covering interrelated but distinct spaces affected by the crises of the time, these novels, when read alongside one another, showcase how the tightly linked economic and ecological failures of the Dust Bowl and Depression shook traditional partisan ideologies of cooperative labor and government intervention. At the same time, however, because not all four novels grapple with the same ecological and economic crises—Waters's novel, for instance, deals with the Depression but its place is untouched by the Dust Bowl—they also showcase a multitude of western experiences with places in crisis, a plurality that has been obscured by the dominance of *The Grapes of Wrath* in critical discussions of western literature of the 1930s. Through shared naturalist and realist episodes and metaphors of uncertainty, loss, and desperation in the face of overwhelming cir-

cumstances—of space, class, and labor—these novels contribute to a more historically precise, zoomed-in literary portrait of those who failed in the West in the 1930s, a strain of American literature still seeking its rightful place in critical discourse and popular memory.[5]

## On Space

Each novel details damaged, overwhelming, and constrictive ecological and domestic spaces that communicate an uncertainty about the future instigated by the Depression and the Dust Bowl. These broken, unreliable spaces engulf the novels' characters in their vastness and in the futility of trying to work productively in them. When, in Fante's *Ask the Dust*, Sammy (one of the novel's peripheral characters) goes to Joshua Tree to die, Arturo, the protagonist, and his love interest, Camilla, go to find him in the vast California desert—a naturalist landscape of inevitable devastation far from Steinbeck's California of fertile hope:

> By dawn we were in a land of grey desolation, of cactus and sagebrush and Joshua trees, a desert where the sand was scarce and the whole vast plain was pimpled with tumbled rocks and scarred by stumpy little hills. Then we turned off the main highway and entered a wagon trail clogged with boulders and rarely used. The road rose and fell to the rhythm of the listless hills. It was daylight when we came to a region of canyons and steep gulches, twenty miles in the interior of the Mojave Desert. There below us was where Sammy lived, and Camilla pointed to a squat adobe shack planted at the bottom of three sharp hills. It was at the very edge of a sandy plain. To the east the plain spread away infinitely. (Fante 1980, 136)

When they arrive, Sammy answers the door, "eyes grey and dazed, the hair in ruins across his forehead. . . . He was tall, gaunt, a cadaver of a man, tanned almost to blackness" (136–37). The overwhelming desert, described in terms that render it both indifferent and hos-

tile, has seeped into Sammy and ruined his health. The description of the desert that precedes Arturo's recognition of Sammy's uncertain future is itself tinged with a dreary apathy that reinforces this uncertainty. And the land is also constrictive in its overpowering, depressing openness. Depicted as an ugly, almost totally open space, its unfortunate features (pimples, scars, listless and desolate qualities) bar the characters and the reader from feeling engaged with or energized by it or their place in it. Later in the novel Arturo looks out over the desert and sees that "[a]cross the desolation lay a supreme indifference. . . . You could die, but the desert would hide the secret of your death, it would remain after you, to cover your memory with ageless wind of heat and cold" (164). The listless, physically desolate Sammy, confined to his hovel, represents the desert in human form and the effect of that desert on the human form.

Moreover, when he begins to lose his health, Sammy goes to the desert to work, where "he lived in a shack, writing feverishly" (116). Health and work are yoked together, and Fante's descriptions of both reflect the desolate landscape. In the context of the Great Depression, Sammy's focus on profit—he is "interested in the financial side of writing more than in writing itself"—also gestures toward a loss of self and choice in the darkness of poverty, reinforced by his shabby condition (138). Arturo himself experiences a similar moment when a drunken woman who lives in the same hotel as he does criticizes his writing and causes him to disparage his situation: "the absurdity of a hopelessly bad writer like myself buried in a cheap hotel in Los Angeles, California, of all places, writing banal things the world would never read and never get a chance to forget" (81). Again, personal situations and living conditions reflect one another in ways that transcend political ideology. When read in the context of Fante's depictions of LA, the dark sense of anonymity and decay becomes even more poignantly biting. LA is a "sad flower in the sand," a place of "frame houses reeking with murder stories" and drab scenery; Arturo recalls one night when

"I went up to my room, up the dusty stairs of Bunker Hill, past the soot-covered frame buildings and along that dark street, sand and oil and grease choking the futile palm trees standing like dying prisoners, chained to a little plot of ground with black pavement hiding their feet. Dust and old buildings and old people sitting at windows" (13, 12, 45). Rather than being the glitzy land of opportunity he loved at first, LA is a drab, dirty, depressing reminder of his personal and financial struggles as a writer. Arturo himself makes that connection when an earthquake literally tears LA apart; he takes the widespread destruction as a sign that his lifestyle and working habits are destructive and must change: "This was the turning point. This was for me, a warning for Arturo Bandini" (99).

The disappointment of California ecology plays a similar role in Babb's *Whose Names Are Unknown*. When the Dunnes, the central family in the novel, decide to leave their Dust Bowl–ravaged home in Cimarron County, Oklahoma, they are lured by the prospect of a friendlier space and better working and living conditions in Imperial County, California—a prospect that does not bring immediate success. Mrs. Starwood, an older neighbor who spearheads the move, dreams that "[m]aybe someday I'll have a little farm in California" but still recognizes the working and financial challenges that lie ahead: "We got to pick a lot of fruit though" (Babb 2004, 124). These dreams are quickly compromised as the Dunnes, Mrs. Starwood, and Frieda (a young woman from their hometown who comes along to California) recognize frightening ecological similarities between California and Oklahoma: "The shadow of the car slid along the east side of the highway, blotting the sagebrush and the cracked dry earth. . . . Jagging crazily through the great desert, the yawning, parched mouths of narrow gullies showed their sandy tongues. . . . Julia leaned wearily against the back of the seat. . . . Her head was tied with a cotton bandana to keep the dust from her hair" (133). Although the dust here comes from the desert climate of Southern California, it wears on the characters' psyches and feelings about space because it reminds them of conditions back in Oklahoma. The California desert, described in naturalist terms as a palpable force of decay and depression, is linked to the hard labor of cotton and fruit picking—"Damn cotton picking will break your back," in Milt Dunne's words—and thus to the difficulties they had in Oklahoma (133). When they move on from the desert, the next town is no better. Calipatria presents "an uninteresting prospect. The gray stone buildings squatted along the dusty streets like tough beetles" (134). Their attitudes toward this space color their perception about future possibilities, as Mrs. Starwood reflects on the distance between their expectations and the truth: "Holy Moses! This is a lonesome-looking place. . . . Suppose we been hearing things again?" (135).

California, in both Fante's and Babb's novels, represents a better hope for the future—as it did for many migrant working families during the Dust Bowl—that is ultimately foreclosed, both metaphorically and literally, by its spatial conditions. The better futures that both the Dunnes and Arturo Bandini sought in California turn into uncertain futures reinforced and reflected by indifferent and hostile landscapes. This loss of future stability points to broader losses of the Great Depression and the Dust Bowl. While every family in the area suffered the effects of inclement weather and hostile land, in these novels such material hardships not only cast doubt on the future but also render relationships among the individual members of the families themselves more uncertain, breaking ties that were thought unbreakable. In *Whose Names Are Unknown*, Milt's father elects to stay behind on the farm in Oklahoma—a decision that depresses him and the rest of the family—and his character is not heard from again. In *Wait Until Spring, Bandini*, Arturo's father, Svevo Bandini, conducts a complicated affair around Christmas that comprises both sexual and class transgression, tearing his marriage and domestic space apart: "The house lost its identity now. . . . The world of inanimate things found voice, conversed with the old house, and the house chattered with the cronish delight of the discontent within its walls" (Fante 1983, 72). In *Ask the Dust*, Arturo's constant poverty and subsequent relentless begging strain his already estranged relationship with his parents. And in *Below Grass Roots*, Rogier's desperate obsession with mining and Pikes Peak literally breaks his family when his son-in-law, Cable, dies because of the effects of mining. In each case the constricting conditions of space figure the irreparable stress placed on family structure during the Depression and the Dust Bowl, gesturing toward yet another loss of certainty—that of the family bond. And filtering these losses through individual actions pushes against the strength of community that other, sunnier narratives of the era portray via the success of the broader political identity of the collective.

Even when California offers relatively favorable working conditions compared to the Dust Bowl's more ecologically unsound spaces, Fante's naturalist depictions of its spatial realities disable a viable working life in that space. Although superficially California's fertile spaces offer better chances for financial and familial success, these spaces are difficult to adjust to and take their own toll on those who inhabit them. When Arturo finds Camilla at the end of *Ask the Dust*, he realizes that "[s]he couldn't stay in Los Angeles. She needed a rest . . . Laguna Beach! That was the place for her" (Fante 1980, 156). And he finds what he imagines is the perfect place, a direct opposition to the overwhelming grind and difficulty of Depression-era Los Angeles: "A tender day, a sky like the sea, the sea like the sky. On the left, golden hills, the gold of winter . . . Camilla's land, Camilla's home. . . . The house I liked was a twin-gabled place, with a white picket fence around it, not fifty yards from the shore. The backyard was a bed of white sand. It was well furnished, full of bright curtains and water-colors" (159). But Camilla fails to accept the conditions of her new home and instead disappears into the desert, where Arturo is unable to find her. As the house stands in stark contrast to every other space of the novel, it represents a spatial salvation; thus Camilla's and then Arturo's departures mark the more gentle landscape as a place to which neither belongs. Salvation, it turns out, cannot hinge merely on location. Instead, the twin-gabled house gives way to the desert, which in comparison has "no roads, no towns, no human life . . . nothing but wasteland for almost a hundred miles" (164). Losing Camilla to the overwhelming, desolate desert—already a place of uncertainty and death in the novel—cuts from his life the possibility of her and the certainty she represents. Moreover, she leaves Arturo's promise of a steady income and quiet life in an actual house, where they could live as "brother and sister," which undermines Arturo's last hope for firm spatial and family structures in the novel (156). At the end of the novel, he "got back in the car, started the engine, and drove back to Los Angeles," which puts Arturo on the move through space, rather than rooted in place. Coupled with his move from the house back to the desert and then farther back to LA, the end of the novel reinforces Arturo's loss of choice and security and his uncertain future on the horizon (165)

If Arturo's final move through overwhelming, unfriendly space symbolizes loss and uncertainty, the Rogier family's rootedness in the same kind of highly detailed space signifies a similar loss of perspective and individual power in *Below Grass Roots*. The title alone suggests that the novel takes shape around spatial entrenchment, especially when read alongside Rogier's return to the mountain at the beginning:

> [He] glimpse[s] again, after an absence of only months, that great Peak rising over the ears of his team; to watch it take shape above the forested slopes of pine and spruce and sparse aspen, above the frost-shattered granite of timberline; to see it stand at last an imperturbable sentinel on the crest of the Great Divide which separates earth and heaven as it does dreamless sleep and wakeful consciousness—to meet it thus, face to face, was to

arouse in Rogier a resurgence of those inexpressible thoughts and conflicting emotions provoked always in a man who returns to a realm which destiny has marked for his own. (Waters 2002, 1)

Rogier sees the Peak literally above all other elements of nature, which accentuates its prominence in his mind. Here the Peak subsumes humanity and the nature around it, marking the mountain early in the text as the most deterministic space in the region. The towns at the base of the mountain similarly compose "not so much a landscape as a state of mind" that reflects the scarring and overwhelming presence of the Peak:

> the high bare hills seamed with gulches, hirsute with gallows frames, smokestacks, and shaft houses, corroded by glory holes and splotched with ore dumps; the shabby little towns cluttering the gulches with squalid shanties and whose stubby streets were blocked by canyon walls or mountainous tailing dumps; the refuse-laden gullies below and the dizzily winding roads and railroad spurs above; the pale sparse aspen groves and dark patches of pines, the clouds filling the canyon; and rising above all, the snowy summit of the Peak itself. (174)

Here the mountain controls the mood and shape of both nature and human-made structures; it engulfs the region in its vastness and casts a decaying shade on the space around it. Rogier even sees the mountain's influence when union strikes derail mining work and bring violence to the area: "Enveloped by black clouds through which protruded only its pale summit, it looked like a ghastly spider waiting in its web. . . . [I]t looked like the bloodless face of a giant underwater squid spewing out its inkish black fluid to poison all it touched" (35–36). Rather than allowing for the viability of communitarian impulses based on shared labor, the Peak envelops and poisons those who live in the space it dominates, turning them dark and violent. The Peak's overpowering presence thus seeps into every aspect of life, especially labor-related issues, foreclosing the kind of proletarian politics common in literature of the period.

Furthermore, Rogier reasons that the land inspires violence because it is "raped and gutted earth that finally had turned on those who thought themselves its masters," lending it an autonomous, naturalist authority that resonates with the acceptance of nature's power—authority that ultimately destroys characters' sense of self (35). As one of those would-be masters, Rogier initially returns to "a realm which destiny has marked for his own," a space that he feels connected to and as if he can control. But ecological reality undermines his senses of ownership, mastery, and destiny and instead overwhelms Rogier so completely that his identity collapses into the Peak: "He had been born for this, geological eras, biological ages ago. Born as an incipient mammal to grow into an individual egohood only to seek and to find at last that universal self which combined within it both himself and the massive Peak whose granite armor he was meant to pierce" (74). Rogier's diminished sense of self relies on the overwhelming force of labor and is divorced from the community of miners with whom he works. By this time in the novel, Rogier ceases to understand himself as an individual outside his obsession with the Peak and its mining—for instance, he notes that both his and the mountain's "future lay in depth" (74). Even earlier, he identifies with the Peak in a particularly disturbing way: "It looked, from where he sat at 11,000 feet, as close as a face in the mirror, one whose features he knew better than his own" (3). In these two moments Rogier yokes his own biology and humanness to inhuman rock, deeply rooting himself as a natural extension of the mountain itself, which is unfriendly and brings no success or pleasure. That link reflects his loss of choice and community: because Rogier believes destiny and biology have joined him to the Peak, he dedicates himself to it with so much of his time and energy that he now does not choose but feels "meant" to pierce the mountain, losing his individual humanity.

Working the mountain's mines successfully of course turns out to be an impossible goal that ruins the family's stability. Ona and Mrs. Rogier dream of moving to town and buying "a fancy place like those in the North End with an iron fence and statues on the lawn," but the desire of Rogier and Cable (Rogier's son-in-law and Ona's husband) to live near the mine and attend obsessively to its needs confines the family to brutal spaces and shakes their relationships with one another (79). When Cable takes Ona and their children to see their new plot of land near the mine, Ona is dismayed: "She could see well enough the dry prairies stretching eastward, brown and unfenced; the rough dirt road crawling so far back to town . . . [she] covered her mouth with a handkerchief and snuggled Leona against her breast to protect her from a dust devil that came whirling across the plains" and advises Cable "we ought to be in town, closer to water and trees and where the children can get to school" (79). Her dislike of the place is a dislike of an unfriendly, difficult land that does not provide the necessities to sustain a family. Moreover, Cable further shakes their familial stability when he insists they abandon that plot to move closer to the mine to another depressing, uncomfortable, and difficult place— one they cannot leave. The new house is "set on the street parallel to the high railroad embankment," and so the "shrill blast of the [train] whistle [and] . . . the piercing scream of brakes" are heard and the "roar of the train [shakes] the house" on the hour (173). Living there is a consequence of the mine that affects the entire family structure—which March, Cable and Ona's son, unknowingly pinpoints one evening while the family sits silent in the living room: "Here he sensed an ungiving bluntness, a tautness in the very air" (175).

Cable's Depression-era obsession with mining the Peak for profit saps him of energy and destroys his sense of self as well as his place in the family. Ultimately the Peak and its work kill Cable; when March is told to go to his grandfather's house so that he does not witness Cable dying, his entrance reflects the tension the Peak places on his whole family: "The boy did not move or speak. He clenched his teeth in a vain effort to stop the echo of a rattle that shook his whole body" (241). Cable's death is explicitly marked by the Peak—behind his death are "the same enigmatic mountains, . . . the same curse that had killed Tom [and] old man Reynolds" (244)—as is Ona's realization that losing Cable means losing herself as well: "Henceforth she was to be not an individual but a part, indistinguishable from those others who had failed to escape their ancestral womb" (243). Family represents not the ties that bind but the ties that constrict, because those ties are rooted to a place that brings ruin and ends in death. Against the grain of popular memories and traditional literature of the 1930s, Cable's death thus illustrates how individuals can become divided over linked ecological and economic hardship, rather than roused to achieve a common goal.

The Dunnes in Babb's *Whose Names Are Unknown* suffer similar challenges and constraints placed on their family structure because they are trapped in and overwhelmed by a place consumed by the Dust Bowl. When the dust becomes particularly heavy at the Dunne farm, Babb (2004, 77–78) calls it "a new attack of nature . . . an evil monster coming on in mysterious, footless silence. It was magnificent and horrible like a nightmare of destiny towering over their slight world that had every day before this impressed upon them its vast unconquerable might." Here she uses naturalist rhetoric similar to that of Waters and highlights the uncontrollable force of space on human life, despite efforts at cultivation. Like Rogier, Babb's patriarchs—Milt and his father—stand between awe and fear of the dust storms. And also like Rogier, this straddling comes about from a sense of connection to and ownership of the land that men individually express early in the novel: "They looked at the land they had planted the day before, and the land they would plant this day, and they felt a sense of possession growing in them for the piece of earth that was theirs" (6). But, again as in Waters's novel, that sense of mastery over an overwhelming space brings uncertainty and failure into their lives. Later Milt's father recalls what living in that space for so long has taught him and paints a very different picture: "I got nothing for my work, and I ain't the only one. . . . I may lose my farm and then there's no place to go. No more new land, no more free gold out west" (101). As the Dust Bowl progresses, outlooks on the present and the future change and reflect the failures of that time and place. Here ownership does not come easy, given present circumstances. Instead it brings a host of problems—failure, loss, uncertainty—to entire families and ultimately undoes the notion of communal work on difficult land.

As the climate and land get harder to manage, the characters' reactions and perspectives get more desperate, reflecting a continued failure of secure living patterns. Lives are scarred by dust and dirt, homes and living patterns upended by the consistency of the Dust Bowl and the relative inconsistency of everything else. Julia, Milt Dunne's wife, keeps a journal of the weather, and her naturalist-like records are poignantly summed up by her only comment on April 5: "Today is a terror" (90). On April 10 she writes,

> Blowing all night again and all day today. Got up at 5:30, very dark and dirty. At nine o'clock a car stopped and people wanted a drink. Looked like bandits with noses and mouths tied up, faces and hair dirty, and clothes covered. They told us people in town were asked over radio to keep porch lights on overnight to aid someone who might have to get out. Said hospitals refuse to operate on anyone unless it's life or death. Some people getting dust pneumonia. 10 a.m. Just lighted lamp, fierce dark at times. Hope those people get where they are going safely. (91)

The poor health and general condition of those whom Julia meets indicate how such a space constrains all who live there. She recognizes the wider scope of these problems too: "It is just terrible for everyone. The drought years are bad enough but this is almost more than people can stand on top of being so poor from the depression and all. . . . If the land is ruined we can't just sit here and starve" (93). Linking the Dust Bowl to the economic troubles of the Depression, she accentuates the devastating link between financial and ecological ruin. The dust is a relentless force that saps certainty from everyone's lives and ruins not just the land and income but families as well; the journal ends when a neighbor, Mr. Starwood, dies alone, trapped overnight in his truck by a dust storm. The event prompts Julia to stop writing: "No use to keep writing on dust, dust, dust. Seems it will outlast us" (95). Her hopelessness here points to the overwhelming insistency of the Dust Bowl, specifically how it can cause even the most hopeful to admit defeat or the most secure community or family to fail.

When Milt and Julia finally decide to take the family, along with Mrs. Starwood and Frieda, to California, their move recognizes that the unforgiving financial and ecological consequences of the Dust Bowl and the Depression ultimately become too much for even the most stalwart: "The never-settled hearts of these pioneer-bred people, working hard to make a lifelong home in an unrelenting land, stirred uneasily and dreamed of newer lands" (62). Milt's father stays in that "unrelenting land" that he identifies as a "lifelong home"—here the land and his dedication to the farm take precedence over his dedication to family (126). The old man thus loses his choice to leave with his family because of his overpowering connection to the land. These losses are foreshadowed in his thoughts on the landscape and his family's property, with which the chapter opens: "The dust was blowing thinly off the field and over the yard like a worn and dingy curtain flapping disconsolately at the window of the world. Through it the old man saw the faded landscape, gray and colorless except for the line of half-dead trees along the creek. *It will be another year*, he thought, *before the high wide plains are green.* He turned away" (125). The desolate, desperate imagery reveals how much his decision is governed by an irrational connection to a constricting landscape that also shapes

The unrewarding and unsuccessful labor in these moments not only signifies the broad failure Rogier experiences when he attempts to mine the mountain but also reflects the more personal, specific failures that accompany hard labor in each novel. Reynolds's death because of an explosion demonstrates how dangerous mining is to individuals when they work alone. His death comes immediately after Rogier finally recognizes the mine's obstinacy: "Rogier nodded. It was the same old story. Gash veins. Low grade ore. Laborious work. And dangerous" (43). Yet this recognition does not mitigate Rogier's insistence that they keep working even after the accident to offset the financial loss they have already suffered. Although Rogier mourns Reynolds's death and "on the perimeter of his thoughts, like a wolf at the edge of firelight, there prowled the specter of an accusation that he might have replaced those old timber sets" that collapsed beneath Reynolds, his guilt is absorbed by and his attention quickly redirected to mining: "Mostly he puttered around the dump and the ore bins, selecting the best samples. These he ground with mortar and pestle, pouring the pulverized ore into a white saucer and adding three or four drops of sulphuric acid" (44–45). Although the physical labor and danger of mining kills Reynolds and brings a temporary halt to heavy labor, Rogier returns to meaningless yet familiar mine-related chores. His return to mining work distracts and distances him from the event, signifying his dependence on work for self-stability and his imperviousness to any communal impulse. Mining is at the root of this disaster and also seems to be its antidote, which highlights the deterministic circular path Rogier must follow. Even though losing Reynolds should serve as an early sign of danger, Rogier's reaction is not to forgo mining but to do more of it. Although failure is staring him in the face, working the mine possesses Rogier, even as success becomes even less possible and Depression-era economics take their toll. As March learns in the midst of these disasters, "not every venture, not every man, is unavoidably marked for success" (198).

In *Ask the Dust*, Arturo is also trapped by his labor—writing—and, as in the case of Rogier, it overwhelms his ability to make his own choices. Just as mining imprisons Rogier through the temptation of success and the reality of disappointment, the isolated pursuit of writing entraps Arturo because it consumes his energy on both ends of the spectrum. His failures—both in writing and in other pursuits—leave him without the wherewithal to choose another kind of work, and his successes overinflate his easily punctured writerly ego. When Camilla rejects him, he responds by working obsessively: "I sat before my typewriter and worked most of the night" (Fante 1980, 108). He continues to channel his energy into work throughout the fall. When he runs out of food and money, poverty "drove me to the typewriter. I sat before it, overwhelmed with grief" (109, 27). Although writing seems to be a coping strategy here, it more closely resembles further punishment: in both cases he writes nothing he can publish, because his sense of failure seeps into his writing. In this way Arturo's personal failure begets a social and financial failure common to Depression-era unemployment: the failure of isolated working situations. In the same vein, when Arturo struggles to write another piece for publication because his poverty and lack of publications depress him, he calls that period "the lean days of determination. That was the word for it, determination: Arturo Bandini in front of his typewriter two full days in succession, determined to succeed; but it didn't work, the longest siege of hard and fast determination in his life, and not one line done, only two words written over and over across the page, up and down, the same words: palm tree, palm tree, palm tree, a battle to the death of the palm tree and me, and the palm tree won" (17).

Whenever Arturo considers the work of writing, he homes in on its difficulty and the energy he must expend to complete it, especially when he writes as a reaction to failure. Repeating "palm tree" obsessively indicates a fruitless labor that produces no profitable result. Only when writing stops being "work" does it bear the marks

of joy and ease. Writing a letter to his editor, Hackmuth feels "easy," and Hackmuth responds by asking to "remove the salutation and ending . . . and print it as a short story for my magazine" (33, 56).

Just as Arturo's sense of self and self-value depend on his largely futile work as a writer, in *Wait Until Spring, Bandini* his father, Svevo, loses his sense of self in his work as a bricklayer. He often needs his labor to feel proud, especially in the context of the Depression, when jobs were scarce and men found it harder to achieve self-worth by providing adequately for a family: "He was a bricklayer, and to him there was not a more sacred calling upon the face of the earth. . . . [N]o matter what you were you had to have a house; and if you had any sense at all it would be a brickhouse" (Fante 1983, 74). To Svevo, his bricklaying is a noble labor that he does with skill and precision, that produces a tangible object, and that palpably represents financial stability. Fante also reflects the reverse in *Wait Until Spring, Bandini*'s younger Arturo, who gauges and judges people by their labor. Angry about his unrequited love for Rosa, he demeans her father as "a Wop coal miner . . . a goddamn lousy coal miner . . . so low down he had to work in a coal mine. Could he put up a wall that lasted years and years, a hundred, two hundred years? Nah . . . he had to go down under the ground and make his living like a damn Dago rat" (50).[6] Here Arturo compares Rosa's father to his own and rationalizes that his father is superior because of his labor, which produces durable structures above ground rather than merely collecting material underground. More specifically, Arturo degrades Rosa's father's labor on the basis of its relationship to space. Salvatore, Rosa's father, must go down—literally and figuratively—to do his work, whereas Svevo is elevated by his work in building brick structures. Here and in *Ask the Dust* the notion of the dignity of labor gives way to unhealthy perceptions of individualistic self-pride that undermine the proletarian novel's traditional associations between labor politics and the gathering and galvanizing of community.

At the same time, Fante uses Svevo's work for and affair with a wealthy widow to accentuate the personal failures Svevo's constrictive labor have brought about. The widow in *Wait Until Spring, Bandini* tries to make conversation by asking Svevo if he knows of paintings and cathedrals she has admired in Italy, but Svevo "had seen none of these.... He had worked hard as a boy. There had been no time for anything else" (176). And again, when she asks him about a writer from his own province, "he found himself unable to say more on the subject" because his work had always dominated his life, even as a young man (177). In the face of these inquiries, Svevo is silent and uncomfortable: "he turned his head in confusion, his gaze following the heavy beams across the room" (177). The only parts of the conversation he can contribute to are those that involve his work—"Did he like to lay brick?" she asks when he is obviously overwhelmed by her cultural knowledge—or otherwise lead him back to his work. When the widow brings up the climate, for instance, "[h]e spoke then tumbling out his torment at the weather" and its effect on his bricklaying (177). This narrow conversation showcases the ways that Svevo's hard labor has failed him and constricted his choices as an individual, preventing him from creating a stable sense of self defined by anything but labor.

When Svevo begins work on the widow's fireplace, he is "[d]etermined that the job should last a full day" to prove his work ethic and proficiency (178). Fante's detailed description of the work he does on the fireplace emphasizes that Svevo's sense of self is founded on exercising a particular skill in isolation: "He had done a careful job: not a speck of mortar was smeared on the faces of the brick he had laid. Even the canvas was clean. ... She noticed this, and it pleased him" (178). The widow's approval strikes a chord in Svevo, who almost tears up when she praises him as "a splendid worker" (182–83). Outside perceptions of work determine his personal assessment of the value of his labor—the compliments he receives on his work are for him, as they were for Arturo, the most important components of his sense of identity. Svevo deliberately does not belong to a labor union, and his reliance on solitary labor to define his worth makes him particularly susceptible to outside control.

We see the consequences when the widow's continued praise draws Svevo from his family and renders his identity as a husband and a father obsolete. He remains at work for weeks instead of returning home, where Maria, his wife, does not appreciate his work. The widow's constant rewards for his work—including getting him a heater to keep his working space warm and a better pair of shoes—reinforce his individual identity as a good bricklayer; after getting the heater, he looks at it and imagines telling her, "You're looking at the best bricklayer in Colorado, Lady" (190). Maria "might sneer" at his labor, and she attacks him for being away at work so much, but in the widow's house "there was no question of his ability" (182–83). Although his relationship to work is superficially more positive than his son's or Rogier's, Svevo's work nonetheless dictates his choices, controls his sense of self, hurts his family's security, and ultimately brings financial and personal failure to his life.

Rogier's entrapment in his work in *Below Grass Roots* also effaces his personal life through isolation: mining Pikes Peak absorbs his attention so thoroughly that it destroys his better judgment, his sense of humanity, and his relationships with his family and his fellow workers. When it becomes evident that the mine will fail and Rogier himself figures the cost to be beyond their means, mining overpowers his sense of protecting the family's financial security: "Damn the expense! He knew what he wanted: the Sylvanite" (Waters 2002, 93). He thus continues to push his family deeper into poverty to satiate his obsession, a figure of how mining dictates his decisions and blinds him to the well-being of any broader community. Similarly, when Reynolds's death forces Rogier to close his mines for a brief period, he thinks not of Reynolds nor his death but of the mountain and the "divinity of its everlasting promise of fulfillment, the diabolic cruelty with which it had blocked his every attempt to plumb its mystery! Yet never for an instant, even now, did it occur to him to give up his search" (58). Even though he recognizes that mining has killed his partner and the mines have thus far resisted his most extensive attempts to turn a profit from a good vein, the challenges he faces only reinforce his determination. In the context of the events of the novel, his single-minded self-determination, expressed as an insistence on the sacredness of the mountain as dominant space, is not a sign of strength; instead, it leaves him no choice but to keep mining despite the costs.

That lack of choice also points to Rogier's loss of self and financial independence in the consistently hard, all-encompassing labor of mining. As mining consumes his life with its rigor, it simultaneously consumes his previously successful identity as an architect: "Of cool, calm Rogier, master builder and contractor for $100,000 jobs, there was now no semblance left" because of his investment in mining (109). Later in the novel, when his crew begins to lose faith in mining, Rogier becomes even more dedicated. At night he stays in the bunkhouse at the mine instead of going home to his family because he is so compelled to continue working after his men leave; he is sacrificing his identity as a friend, fellow worker, husband, father, and grandfather to maintain a "relationship" with the mine. His obsession haunts him even at night; he cannot sleep because "through floor and earth and granite, from the deep heart below, would come the measured rhythmic beat of the cosmic pulse of the Peak. With its throbbing in his aching head, he would get up, wrapped in blankets, and stare out the window" (211). In Waters's naturalist depiction, the mountain and its mining prospects have literally gotten into Rogier's head and changed his priorities, sense of self, and sense of reason. And mining not only keeps him up at night, it also swallows him during the day. He "prowled alone through abandoned drifts, stopes, and cross-cuts. And the deeper he descended the more secure he felt. . . . He could feel its rhythmic beat, feel it close around him and adhere with the familiar and comforting illusion of adding to him another strata of being" (212–13). Here Rogier needs to be in the presence of the mine to feel stable, even when that stability is an illusion. He becomes more and more individualistic, delusional, and obsessed with mining toward the end of the novel. Rawlings, his partner after Reynolds, notices the change in Rogier's behavior as the mine continues to fail and as that failure undoes him: "But what was wrong with Rogier, to be so blind to the obvious? Rogier, he observed, was more nervous and erratic than ever before. . . . And what was worse, he was gone for days at a stretch—up to his blessed mine in the mountains" (225). Failing prospects at the mine do not discourage Rogier nor indicate that he should return to architecture; instead, because he has lost all sense of himself as a being separate from the mine, he has no choice but to pursue his obsession at all costs, which in turn effaces the little sanity and security he has left.

Rogier isn't the only one in the novel whom mining destroys; his entire family suffers in one way or another because of the overwhelming power of that labor. Most telling is how mining comes to ruin Cable and Ona's life together and their lives as individuals with personal interests, needs, and history. Before Cable goes to the mine to work full time, he visits the Indian reservation where he grew up to reconnect with his roots. There he feels alive and at home, but once he returns to the mine, the work makes him forget his Indian roots and respect for his people's traditions; when he condescendingly offers the reward of his mining—"Gold. Big nuggets"—to an older Indian, the reply is harsh: "The old Indian gave him a penetrating stare and grunted. . . . [H]e picked a lump of dirt the size of a marble and handed it to Cable. 'Gold no good for Indian. This more better'" (216). Cable's response is ambiguous and denotes an uncertainty with himself he did not feel on the reservation: "Cable laughed. Slowly his face changed as he crumpled the dirt between his fingers. 'No, no good for an Indian'" (216). Cable here recognizes how far he is from his roots and those to whom he once felt connected, yet that realization does not dissuade him from mining, the pursuit of which only tears him from the communal work and atmosphere of the reservation, pulling him ever farther away. Ona's earlier objections to his mining and her sense of what it will do— when her father insists that Cable should mine, "she felt impending a disaster that would rend her apart" (85)—thus foreshadow how mining will undo Cable and his network of connections, fulfilling her fear of an uncertain future with an insecure family (190). After Cable's death, Ona's isolation prompts her to think of all those connected to or in her family who have been destroyed by mining. It "seemed to her that the pattern of life in this gaunt old house never changed" (244). Reflecting on her own family at the novel's close, Ona concludes that she along "with March, Leona, Nancy, and Mrs. Rogier were imprisoned hostages to Rogier's monomaniacal search for gold in the Sylvanite, come what might" (244).

The first part of *Whose Names Are Unknown*, set in Oklahoma, conforms to this paradigm. In Cimarron County, the difficulty of compulsive labor in an unfriendly landscape to which farmers are deeply attached dictates choice and breaks families apart, ultimately leaving the Dunne family and others around them facing an uncertain future. When Milt wants to try wheat farming on their drying land, his father objects until their usual crop of corn fails to grow in the encroaching Dust Bowl conditions: "The old man finally gave in. Life could not be any harder than it was or money more scarce" (Babb 2004, 3). And again, later in the novel, when older farmers discuss the ecological problems leading to the Dust Bowl, they mourn the current difficulty they have with farming, given how they have changed the land over time: "We've been here for years and the dust wasn't so bad before the land was mostly all broken," one points out. "The wind is bad enough anyway without blowing our wheat out." Another agrees, noting what they've learned from their time working the landscape: "And we need trees. My wife said we ought to plant trees because the place was unnatural" (97). A third attempts to distance the dust from the poor farming practices that produced it and instead indicates a lingering hope for the land that is still tinged with uncertainty: "We got a fine country, big and rich as you can find anywhere in the world, I reckon, and if things were right we'd be getting along fine" (98). These disagreements over the shape of labor on unprofitable land preclude any movement toward the narrative trope of farmers joining to work together to pursue common survival. Community action remains beyond the reach of those who traditionally work alone.

Part of the reason these men are left without choice is because their identities and sense of personal success are yoked closely to work they know well and that was shaped by the land before it changed, which blinds them to the ecological and financial challenges of farming in the southern plains during the Dust Bowl. Even as it becomes more and more obvious that the Dust Bowl makes their labor impossible, Milt hangs onto his identity as a self-sufficient farmer and still feels that "nothing was quite like the satisfaction he felt after he planted or harvested a crop. *This kind of feeling is one of the things a man lives for . . . the feeling that I made something, I made something with the soil, together we made a crop grow in order and loveliness*" (58). Similarly, Milt and his father "looked over the land they had planted the day before, and the land they would plant this day, and they felt a sense of possession growing in them for the piece of earth that was theirs" (6). But it is this sense of pride and ownership that deprives men like Milt and his father of choice. Their "sense of possession" makes them feel inherently tied to the land, as if it is their responsibility to continue to labor even when failure is on the horizon. That their senses of accomplishment and identity are tied up in this work makes continuing despite all odds a matter of individual pride and stability that proves rightful ownership of space. Even though the output of farming declines as they continue to grow crops in Cimarron County, the novel's farmers feel that their futures are certain when rooted in a labor they trust will return to normal. Like the other male protagonists discussed in this chapter, these men who lose themselves—and perhaps even hide from the certainty of failure—in work that is familiar yet failing are thus compelled to be isolated farmers even in the midst of terrible conditions.

This need to stand and work on familiar ground pulls apart multiple families in *Whose Names Are Unknown* and so gestures toward an uncertain future in that place, which reflects the era's linked financial, social, and spatial insecurity. Families run into trouble even before they are formally constituted, which further casts the shadow of ecological failure onto community and the future. When Anna and Max, a young couple engaged to be married, talk about the future, their conversation is tinged with uncertainty and orbits shaky family structures: "And now what have we got? . . . My wheat ruined, so I've lost my start. We can't get married on nothing, and things are even shaky with the folks. Yours are still safe; I'd be taking you from something sure, and I can't do that" (106). For the younger generation to talk directly about the uncertainty of the future foreshadows the long-lasting linked environmental and economic damage the Dust Bowl and Depression caused. These novels imagine how, as the financial setbacks of the Depression moved across the country, the work and working identities of those living out West were compromised by not only environmental restriction but class limitation as well.

## On Class

In each of the novels discussed in this chapter, class lines function as limiting forces that lock characters in spaces and to forms of work that themselves become yoked to particular, often failing economic orders. Class mobility is thus not only impossible, but striving for it ends in multiple losses, especially when that mobility is pursued by individuals and not communities. In other words, living and working patterns both reflect and reinforce class status; labor in space is tied to particular classes, as when Arturo calls Rosa's father "a goddamn lousy coal miner . . . so low down he had to work in a coal mine," using the space of his labor to accentuate his low-class status (Fante 1983, 50). This feedback loop calcifies classes and their divisions spatially, which calls into question the possibility of class mobility. More than just a reflection of the economic stasis of the Depression, however, this lack of mobility also suggests that class effectively inhabits characters regardless of socioeconomic status. And that lack of mobility is doubly reinforced when the characters of each novel flirt with people and objects from classes other than their own; those moments of class transgression, especially when they result in the illusion of gaining social capital, are followed by personal and public losses.

In Fante's *Ask the Dust*, Arturo's obsession with money, what it can purchase, and how it conveys status reveals inflexible class lines that persist despite outward appearance—an inflexibility that haunts and harms individuals and their relationships with one another. When Arturo meets Camilla, he disparages her choice of shoes because they "emphasize the fact that you always were and always will be a filthy little Greaser" (Fante 1980, 44). Although Arturo uses her shoes in part to degrade her nationality, he also notices that they are dirty and old, which reflects her lower-class status.[7] Camilla buys new shoes in response, which only reinforces this association between ornamentation and class. However, while her "new white pumps, with high heels," are clean and nondescript and indicate that she possesses purchasing power to better her situation, she ultimately trades them for her old shoes, which reaffirms her persistent lower-class identity (60). This series of choices emphasizes that when individuals make isolated class-based decisions, those decisions often end in further alienation and failure. Fante reinforces this connection between the outward image of class status, especially in terms of clothing, and personal finance when Arturo earns some money by selling his letter-turned-story to Hackmuth:

"It was the finest suit of clothes I ever bought, a brown pin-stripe with two pairs of pants. Now I could be well dressed at all times. I bought two-tone brown and white shoes, a lot of shirts and a lot of socks, and a hat. My first hat, dark brown, real felt with a white silk lining. . . . I changed behind a curtain stall, put on everything new, with the hat to top it off" (58). Here Arturo's sense of success is reflected in the outward signs of that success: nice clothes. However, just as Camilla's flirtation with an object of the upper class does not last long, Arturo grows uncomfortable in his new clothes, and when he looks in the mirror, "[t]he image in the glass seemed only vaguely familiar":

> All at once everything began to irritate me. The stiff collar was strangling me. The shoes pinched my feet. The pants smelled like a clothing store basement and were too tight in the crotch. Sweat broke out at my temples where the hat band squeezed my skull. Suddenly I began to itch, and when I moved everything crackled like a paper sack. . . . I pulled everything off, washed the smells out of my hair, and climbed into my old clothes. They were very glad to have me again: they clung to me with cool delight, and my tormented feet slipped into the old shoes as into the softness of Spring grass. (59)

Both Arturo and Camilla try on clothing associated with the upper classes, but neither can sustain the illusion. They remain locked into their lower-class outfits and thus the lower class as well. Although the failures here are personal and minor, they nonetheless recall the broader failure of family at the end of the novel, when Camilla and Arturo separately desert the beautiful middle-class cottage Arturo rents on the beach for far more uncertain, lower-class spaces. Especially in light of the fact that Arturo returns to LA after that failure, such episodes indicate that gestures and mobility toward the upper class are illusions that fail, have painful consequences that ruin communal relationships, and only reconfirm lower-class status.

Similarly, in *Below Grass Roots* the Rogiers set their sights on the class ascendancy mining could bring, if it were profitable. Yet the novel imagines no labor to be profitable during the Depression, especially physical labor out West. Mining, rather than producing excess wealth or changing class status, barely makes enough money to fund itself; instead, it dashes hope and threatens financial and individual security. Particularly after Cable leaves for the Indian reservation, Rogier "was feeling a squeeze": he cuts Ona's monthly allowance in half and writes Boné, his nephew, for an investment because "[t]o sink the shaft would be expensive"; this sort of communication is all he has with Boné, and it casts him as little more than a financial resource (126). This is not the first time mining has cost Rogier more than he has available; when Ona and Cable marry, "[t]he wedding bills kept comin in. . . . And yet all these were but the last embroidery on the immense tapestry of Cripple Creek debt Rogier has woven: pumping equipment for the Gloriana, hoist machinery shipped to the Magpie, supplies drawn by Reynolds from an Altman store, and an overdrawn account on a Victor bank" (56). Even without the wedding expenses, the Rogiers' finances are unforgiving, and mining thus binds them to the working class. Mrs. Rogier recognizes this as it becomes apparent that their financial troubles will never cease:

> To give up her last lingering hope of moving into a mansion in the North End was for Mrs. Rogier a feat of renunciation accomplished without bitterness or regret. She sat rocking in front of the window, counting off on her fingers the ragtag and bobtail of town who had struck it rich at Cripple Creek . . . more than forty who had become millionaires and were now the cream of North End society! Why was it that Lady Luck had led these men to fame and fortune instead of Rogier, so much smarter and more deserving[?] (57)

Here mining and its failures have chained the Rogiers to their Depression-era working-class life, rather than providing the wealth they imagined.

Moreover, Rogier's own thoughts about the effect of such repeated failures on his family indicate both the false allure of mining and the ultimate financial hopelessness it yields, as well as how those facts bind families to unsteady futures and thus undo them. He thinks of his children, who have witnessed and lived through mining's "hopeless incertitude"; they are "children tinged with the bitterness of the wealth and luxury at their hands' reach but forever beyond their grasp, and touched by its splendor too. Children of that soil who hated it and yet were bound to it forever. Who loved it and were driven from it by the same blind fury that brought their fathers. . . . They were the poor and their lives would enrich the earth. They achieved no dreams" (65). Again, as the marker of the future, these children indicate a loss of the security and certainty—financial and personal—that labor promised. The financial difficulties alluded to here are like the financial difficulties that prevent Mrs. Rogier and Ona from achieving their dream of living in the North End. Working on difficult ground may have a tantalizing sheen, but that sheen is dulled by socioeconomic failure. That these children would "enrich the earth" but "achieve no dreams" for themselves roots these losses of hope and class ascendancy in the soil to which their families are inextricably linked. The lower class of which these families are part thus functions like quicksand that ensnares the individual: the labor of mining makes it impossible to achieve class mobility, a figure of the Depression-era conviction that physical labor in this kind of rural region could not lead to success.

Like mining, bricklaying in *Wait Until Spring, Bandini* widens the gaps among classes via labor. Svevo's work for and affair with Effie in her mansion only reaffirm this fact—instead of helping Svevo climb the social ladder, her social capital only tears his family apart and accentuates his personal lower-class status. Fante narrates the affair from the outside to establish the class dynamics of that relationship: he first introduces the widow, Effie Hildegarde, as a member of a class much higher than the Bandinis. While buying groceries on a credit account the family cannot settle, Maria learns that Mr. Craik, the grocer, saw her husband "up around Effie Hildegarde's house . . . [she's] got lots of money . . . [o]wns the street car company . . . [o]wns lots of real estate in this town" (Fante 1983, 105). Not only does that scene cast a shadow on Svevo's actions—Maria does not know where he is, and he is with another woman—it also draws a sharp line between the Bandinis' poverty and Effie's wealth. The same thing happens when Arturo and August, walking home from school, spot Effie and Svevo in Effie's coupe. The boys argue about whether or not to tell their mother and whether or not their father is wrong, and their arguments come down to class difference. While August is upset over this first glimpse of the affair and defends his mother—"Just because Mamma hasn't got good clothes"—Arturo is proud of his father for catching the attention of a wealthy woman and grows angry at August's disapproval: "You're just like everybody else. Just because Papa's poor" (121, 122). August acknowledges but does not disparage his family's poverty, while Arturo disparages it and approves of his father's temporary class mobility. And even though Arturo's criticism is complicated by his dedication to his own family—"this was Effie Hildegarde, one of the richest women in town. Pretty good for his father; pretty swell. She wasn't as good as his mother—no: but that didn't have anything to do with it"—his admiration for his father's class-jumping trounces shame for his adultery and his failure to be a good family man (125). Again, sharp class lines are drawn to separate Svevo from both his family and from the upper class in the novel, which in turn hints at the inflexible class identities that come to haunt the affair.

Svevo's only role in Effie's fine house is to service her and reconstruct the fireplace—a luxury that showcases wealth—and because that job fixes a non-necessity, it renders Svevo's work a non-necessity by association. His labor is thus downplayed in comparison to the wealth it begets for others. Money is the centerpiece of this affair, and thus the affair takes on the hue of class transgression.

The results of transgression are devastating. When Effie grows tired of Svevo's reluctance to take her hints, she draws him into the bedroom, has him pour her a glass of wine, and lies down on the bed. As she lures him closer, Svevo's discomfort grows: "He could not be sure of himself. He squinted his eyes as he watched her. No—she could not mean it. This woman had too much money. Her wealth impeded the imagery. Such things did not happen" (198). When he initially refuses her, unsettled by the tang of transgression surrounding the encounter, Effie taps into that class-based unease and calls after him, "You fool! . . . You ignorant peasant." It is this insult that brings him back to the bedroom to indulge her fantasy and reclaim his own power, despite his lower-class status: she "cried with ecstatic pain, weeping that he have mercy, her weeping a pretense, a beseeching for mercilessness. He laughed the triumph of his poverty and peasantry. This Widow! She with her wealth and deep plump warmth" (199). The power of class not only incites Svevo to return to Effie—he wants to prove his worth despite being poor—but also drives Effie's desire for Svevo. Their affair exists in the gap between their class statuses and so satiates a desire they both have for class novelty. Both use the affair to participate in class transgression—an experiment that reveals in yet another way how class divisions spawn isolation rather than community.

While Svevo works in her house, "a place where he did not belong," Effie sustains their affair by wielding her class power as a consumer to accentuate the restrictions Svevo's lower-class identity produces. To showcase his constricted power and choices, she dons nice dresses, buys Svevo expensive gifts, and initiates "[a] strange rendezvous. No kisses and no embraces" (200). Effie never pays Svevo a regular wage beyond these gifts, which renders him financially dependent on her and binds him to her space. Although he imagines that eventually "[h]e would leave, never to return. In his pockets would be money," Svevo's lack of capital reveals that his sense of individual and class power is false. Instead, objects and habits of upper-class life tantalize Svevo and beguile him into remaining under Effie's control:

> Meantime, he liked it here. He liked the fine whiskey, the fragrant cigars. He liked this pleasant room and this rich woman who lived in it. She was not far from him, reading her book, and in a little while she would walk into the bedroom and he would follow. She would gasp and weep and then he would leave in the twilight, triumph giving zest to his legs. The leave-taking he loved most of all. That surge of satisfaction, that vague chauvinism telling him that no people on earth equalled [*sic*] the Italian people, that joy in his peasantry. The Widow had money—yes. But back there she lay, crushed, and Bandini was a better man than she, by God. (202)

While gender and nationality play roles in Svevo's analysis of their affair, class lies at its heart. Effie's wealth draws Svevo to her, and his poverty draws her to him. And although he leaves "certain he would not return," Maria's violent outburst drives him back "in less than an hour" (208). Without the means to support himself and without the support of his family structure, Svevo must return to Effie for protection, which gestures toward the power her class stability grants her over him. Here, class's impact is squarely on individuals' sense of themselves and personal relationships to one another, rather than on any kind of larger communal belonging.

The novel ends on an uncertain note as Svevo and Arturo walk away from Effie's house: Svevo tries to reassure Arturo that all will be right come spring, but a single snowflake falls on his hand. Although the class transgression of his affair is behind him, his own poverty, the lack of organized community support, and the difficulty of his work paying off all stand in front of him, which emphasizes the uncertainty of the future for the lower class. Indeed, in light of the ending, Svevo's affair looks like a desperate attempt for certainty in a space and climate unfriendly to his work, and so his income and his attraction to Effie's lifestyle lure him to a security his own class and its limits cannot provide.

Rogier experiences that uncertainty of personal and familial lower-class living patterns in *Below Grass Roots*, especially as mining saps more and more of his family's money and pulls restrictive and damaging class lines tighter around them. But rather than just experiencing it, Rogier amplifies that uncertainty and the family instability it brings when he tries to draw his family financially into mining. Attempting to convince his nephew, Boné, to go into business with him, Rogier offers the same empty promises of individual success that he falls for: "If the Sylvanite runs into a blanket vein you won't ever have to worry, any more than Cable and Ona. You'll be independent for life!" (Waters 2002, 104). This sentiment rings false, especially in light of Ona's prescient anger over her father's push to bring Cable back into mining: "mining is a risky and expensive venture. I really wish you'd keep out of it. . . . [Cable] hasn't got any business in it. . . . He's got me and the children to look after. He can't afford to take any chances" (84–85). Ona's focus on how the financial cost of mining takes a personal toll yokes the two together, implying that if one fails, the other follows suit. Moreover, her concern for the future of her family indicates that mining is poison for the kind of familial security she expects for herself and, most importantly, her children.

Rogier's pleas to Boné thus showcase only the desperation mining evokes in men when it comes to financing ventures. Rogier is willing to bet his family's happiness and the certainty of their future on labor that does not turn a profit. At this point in the novel, mining has pushed the Rogiers deeply into the lower class—as physical, rural work tended to do during the upheaval of the 1930s in the West— and Rogier's begging for money from his nephew demonstrates how his obsession with the mine has blinded him to the even broader national troubles and limits of class, making those troubles and limits all the more evident to the reader. When Cable tries to explain to Rogier how much financial strain the mine has put on their family— "This is a business we've got to make pay" (171), he says—Rogier responds angrily and without empathy for or even attention to his family's situation. Instead his attention is on the work of mining: "Business! Who told you this was a business? This is a mine, and more too. It's a shaft to Hell if I can get it there! There's going to be no fool business cluttering up the Sylvanite. Get that through your head" (171). Rogier attempts to refute the notion that mining is a collectively experienced business, preferring to understand it as a deeply personal, individualistic enterprise. That attitude, combined with the near certainty of failure, guarantees that his commitment to mining will bring disaster to his family.

The section of *Whose Names Are Unknown* set in Oklahoma follows a similar pattern. The Dunnes are limited by their lower-class status, which is itself reinforced by the financially unproductive nature of the labor to which they are accustomed. The book opens with the depressing financial facts of trying to grow crops in Cimarron County during the Dust Bowl: "The average for any crop in this drought country was two out of every four or five years, the rest being outright failures or just enough harvest to get by with pinching" (Babb 2004, 3). Because the men of the novel are unable to leave their individual plots of land and isolated labor even when both fail to produce capital or resources, their reluctance to find other employment or another space with better opportunities points to losses of confidence and stability that the Dust Bowl's widespread ecological and employment failure caused. In one particularly telling moment, Julia and Mrs. Long, one of the Dunnes' neighbors, converse about their current situation and reveal an awareness of the gravity of widespread ecological and economic decay. Julia thinks, "*It is pitiful the way people have to fight nowadays to make a bare living. . . . Which way is a poor man to turn if there isn't even work and honest pay?*" and Mrs. Long "interrupted Julia's thoughts as if she felt them meet her own bewildered questioning": "'We wouldn't think of leaving here if it wasn't for the drought and the depression. Ordinary times we like it well enough and it's healthy country. Drought'll come to an end, I reckon, always has before, but this time the depression don't end. Nearly ten years long now. My kids never lived in good times. I'm scared sometimes they won't have good health and won't get an education. I always wanted 'em to know something and be what they want'" (56–57).

Julia's despair over the situation she sees unfolding in front of her gestures toward the crumbling of the future that class entrapment begets when labor fails to make money. Julia sees the future as uncertain and hopeless, but Mrs. Long, in her defense of leaving Oklahoma, indicates that there is a better chance of a more certain future elsewhere. Mrs. Long's willingness to leave well-known but failing land thus indicates a growing realization that the currently hostile conditions of Cimarron County are not worth working in, despite the familiarity of and consequent comfort in that space. Like Ona's concerns in *Below Grass Roots*, Mrs. Long's worries about her children's future become the guiding reason to leave for California, where labor patterns and the land are different and could improve their class status.

Finally, after witnessing so much failure, Mrs. Starwood, Frieda, and Julia insist they get out of Oklahoma and go to California, following the Longs' trail to a potentially better life for them and their children. Although cotton picking in California is difficult—"Damn cotton picking'll break your back," Milt comments—and means living in temporary housing at job sites, it holds more financial promise and so offers a chance at a better and more secure future than planting crops in Oklahoma. Leaving Oklahoma also puts the implications of that future in the forefront of the Dunnes' minds. Although "[t]he whole family had to work in the prunes if they were to make even two dollars a day . . . school was important" and takes precedence over making money when it comes time to send the children off (164). Unlike in Oklahoma, where school became impossible because of dust storms and labor requirements, school in California is a necessity and does not get pushed aside, which registers a broader view of future prospects for working and living. The repeated and constrictive tolls the Dust Bowl has exacted on Cimarron County bar characters from envisioning a different future, whereas California's potential opens up the possibility.

This commitment to education and the children's future also indicates a broader change in the novel's perception of possibility when the Dunnes move to California. Unlike Oklahoma, where particular labor done on repressive land chains them to one particular class, in California class mobility is possible as a collective. The Dunnes, along with Frieda and Mrs. Starwood, join a group that wants to start a union to protest the unfair treatment of laborers at the picking camps. In Oklahoma such a move would have been impossible, as the farmers functioned as individuals, tending their own individual plots of land. However, in California the fruit pickers band together and use their community's social capital to better their economic capital. The spatial change from Oklahoma to California thus breaks the cycle of an overwhelming, unfriendly, land-constricting labor and class system and so allows for more working and financial possibilities. Milt anticipates this transition when driving from one camp to another and thinking of the unfair labor camps; in contrast to his focus on money back in Oklahoma—a focus that always entailed calculating how much crop growing would make in a given season—his reflections in California take on an ethical tone: "It was money, maybe—money enough to hire another man. There was something else behind that, which let a man get money enough to harden his heart and forget the humanity of man" (168). For the first time Milt considers the implications of individual gain and not just the need for it—a recognition that would have been impossible under the constrictions of living and working in Oklahoma.

This new kind of relationship to money enables the Dunnes to participate in forming a union in California and challenges the familial and community failure the other novels document. Because the union is a community project, it encourages the development of a strong "family" that uses labor as a crucial but flexible element in maintaining a life, rather than submitting to labor that does not bring financial or structural support. Asking not just for better rates for one season but looking to improve conditions for the longer term, another specifically proletarian gesture toward the future, the union would provide "[b]etter hours, better wages, better living conditions" (174–75). Here the union promises a kind of group education—itself linked to the future—that would support the laborers standing up for themselves and their living standards as a cohesive and powerful group. And although forming the union is not a smooth or easy process—government-backed labor initiatives and unions formed during the Dust Bowl ultimately failed, and at the end of the novel many key union members, including Milt, are in jail—it is something the Dunnes are wholly committed to, as are many other members of their labor camp, which strengthens family and community bonds.

Yet the novel's uncertain ending on these terms does not exclude the possibility of failure, which, I argue, makes it distinct from Steinbeck's hopeful ending. Babb indicates that sturdy relationships could lead either way: "One thing was left, as clear and perfect as a drop of rain—the desperate need to stand together as one man. They would rise and fall and, in their falling, rise again" (222). Her attention to the certainty of "falling" counteracts the one-dimensional story of the triumph of the human spirit to which this novel could be reduced. Ending on such an uncertain plot and rhetorical note gives Babb the opportunity to remind her readers that failure was an inevitable component of the Dust Bowl and the Depression, even when removing the chains of space and labor changes relationships to class and offers families more potential to meet more than minimal needs. This uncertain ending also reminds the reader that the naturalist bent of the novel includes the possibility that fatal landscapes could continue to isolate individuals from communities. Indeed, the title of the novel itself refers to a vaguely worded eviction notice to workers "whose names are unknown," which again reinforces the danger of individuals becoming splintered off from one another and from any communal effort to improve working conditions (219). While we are prone to read Babb as another Steinbeck—the initial reason her novel was refused for publication in the 1930s was that it supposedly replicated *The Grapes of Wrath*—her ending precludes that too-easy assumption by reminding the reader to take seriously the possibility of failure.

When read as a group, *Wait Until Spring, Bandini, Ask the Dust, Whose Names Are Unknown*, and *Below Grass Roots* offer fine-grained realist and naturalist perspectives on the harsh reality of lived experience to tell a story of communal and familial failure and uncertainty in the Dust Bowl and Depression era that critical and popular memory often overlooks in favor of narratives about the triumph over adversity. Moreover, those depictions diverge from proletarian literature's emphasis on the dignity of labor and community organization, instead zooming in on individual isolation in the face of overwhelming ecological, economic, and working conditions. Together they imagine how labor in the West gives rise to fixed class systems and a corresponding lack of class mobility unique to this environment. Although the union may succeed, Svevo's family may repair itself, Arturo may find another love and another writing cottage, and Rogier may strike it rich at the mine and save his family, the failures experienced along the way are not easily forgotten, forgiven, or likely to be put right. The widespread losses of labor, class security, and spatial rootedness generated by the unforgiving socioeconomic and environmental dimensions of the Depression and the Dust Bowl haunt these narratives and foreclose the rene-gotiation of class difference and private lives through the dignity of labor to which proletarian literature often aspired. Instead, these novels explore how identities shaped by the convergence of labor, class, and space reveal the constrictive effect of those three elements' specific historical interdependencies in the Depression-era West.

# 4 He Was a Good Cowboy

Identity and History on the Post–World War II
Texas Ranch in Larry McMurtry's *Horseman,
Pass By*, Elmer Kelton's *The Time It Never Rained*,
and Cormac McCarthy's *All the Pretty Horses*

If you asked most people which figure represents the "authentic" American West, many would pretty quickly respond "the cowboy." The image of a rugged man on horseback, heels down in worn leather boots, gun slung across his hip or back, Stetson on his head, riding off into the sunset, is a familiar one that American culture loves to capitalize on—for cigarette and car sales, for lullabies and campfire songs, for fashion and film. As the late Lawrence Clayton (2000, 206)—whose personal, historical, and biographical ethnographies and academic studies of ranching life are among the most respected in his field—once wrote, "The mythic figure has an appeal we cannot deny." But how can a mythic figure of the cowboy reflect the "authentic" West? What does the cowboy even mean in a context in which, as the collection edited by William R. Handley and Nathaniel Lewis (2004, 1) shows, the concept of authenticity has been so widely used "to invent, test, advertise, and read the West" more broadly? And if the cowboy is so entangled in both the historical and mythological representations of the region, where did this figure come from? And where has he gone?

This chapter seeks to excavate some of the bones underneath the cowboy's long road to becoming a cultural icon of the modern U.S. West. More specifically, I mean to sift through the cultural, historical, and socioeconomic stories layered underneath the seemingly uncomplicated literary representations of ranch work in the decades following World War II. I put forth three interrelated questions. First, what constituted the actual ranching labor done by cowboys and cattlemen in this period, and how is such labor depicted in the fiction of the latter half of the twentieth century? Second, what can these novels tell us about how ranch labor provided the bedrock for class systems in the workplace and how the performance of those class systems shifted both over time and in(to) other social spaces? And finally, how did these cowboys, cattlemen, and ranchers—real and fictional—organize, mediate, and reflect on the social and environmental spaces in which they worked?

Many of these questions pivot on Janet Zandy's (2004, 113) suggestion that physical labor and its literary representations carry a cultural weight that must be interrogated on its own terms. Even more acutely, however, these questions respond to a distinction that John R. Erickson (4–5) nicely sums up in *The Modern Cowboy*: "The cowboy I know is a working man. He is defined by his work, which should not be confused with the term 'job.' Cowboy work is more than a job; it is a life-style and a medium of expression. Remove the cowboy from his working environment and you have someone else, someone who resembles a cowboy in outward appearance but who, to one degree or another, is an imposter." Readers might object to Erickson's often nostalgic defense of what he prefers to call the "traditional" cowboy, but he is hardly alone in his sense that cowboy identity is primarily a working identity. It is in this light, then, that I examine the cowboy as a figure of labor so as to resituate him in the literary canon of the western.

"Resituate" might seem inapt to those who believe that cowboys are already securely placed. And yet they actually have come to occupy quite contested terrain in western literary studies. Melody Graulich (2007, 187) writes, for instance, that "the 'cowboy' identity is a commodity, transportable anywhere," while Christine

Bold (1987) often reads the western as if it were little more than an emblem of consumerism in the modern literary marketplace. And Jane Tompkins (1992, 13) argues, albeit rather scathingly, that the cowboy "posits a world without God, without ideas, without institutions, without what is commonly recognized as culture, a world of men and things, where male adults in the prime of life find ultimate meaning in doing their best together on the job." What these studies have in common, however, is the idea that an uncritical focus on the masculine cultures of the West would, as Krista Comer (1999, 33) puts it, run "the risk of replicating a mythic white-male center" and a rather misogynistic, insular, and intolerant one at that. The challenge instead is to situate the laboring cowboy in a diverse constellation of dynamic and plural Wests. That is, rather than simply rehearsing the familiar mythology of the cowboy, we need to pay close attention to the subtle textures of his labor and to locate them within specific, diverse western socio-ecological spaces that demand particular *kinds* of work and social structure. This approach will reveal the multiple class and environmental fault lines beneath the history of the cowboys, ranchers, and cattlemen who populate this chapter. Cowboys, ranchers, and their labor are both ultimately shaped by history *and* ultimately idealized as well: they are men who are deeply invested in their carefully cultivated ranches and farms, men whose identities are intricately interwoven with local culture, broader national movements, and nostalgia for both their work *and* the history of that work.

To explore this story, this chapter turns to the literary habits and historical contexts that accompany labor in Larry McMurtry's *Horseman, Pass By* (first published in 1961), Elmer Kelton's *The Time It Never Rained* (1973), and Cormac McCarthy's *All the Pretty Horses* (1992). My goal is to tease apart the reciprocal yet thorny relationships among the cowboy, his labor, and the socio-economic and ecological landscape of Texas in the decades immediately following World War II. These novels filter representations of labor and class on the ranch through the lens of the very real historical and ecological circumstances of Texas from 1945 to 1965; they situate their cowboy protagonists in a shifting and often hostile socioeconomic landscape. At the same time, these representations respond to older notions of cowboy labor that cherish the noble, hard work of an individual on a ranch—an ideal that ranchers and cowboys are reluctant to give up. Although written across a span of thirty years, these three novels concern only seven years among them: *All the Pretty Horses* is set in 1949, *The Time It Never Rained* in 1956, and *Horseman, Pass By* in 1954. This period encompasses the unique combination of spatial, political, ecological, and cultural changes Texas underwent as a result of the rapid industrialization necessitated by World War II, as well as the environmental effects of an infamously long drought in the region in the 1950s.

Meanwhile, all three texts document the simultaneous financial and structural decay of the ranching industry through the eyes and the bodies of their protagonists. McMurtry's Homer Bannon witnesses the loss of his cattle and land as a result of a devastating outbreak of hoof-and-mouth disease that financially ruins him; Kelton's Charlie Flagg experiences the destructive force of the long drought firsthand as a ranch owner; and McCarthy's John Grady Cole faces the death of his grandfather, the ensuing loss of the family ranch, and the destruction of that legacy when he moves from Texas to Mexico. Although not untouched by nostalgia, these protagonists experience the sense of futility (and sheer loss) of their ranching labor while simultaneously seeking to pursue and preserve it. As this double-sided act of preservation and mourning becomes a public matter, its cultural and historical debris comes to the surface; as it does, these cowboys discover how their work identity had been tied to the ranch's class system. Each novel thus bears witness to the intricate interdependence of labor, class, space, and identity in the cowboy's West.

By focusing on the cowboy as a figure of labor who participates in structured spatial and work systems, we can uncover the locus of class stratification within the crossroads of natural and constructed landscapes. Moreover, the idealization of a lost working identity in these novels unveils the intricate way the memorialization of community history continues to inform class stratification and limits class mobility even in the present day. All three novels examine, through both historical and contemporary lenses, how those who work on ranches manipulate and redefine several markers of class status—clothing, owning and developing land, livestock ownership, and horseback riding skill, among others. These physical markers simultaneously draw from nostalgia and reflect the changes wrought across the landscapes in which these cowboys and ranchers live. Rather than reflecting a unitary notion of "the cowboy," representations of ranch laborers in and out of work shed light on the changing terms of success, class mobility, and spatial belonging in the West as the industry took shape in the years following World War II.

## On History, Nostalgia, and the Cowboy Mythos

Because the conventional model of the cowboy is both a fictional and a historical construct, the challenge of studying cowboys is in part etymological. The term "cowboy" originally described adolescent and young adult males who in the nineteenth century were employed by ranchers to drive, brand, castrate, and care for cattle herds. These cowboys were not landowners; indeed, they rarely remained at one ranch for longer than a season and were often associated in the popular imagination with vagrants and drifters—dangerously mobile men who posed a threat to organized, familiar (and thus feminine) domestic space. As Paul H. Carlson (2000, 3) suggests, quoting William Forbis, "real cowboys" in the nineteenth century had indeed been "dirty, overworked laborers" who "'fried their brains under a hot prairie sun.'" However, with the advent of barbed wire and the subsequent end of the open range in the 1880s, cowboys dropped in number and so slipped into a collective mythical memory that celebrated their most commercially alluring—and superficial—qualities: freedom, masculinity, and dominance over nature.

This image gained significant cultural traction through the early to mid-twentieth century, as romanticized versions of cowboys and ranchers took center stage in Wild West films, cowboy pulp novels, spaghetti westerns, long-running TV shows such as *The Lone Ranger*, and more. This shift—from practical workers to objects of a consumerist fantasy—galvanizes the most common readings of cowboys, even when they are attacked as idolized representations of ecological, social, and racial exploitation, patriarchal values, or national expansion. This critique, one might add, persists in literary studies, despite contributions such as Paul Carlson's (2000) collection *The Cowboy Way*, Jacqueline Moore's (2009) collection *Cow Boys and Cattle Men*, and J. W. Williams's (1999) *The Big Ranch Country*, all of which document, in close detail, the dynamic and complex real-life circumstances and identities of those who have worked on ranches. Nevertheless, even these fine books still focus primarily on the 1880s through the 1930s. As such, by "archiving" the cowboy and only gesturing toward future changes, they risk reinforcing the very nostalgia and mythos they help to dismantle.

My larger point, however, is not the familiar one—that a one-dimensional, essentialized, and unchanging view of cowboy labor risks overshadowing ranchers and cowboys who came after the ideal had fallen into the past. On the contrary, it is that this approach might lead us to dismiss the cowboy mythos as merely anachronistic, when in fact I will argue here that it continued to suffuse cowboys' own sense of their work. Carlo Rotella (2002, 8–9) makes a similar point about the memorialization of blue-collar work in the Rust Belt well after that region's heyday of heavy industry: "Reacting to the aging of industrial urbanism and especially to the departure of factory jobs from the Rust Belt in the latter part of the twentieth century, trend spotters have been perhaps overly quick to attach a nostalgic aura to good hands and body work. . . . Separating the virtue from the work ethic to which it inheres, this use of 'blue-collar' eulogizes actual blue-collar labor in such a way as to end up prematurely dismissing it as an anachronism."

In much the same way, the nostalgic idealization of the cowboy's "hand and body work" was very much present in the actual labor of the ranch (and the minds of those who undertook that labor) well into the twentieth century: the "belief that strong hands doing skilled work had built particular ways of life infused with value" (Rotella 2002, 3). The craft and execution of skilled labor in this way became metonymic for an inheritance that carried with it a commitment to "an honest day's work" slowly slipping away. Ranch labor was thus realized, reshaped by history, *and* idealized within a thick nexus of memory and lived experience of the present; indeed, nostalgia sustained that present, even making the work possible. That being said, this self-mythologizing is neither one-dimensional nor straightforward. It does not negate the gritty, unpleasant reality of ranching work; cowboys often do see themselves doing a rapidly disappearing job, but it is one that no one else wants to do. (That perspective is especially present in the writing of McMurtry or Kelton, both of whom had worked and lived on ranches.) Put simply, in a phrase that finds itself echoed, with slight alterations, in almost every book and article one reads about modern cowboy labor, "It's dangerous, dirty work, but someone's gotta do it."

If, then, a cowboy is the work he does, we also have to recognize that there actually had been two kinds of "cowboys": working ranch hands and "cattlemen" (rancher-owners). Fifty years prior to World War II, the social differences between cattlemen who owned the ranch and their hands had been palpable. As Moore (2009, 3) writes, "there was a clear class distinction between cowboy and cattleman [in the late nineteenth century]. A cowboy was a hired hand who worked cattle on horseback on the ranch and/or up the trail, but who occasionally did other work on foot for the ranch such as repairing fences. Conversely, a cattleman was simply a ranch owner or manager who employed cowboys" (3). Erickson (1981, 5) puts it even more bluntly: "There is one difference between them that goes right to the heart of the matter . . . the rancher can take the day off or go into town whenever he wishes, but the cowboy can't." Moore (2009) expands on the cultural and historical roots of this distinction:

> The cattle industry is an integral part of the history of American expansion in the nineteenth century. On the edges of the frontier, cattlemen were the forerunners of Anglo civilization, and were responsible for building new towns and ensuring economic growth. They were useful citizens. But the cowboy was a nostalgic figure from the start. In the nineteenth century view of the inevitable March of Progress, his job was to tame the frontier for the next wave of productive farmers, and then fade away into history. He was a man outside of time. (6)

As Moore suggests, from the outset cowboys and ranchers or cattlemen seemed very nearly distinct breeds, men needed for distinct tasks that yoked each to a particular social class and cultural use and, in turn, their representation. However, by the mid-twentieth century, these socioeconomic distinctions had begun to give ground, as the twin forces of industrialization and urbanization chained both figures to the labor of the ranch and, in ways we have not appreciated, sometimes eroded the class distinctions between them.

Post–World War II West Texas experienced a particularly illustrative convergence of socioeconomic, industrial, and environmental effects that bore down on both the ranches and those who worked them. Of course the drought experienced by West Texas was matched by a similar one in southeastern Texas; Southern California also had to adjust to the pressures of farm mechanization, while Wyoming grappled with socioeconomic globalization long before its ranches embraced the steady income of dude ranching. But West Texas was the place where all these transformations came together. Because Texas had lagged behind much of the country during the Industrial Revolution, because its own modernization occurred during a financial boom that drove much of its population into the cities, and because this urbanization dovetailed almost perfectly with one of the worst droughts in West Texas recorded history, these ranches found themselves at a crossroads that seemed to demand one thing yet only allowed for the opposite. While the rest of Texas was modernizing—and while new agribusinesses were devouring investment cash—West Texas could only crawl along, its ranches negotiating subsidies from Washington DC to feed their dwindling, frequently starving cattle stock. And while drought and isolation and technological lag beleaguered these ranches, these changes still demanded—loudly—"someone's gotta do it."

Following the rapid industrialization accompanying World War II and the environmental effects of the long drought, the two-decade postwar era became, in the words of Don Graham (2003, 2), a "period of radical transformation in [Texas's] population and economy, when the whole state was changing." An article in the Texas State Historical Association's *Texas Almanac* zooms in more closely on the ranching industry:

> World War II and its manpower shortages forced drastic changes upon the ranching scene. Much of the workforce went into military service. Ranchers had to streamline operations for efficiency, automating wherever possible, cutting pasture sizes, substituting machinery for manual labor, pickup trucks for horses. Most of these changes became permanent, for much of the pre-war manpower never returned. Former cowboys found higher paying jobs in the oil fields and in town. Many innovations appeared in

the first decades after the war: crossbreeding, artificial insemination and computerization being only a few. . . .

A seven-year drought in the 1950s drove home severe lessons in range management, bringing a greater awareness of proper stocking rates, encouraging rotation grazing, grass reseeding, new methods of brush control. (Kelton 2007, 5)

The broader history of Texas during and after World War II reflects similar trends. In his *Gone to Texas: A History of the Lone Star State*, Randolph B. Campbell (2003, 405) traces population density changes that "completed the transition from [Texas's] overwhelming rural past to a predominantly urban present": "by 1950, for the first time, a majority (60 percent in fact) of Texans lived in towns and cities of more than 2,500 population." This transition reflected a number of changes:

The urbanization of Texas, starting late but proceeding faster than the American norm after the 1940s, proceeded on several planes. The automobile sent the first growth to the small cities and towns. Then, suddenly, the new metropolis started to suck the countryside dry . . . as the counties became more and more depopulated, many of the small, rurally situated towns began to wither. Their market was drying up. . . . In most Texas small towns established business declined; young men looked for opportunity elsewhere; numbers stagnated, then slowly declined. (Fehrenbach 2000, 674)

Across the state, vast spatial and socioeconomic changes were having their impact on lifestyles and patterns of work. As small towns—like those featured in the novels discussed in this chapter—lost their populations and businesses, ranchers began to rely more and more on industrial-sized output to cities to subsidize the local business they had lost. Beginning in the late 1940s and early 1950s, "machinery rapidly replaced most farm labor, changing the countryside"

(666). "Cattlemen," Erickson (1981, 183) tells us, "discovered they [could] produce finished beef more cheaply, more quickly, and more efficiently in a factory than on a ranch."

This transition to machinery "marked the transition from farming to agribusiness," a move that itself gestured toward "a model for a totally mechanized and confined cattle industry" (Campbell 2003, 408; Erickson 1981, 183). Labor shifted from traditional manpower to farm equipment like "tractors, disc plows, steam-powered brush-clearing equipment, and giant combines and harvesters," in part to meet growing industrial expectations of output (Fehrenbach 2000, 665). On the surface these changes brought the improvements Erickson notes were necessary to running a ranch after World War II: increased productivity, greater economic gain, and consistent efficiency. As Graham (2003, 221) writes, "Modern technology has transformed some of the old ways of the vaqueros. Rounding up three or four hundred cows, for example, used to take about a week's work performed by fifteen cowboys. With three helicopters (contracted with outside companies), the task can be accomplished in about three hours, and the entire job of branding and doctoring the cattle can be done in about two days."

Yet there was a cost to all this modernization. Along with greater output, mechanization reduced the number of men working permanently on any given ranch (Clayton and Clayton 1985, 28). The men who did remain lost much of the work that once furnished so much of their identity. "Unfortunately for the cowboy," J. W. Williams (1999, 7) would write, "each one of these advances and devices allows the ranch to do the work with fewer men. Although the horse remains the emotional center of ranching, the machine—pickup and stock trailer, bulldozer, helicopter, backhoe—does much of the work." An account of the King Ranch during the 1980s reflects on the emotional toll these kinds of changes could eventually exact from, for example, the foreman of a ranch, like Stephen "Tio" Kleberg:

All Tio wanted to do was ranch. He was happiest on horseback when the worries of a balance sheet vanished in the feel of a good horse cutting off a recalcitrant calf's wayward progress. . . . But Tio was a throwback to the old days. Tio on horseback was what King Ranch was supposed to be. . . . The horse and its rider [Tio] were working cattle in the old way, in the brush and dust. . . . They were laboring on King Ranch in the time-honored manner of the old vaqueros and cowboys going back to the days of the ranch's founding. . . . [But new] conditions forced Tio off the ranch and onto the board of directors—meetings instead of roundups, days spent on golf carts instead of on horseback. (Graham 2003, 216)

Like the cowboys and ranchers decades earlier, Tio feels most at home on a horse, doing the same labor as those who came before him. But once this connection to the history of work was severed, that working identity would suffer. As Erickson (1981, 184) sadly recounts when he remembers seeing a young, now-modern cowboy working on a feedlot instead of a ranch, "He sat in a new saddle, with a big daily horn wrapped with strips of rubber, a breast harness, and a roping cinch, but he carried no rope. Neither did the other men on the crew. And I thought to myself: 'Well, cowboy, they've taken away your rope. Tomorrow they'll take away your horse and issue you a four-wheeler.'" (But four-wheelers can't cut calves like a good quarter horse can.) Or, as Kelton's (1973, 312) protagonist Charlie Flagg puts it, "'The cowboy-rancher has had his day, Big says. It's a bookkeeper's world from here on out.'"

Kelton's clever use of the term "cowboy-rancher," however, again suggests that during this period the lives and work of cowboys and cattlemen ironically came to much more closely mirror each other. Cowboys and ranchers alike began to see themselves as doing a unique, dirty, and well-loved job that was rapidly losing financial stability. A good example is provided, as Clayton has written, in the memoir entitled *The Big Ranch Country*, by J. W. Williams. Williams witnessed ranching go through a major transformation after World War II, as ranchers mechanized their operations, and it was a change that meant fewer and fewer cowboys were needed to do the work (Clayton and Clayton 1985, 3). And then the Big Drought caused even more ranchers to retreat from West Texas. Cattlemen continued to own ranches and employ cowboys, but beyond that distinction the class lines blurred. The ranching literature of the day suggests that neither of these characters from this era had the time or luxury to go into town for a break or dance the night away at a dance hall. However, this erosion of class differences did not mean that the ranch functioned as a classless workplace. Instead, it was that the performance of class identity and class stratification on the ranch now proved to be both malleable and static, especially for a younger generation. As the Claytons (1985, 54) elegantly reflect in their biographical ethnography, *Clear Fork Cowboys: Contemporary Cowboys along the Clear Fork of the Brazos River*, the paradox was that "[c]owboying ha[d] changed, but cowboys ha[d] not."

Faced with a drastically changing work landscape, both cowboys and ranchers would seek out other outlets for the identities and work they assumed they would always have. Between 1950 and 1970, for example, the rodeo rose in both regional and national popularity at an unprecedented rate. As we will see with McMurtry's, Kelton's, and McCarthy's younger protagonists, with less to do on the ranch, the sons and daughters of traditional ranchers and cowboys participated in rodeos and similar events that ameliorated the sting of loss while simultaneously revitalizing crucial components of ranching and cowboy identity. Now the alluring fame and shiny rewards bestowed on the rodeo star momentarily distracted participants from the loss of the actual work the show came to represent. In the novels depicting this period, the rodeos and other performance-based venues act as central stages for, and sites of codification of, the performance of class identity right as that identity seemed to be collapsing back home on the ranch. Here young would-be cowboys and ranchers could reaffirm their identities and class status by literally performing their talents at ranch work. Indeed, those who performed the best—usually, those with the most training and the most expensive horses and gear (in other words, sons and daughters of ranch owners)—could reestablish their family's elite status. In each novel, demonstrations of wealth in the form of clothing, trailers, and other commodities are commonplace at the rodeo and lend class status to those who can afford them—because being a rodeo hero, it turns out, is not cheap. But without real ranch labor to prove one's skill, the articulation of class identity and class status at the rodeo could become an ultimately empty performance.

## On Labor

It is from within this composite historical, cultural, and political framework that I read late twentieth-century cowboy literature as a site of identity production and negotiation. Both the rhetoric surrounding labor and class and the scenes that detail them interrogate the continued aftereffects of change from the late 1940s through early 1960s. As Betsy Klimasmith (2005) argues, literature is a laboratory that tests the very real consequences of historical transformation; novels like *Horseman, Pass By*, *All the Pretty Horses*, and *The Time It Never Rained* can unveil the intricate way regional history and socioeconomic experience came to affect cowboys' lived experience. Meanwhile, these novels reveal the way cowboys and ranchers confronted the forces weighing so heavily on how they conceptualized, how they *thought about*, their life and work. Focusing on this specific regional and cultural history and tying it to broader national movements sketches a rhetorical map of the West that so often locates Texas as the heart of cowboy culture and labor.[1]

So I return to my original question: What happens when we read the cowboy as a figure of labor—as Blake Allmendinger (1992, 3) suggests, by beginning with the idea that a "*cowboy* is defined by the work that he does"? When read alongside the historical context I have described, the protagonists of both *The Time It Never Rained* and *Horseman, Pass By*—landowners who tend to their own stock— look a lot like working cowboys. Similarly, McCarthy's protagonists embody the more "traditional" cowboy: drifters who move from ranch to ranch as work demands (or because they are evading the law). Work in each novel is more than a necessity; it grants each text's cowboy protagonists identity and an intimate connection to their land and its patterns.

However, as each novel also makes clear, that labor is not an activity necessarily to be envied. While older novels may have, as Jane Tompkins (1992, 12) has argued, transformed hard work "from the necessity one wants to escape into the most desirable of human endeavors: action that totally saturates the present moment, totally absorbs the body and mind, and directs one's life to the service of an unquestioned goal," the post–World War II cowboy novel draws on a much more precarious context. When in 1950 the census revealed that more Texans were living in urban centers than rural spaces and that the long drought had begun, cattle prices plummeted and ranch after ranch declared bankruptcy. For those who remained, work was not an escape or a desired activity so much as a grueling necessity that barely kept ranchers and cowboys afloat. As Kelton's (1973, 257) Charlie Flagg remarks of the labor necessary to keep his ranch functioning during the drought, "Now there was no longer any fun in it; now it was an ordeal."

Rather than taking pride in their work, Kelton's, McMurtry's, and McCarthy's ranchers and cowboys often feel ashamed of or depressed by the labor the new environment demands. Bound by a sense of ownership and responsibility, as well as the memory of the joy that labor once offered, ranchers soon become the laborers who had previously done the tough physical work of the ranch. Ironically, then, these ranchers now want to arrest the kind of capitalistic development that enabled them to claim their ranches in the first place. The kind of work they covet—the ranching and cattle herding that lends value to their identities—is now predicated on stopping the growth of their ranches, because that movement (previously associated with national expansions and empire) is only contributing to the accelerating mechanization of their labor. Indeed, in each novel, if the West continues its growth, the end result is actually likely to be an economy more focused on oil, and these cowboys will be out of a job.

Each novel showcases that transition through a series of catastrophes that come to represent change in West Texas. For instance, in McMurtry's *Horseman, Pass By*, once a vet has confirmed the outbreak of hoof-and-mouth disease in Homer Bannon's cattle and the government has ordered a full quarantine of his ranch, the labor that now remains to be done is drastically altered. Rather than engaging in the work of the past, which included rounding up cattle for branding, castrating, milking, or selling—all of which had made the ranch profitable—the cowboys must now turn to the depressing task of rounding up cattle for testing, isolation, and eventual slaughter, a job that will deplete the ranch of its resources. The novel's depictions of this new work are often monotonous, unglamorous, and plain; these sections lose much of the nostalgic recollection characteristic of the rest of the novel. In a simultaneously tedious and harrowing event that reflects this atmosphere, for example, Lonnie, Homer's grandson, remembers running a particularly difficult cow through a chute and into a holding pen for the government vets to test for the progress of the disease: "We surrounded her and finally she stuck her head in like she meant to go. When she did I run up behind her to shut the gate. Then she turned back through herself like a bobcat and went charging down the west wall of the pen. As she went by me she threw out a big cracked hoof, and I spun away from it like I had from a thousand others. Only I spun a fraction too slow, and it caught me on the hip" (McMurtry 1985, 61). This mistake knocks him unconscious. Lonnie's narration of this moment—its rhythmic regularity, its snapshot-like quality, and its critical distance from itself—underscores the regularity of this work and the mechanical routine and precision that accompanies it. At the same time, the clarity and candor of this moment challenge Tompkins's formulation, quoted earlier. The haze of nostalgia has been stripped from this scene to reveal the tension within direct, physical work with cattle. (In other words—as I can say from experience—it just sucks to be kicked.) This grainy tension—between labor as a rhythmic, familiar comfort and a dirty, detailed source of pain—remains unresolved in McMurtry's novel.

However, the subsequent losses on the ranch shift the tenor and shape of work too. When Homer is ordered to execute his infected herd, and his nephew Hud suggests that oil derricks might take its place, Homer's strange emotional outburst stands in stark contrast to Lonnie's unemotional narration:

> [T]here'll be no holes punched in this land while I'm here. They ain't gonna come in an' grade no roads, so the wind can blow me away. . . . What good's oil to me. . . . What can I do with it? With a bunch of fuckin' oil wells. I can't ride out ever day an' prowl amongst 'em, like I can my cattle. I can't breed 'em or tend 'em or rope 'em or chase 'em or nothin'. I can't feel a smidgen a pride in 'em, cause they ain't none a my doin'. Money, yes. Piss on that kinda money. . . . I want mine to come from something that keeps a man doing for himself. (105–6)

In this moment the change from cattle to oil reverberates in multiple registers—ecological, emotional, and socioeconomic. Hud suggests oil as the obvious answer because of the financial stability and profit it promises. Indeed, when Hud inherits the Bannon cattle ranch at the end of the novel, he begins to turn it into an industrial oil field. (He has already been spending his time and money in a more glamorous locale, a city.) But to Homer, riddling his land with holes would leave him torn and incomplete, only capable of supporting a sterile and alienating kind of labor. Even if he became an oil baron, labor would not be something he did, but something about which he would merely think, abstractly; the potential loss of physical involvement frustrates his sense of purpose even if it promises upward class mobility. To Homer, a cowboy's class success is not measured wholly by visible demonstrations or even the accumulation of wealth but by the active purpose and practice of the labor on the land.

The close connection between labor and landscape is fore-grounded in *The Time It Never Rained* as well, when Charlie faces the changes the dry winter has forced on his ranching practices:

> Winter wore on relentlessly with a constant series of cold, dry winds that droned a dusty dirge across the hills and prairies, robbing strength from the thinning livestock, seeking out and stealing any vestige of moisture that might still cling in hidden places. Out of necessity, feeding became heavier; it took fifteen sacks of cake a day rather than ten to keep the cattle from show-ing their ribs. It took longer now to circle the pastures and see that the sheep and cattle received extra protein to supplement the meager dry feed they still managed to rustle on the range. Charlie and Lupe each went in their separate pickups now, split-ting the work because there was so much of it. (Kelton 1973, 127)

Similar to the scene where the cow kicks McMurtry's Lonnie, Kelton's pace here is even and rhythmic, producing a monotonous and dreary effect. And while Kelton's prose is slightly more ornamental than Lonnie's narration, the alliteration of "dry winds that droned a dusty dirge" and only "vestigial" moisture paint the image of West Texas's arid landscape as a site of desolation. Likewise, the labor on this land-scape is "arduous, unrelenting work" that will continue only because there is no financial way out of the predicament in which Charlie and the other ranchers find themselves (282). Kelton's cowboys work against the drought's aura of inevitability. Nancy Cook (2007, 235; emphasis added) also points out the distinction, describing the cost of owning and running a ranch, both personally and economically: "there is no pretense about making a living here—this is where one *spends* a living."

Kelton subtly captures that tension between the physical work of the ranch and its idealization when Charlie must castrate a horse belonging to Manuel, the son of his foreman, Lupe Flores. Although it would be tempting to read this scene as reprising the racial inequality between Texas ranch owners and the Mexican laborers they hire, Kelton's novel refuses that stereotype. The Mexican laborers in Kelton's novel are neither racist caricatures nor the representatives of a romanticized Other. Rather, Charlie frequently defers to Lupe's expertise in running the ranch and feeds weary and hungry illegal immigrants before advising them on where to find work and avoid the border patrol. Moreover, this particular scene focuses on the practical necessity of gelding a horse that is destined to work on a ranch. Kelton depicts the castration of the stallion not to signify an act of racial tension and oppression but to showcase another crucial component of working ranch life: ensuring that you can manage the animals on your spread. As Charlie tells Manuel, "'If we leave [the stallion] as a stud he won't be much 'count for you to ride. If we geld him you can make a good usin'-horse out of him'" (Kelton 1973, 151).

As such, the episode is striking for its stoically procedural treatment of the castration itself. That is, the prose is steady and unadorned, as if it were written for an instruction manual rather than a novel:

Then he told José in Spanish to rope both the colt's forefeet. José swung the loop and laid it easily around the feet as Manuel stepped back and the colt moved forward. . . . José jerked, and the colt went to its knees. Charlie Flagg gave its shoulder a hard push; it went down heavily on its side. José pulled the forefeet back and took a wrap around the left hind leg, pulling it and the forefeet tightly together. He took a couple more wraps, these around all three legs, and made a tie. (152)

Much like McMurtry's depiction of running the cows through the chute to be tested for disease, this task is nearly mechanical yet still performed by human hands. Both José and Charlie contribute equally to the process, showcasing not the dominance or talent of either but the necessity of having all present participate in the work that needs to be done. Similarly, Kelton does not depict the horse as an emblem of wildness. Rather, Charlie coaches Manuel to "'[p]et him. . . . Talk to him so he won't hurt himself'" (153), and the rest of the castration is done via a quick routine that limits its pain. These three men are here doing the work to be done—work that Charlie commences with a reluctant, "'Best we get it over with'" (152).

## On Class

A *New York Times* best seller and one of McCarthy's most popular novels, *All the Pretty Horses* owes a significant debt to its literary antecedents, as well as to dime westerns and the cowboy legend. But something strange happens between the publication of McMurtry's and Kelton's novels and McCarthy's roughly twenty-five years later. Or, more accurately, some*one* strange happens. That someone is John Grady Cole, McCarthy's young protagonist. Unlike Charlie Flagg and Homer Bannon, Grady has no ranch to rescue from almost certain financial and spatial ruin; instead, his parents are divorced, and while his father nostalgically gives him a new saddle as an early Christmas present, his mother has moved to the city to be an actress and has decided to sell the family ranch. Grady's inheritance amounts to a romantic but ultimately futile gesture toward a working lifestyle that his mother has replaced with more lucrative performance in an urban center. And so, even if there are no depictions of hard labor in McCarthy's novel, Grady's lineage nicely frames what there *is*: the performance of labor that belies a preoccupation with money and class. McCarthy's (1992, 17) text thus stages what happens to those ranchers when Texas undergoes a complicated social, cultural, economic, and political shift that leaves them largely without their labor but with the memory of that labor—a shift that sits behind the Cole family lawyer's austere warning to a despondent Grady: "'Son, not everybody thinks that life on a cattle ranch in west Texas is the second best thing to dyin and goin to heaven. . . . If it was a payin proposition that'd be one thing. But it aint.'" As Sara Spurgeon (1999, 25) has argued, the novel is "an elegy for a romanticized way of life, a code of honor, a mythical world birthed and brutally murdered . . . the world of the cowboy"—a world that is, as it turns out, based on a mythic figure that "is bound to crumble, for it is hollow at its core and stripped bare."[2]

Nevertheless, to make the case that *All the Pretty Horses* serves to display and then dismantle crucial elements of the typical western and the romantic cowboy mythos, largely through Grady's failures, critics must find the cowboy lifestyle inauthentic—as Spurgeon argues, "hollow." And, in many ways, it *is* hollow—the glamorous, romanticized image of the cowboy riding off into the sunset (how the novel ends) seems little more than a memory constructed by men who have lost their sense of purpose. But there's more weight and depth buried under that seemingly hopeless dream than we typically think. The very absence of labor in McCarthy's novel actually gestures toward a larger loss that leaves room for the class tension that resurfaces in its aftermath.

Laborless and thus unmoored without the kind of working identity so crucial to McMurtry's and Kelton's protagonists, McCarthy's John Grady Cole and his best friend, Lacey Rawlins, leave Texas for Mexico to find and experience "authentic" cowboy labor on a ranch.[3] When they arrive on the Hacienda de Nuestra Señora de la Purísima Concepción, Grady quickly rises to local fame for his superior efficiency in breaking young, wild horses: "the vaqueros seemed to treat them with a certain deference," McCarthy writes, and when Grady and Lacey arrive to work more horses, "there were some twenty people standing about looking at the horses . . . and all waiting for them to return" (McCarthy 1992, 105). Here Grady earns respect on actual ranches because he handles breaking horses with a grace and skill supposedly "authentic" cowboys respect. This respect in turn earns him class mobility when Don Hector, the owner of the hacienda, promotes him on the ranch.

Yet on closer inspection Grady's horse-breaking resembles a performance of class more than labor as such. As word of Grady's work spreads and his audience grows, McCarthy's prose fashions the ranch into a stage and the horses and Grady into actors: "Someone had built a fire on the ground outside the potrero and there were something like a hundred people gathered, some come from the pueblo of La Vega six miles to the south, some from farther. He rode the last five of the horses by the light of that fire, the horses dancing, turning in the light, their red eyes flashing" (107). A makeshift rodeo, this scene sits at the vexed intersection of lived experience and historical memory. Like the rodeo stars who use fame in the spotlight to replace the work they once had reason to do, Grady's breaking becomes a nostalgic, staged affair. The audience Grady draws actually do have to work—indeed, he should not have an audience at all: the laborers he draws merely attest to the lack of work available for them. Those who come to watch are impoverished—many out of work—and thus Grady's performance positions him in a constructed class status above his audience. On the one hand, he is more talented at and vital to ranch work than those who watch; on the other, he merely plays the role of a staged distraction that memorializes the work many in the audience once did. Literally, this is a poor-man's rodeo performance.

In the same vein Grady's promotion by the ranch is undercut by the way Don Hector's house reveals the now-constructed nature of cowboy authenticity: "They sat at a long table of english walnut. The walls of the room were covered with blue damask and hung with portraits of men and horses. At the end of the room was a walnut sideboard with some chafing dishes and decanters set out upon it.... Don Hector reached behind him and took a china ashtray from the sideboard and placed it before them and took from his shirtpocket a small tin box of english cigarettes and opened them and offered them to John Grady and John Grady took one" (112–13). Here the wealth in Don Hector's house demonstrates a class difference that makes Grady uncomfortable. Rather than an "authentic" rancher, Don Hector is a businessman who reaps the benefits of his capital investment, which is furnished by work that feeds off the desire of Grady, and those like him, to experience cowboy labor. His wealth also showcases how integral the West is becoming to the global economy. Don Hector needs cowboys like Grady, who seek out and memorialize the labor of the ranch, to support his wealthy lifestyle.

However, because the ranch and its working order are based in class difference and labor stratification, that order ultimately fails Grady after he begins an affair with Don Hector's daughter. Grady is arrested under the pretext of having stolen a horse. Just as the class mobility Grady has aspired to is revealed as false, class transgression (the affair) leads to punishment by the law. Maintaining a strict hierarchy through his bloodline is one way Don Hector can continually remind those who work for him of their subordinate status. Even though he may also work the ranch, Don Hector, conversely, will not allow others to mimic familial membership. McCarthy thus suggests that class is not only a status that one inhabits and enjoys through financial success. A ranch also sets class lines that cannot be crossed.

At the same time, Kelton's story of Charlie Flagg's struggle with self-representation reminds us that when the capital stability of the ranch is under the pressure of ecological and economic deterioration, class lines cannot be sustained in the same way. Early in the novel Kelton (1973, 20) stages a tension between ranching as pleasurable work and ranching as profitable business: "But later when [Charlie] went into ranching for himself he quickly found it was difficult to show much profit on that kind of cattle or that kind of operation. These blooded Herefords were poor sport but far more negotiable at the bank." Although he would rather raise cattle, here Charlie recognizes the gulf between ranching as enjoyment and ranching as a source of profit. His discomfort with the financial promise yet physical ease of raising Herefords reflects, again, the way cowboys and ranchers thought of their work in both nostalgic and realistic terms. Charlie wants to reexperience the difficult yet invigorating challenges of the past, and he understands that his ranch will quickly go under if he does not adjust to new economic demands. Success at the bank, now a domesticated and more artificial success, does not possess the cultural weight of physically working the ranch— and being able to reflect on that labor.

The line that Kelton draws here between kinds of labor is also manifested in the way cowboy work presents on the body. The Herefords stand for the kind of abstraction from the landscape that the town's young deputy also represents; Kelton describes him as "dressed in a neatly tailored Western shirt and tight legged cowboy pants, shiny high heeled boots and a nicely creased Stetson hat," whereas Charlie "wore a nondescript straw hat beaten badly out of shape and a pair of old black boots, his baggy khaki trousers stuffed carelessly into their tops" (7). What's at stake here is not the appearance of authenticity—which, as Nathaniel Lewis (2003) and others remind us, is a false barometer of westernness—but practicality. Charlie's clothes lend him class purchase not because they gesture toward an "authentic" relationship to the West but because they gesture toward the working relationship he has cultivated on his ranch. Still, it would be misleading to say that the novel's rough-hewn cowboys enjoy some kind of privileged connection to nature—indeed, their failure in the face of the drought magnifies their tense, complicated, often misunderstood interdependence with the natural. It is more that their work encourages a kind of necessary, mutable awareness and respect for what the land can provide. As Charlie reflects when economic instability drives younger cowboys to overgraze their already dry land, "Continued long enough, this abuse would make barren desert pastures that once had grown tall grass. . . . [H]e felt a deep and binding obligation to the land itself. . . . To see it bleed now brought him grief; it was like watching a friend waste away with terminal cancer" (Kelton 1973, 294-95). As the land slips away, work identity *and* the memory of that work figure viscerally in the rancher's sense of self.

In Kelton's novel, however, successfully tending to such labors ultimately proves to be beyond the cowboys' reach. When it becomes evident that Charlie and his community of ranchers must petition for federal aid to offset their losses, the cause only highlights new tensions within the conflicting reality of work and the memory of what that work used to be. The community gathers at Charlie's house to discuss the inevitable. When Charlie suggests that Prentice Harpe, a fellow rancher who does not work his own cattle, go to Washington as their representative, Harpe refuses Charlie's request with an eye on the self-representation of social status: "'I'm a drugstore cowboy. They'd sense it right off. We want somebody who *looks* the part, somebody who's always been a cowman, somebody who's got *ranch* burned onto him like a brand burned on a bull. We want a man who—when he walks in there—will make everybody say, "Now there is the genuine article." You're the one for that, Charlie. You've got *image*'" (269). While each rancher has equal need for federal aid, Charlie's years of cowboy labor and experience "brand" him, a play on words that both links him to the animals he owns and signals the permanent scarring such labor can leave on one's body. And while Charlie's fellow ranchers and cowboys view this "branding" as a marker of class status gained only through years of hard work, to politicians in Washington DC—outsiders—this branding creates a potent visual reminder that even those in Washington would be unable to deny. Here manipulating and relying on the very romanticizing their work effaces, Kelton's ranchers, and especially Charlie, represent the knotty intersection of realized and idealized, environmental and social, that constitutes the cowboy's class status.

But again, the process of accepting that federal aid is a painful one. "Give us rain," Kelton proclaims early in the novel, "and it makes no difference who is in the White House" (4), thus suggesting the power of nature over that of politics. Ideally Charlie and his fellow ranchers would work without government aid or interference, and thus pride in private work is mapped onto shame about public funding even when that feeling is undeserved. Early in the novel, in fact, Charlie and another rancher, Page Mauldin, have discussed the politics of accepting government money to offset the cost of grain and feed. When Charlie resists this help, Page explains the actual financial and political logic behind his decision: "'We ain't paupers, Charlie; that ain't the point. Most of the people who get government money ain't paupers. It ain't given to us because we need it; it's given to us because somebody needs *us* . . . they need our vote. So everybody's gettin' it, and you're payin' your tax money for it. Only way you'll ever get any of that back is to claim what's comin' to you'" (58).

Here Page homes in on the complicated political and emotional regret that accompanies accepting governmental help. In the interest of individual financial growth and his class standing, Page advocates for federal aid because it will enable him and ranchers like him to survive (while noting that politicians benefit as well). Nevertheless, Charlie's response recognizes the fear that accepting government aid would jeopardize the romanticized "authentic identity" he has unknowingly cultivated: "'That ain't the way I was brought up, or you either. . . . We was taught to believe in a man rustlin' for himself as long as he's able. If you get to dependin' on the government, the day'll come when the damn *federales* will dictate everything you do. Some desk clerk in Washington will decide where you live and where you work and what color toilet paper you wipe yourself with. And you'll be scared to say anything because they might cut you off the tit'" (58–59). Charlie says he was "taught to believe," a phrase that unveils the role of memory and history in sustaining the cowboy's working identity. As Charlie's complicated position reveals, current circumstances have forced him to relinquish an "authentic" identity that was, in the way he had been brought up, already a "reality" made by memory-work and sustained by its labors.

On Space

That history—and the memory of that history—is also written onto the space these cowboys and ranchers inhabit. Spaces both for work and for leisure, the ranch and the open reaches of West Texas offer these laborers purpose and home. In all three novels, therefore, space is like cowboy labor itself—both realized and idealized, shifting under the weight of new environmental and economic pressures and offering a stage onto which cowboys and ranchers can project visions of themselves they never really had in the first place. Like cowboy labor—once it had been romanticized as the exciting pursuit of cattle, lasso in hand, shouting "yee-haw"—the spaces of the literary West increasingly became gritty urban-industrial landscapes after World War II.

Shifts in labor, in other words, registered on the landscape itself, as Texas oil fields replaced cattle herds and rows of corn. The war effort required a new urban workforce. The departures of people destined for the military and the factories, combined with the effects of drought and mechanization, led to an overall decline in farm population.[4] As the family or individually run ranch became an even harder venture to support, oil became the predominant resource and, consequently, the principal source of income in the state. (Oil displaced cattle and corn for the first time since Texas had taken its place in the national economy.) As a result, new spaces were etched into Texas: rural spaces were now ornamented by mechanical labor and urban spaces by a more industrial infrastructure. Oil fields glittering with metallic oil rigs, trucks for ranch work, and trains for transportation represented a new phase of structural capital flowing into Texas.

And it is precisely in the gap between these developments and the older stages of capitalization—originally driven by Manifest Destiny, homesteading, and more—that the cowboys and ranchers in these novels find themselves. As the labor they memorialize— and in many respects continue to perform—becomes all but pragmatically obsolete and ecologically impossible in post–World War II Texas, the land of these novels undergoes changes as well. The environmental crises in Kelton's and McMurtry's novels mirror the complex political, structural, and economic devastation their ranches face; the two plights become metonymic for each other. That is, the reshuffling of space and socioeconomics both undermines the identity of those who remain tied to the finances and labor of the ranch and transforms the lives of the younger men and women for whom ranch labor is no longer an option. The result is a twinned shift of identity and space: the younger cowboys in *The Time It Never Rained*, *All the Pretty Horses*, and *Horseman, Pass By*, in a desperate attempt to salvage the skills and familiar base of knowledge they have in a society that is charging headfirst into modernization, look to urban centers for work as "spectacle cowboys" in the local rodeos.

As I have already suggested, John Grady Cole's breaking scene soon becomes a rodeo performance that etches deeper class lines between laborers on the ranch. Additionally, Grady discovers that the real Jimmy Blevins—the name assumed by the young cowboy he and Rawlins encounter on the way to Mexico, and who is the best shot and rider of the three of them—is a western radio minister who broadcasts across the globe. Together the two versions of Jimmy Blevins comprise both the traditional cowboy and the modern performance version—one, at the end of the novel, dead because of conceptions of vigilante justice that recall the Wild West, the other alive and well and reaching "[t]he whole world [with] a voice . . . like a instrument" (McCarthy 1992, 297). Meanwhile, each novel draws together its urban and rural landscapes by showcasing and then foregrounding the passage of time on spaces coded by particular kinds of work. When read alongside one another, these scenes create something like a series of *tableaux vivants* that blur the line between nostalgia and the cowboy's new present.

McMurtry's *Horseman, Pass By* might seem to contain relatively few detailed descriptions of the Texas landscape. The two earliest panoramas are Lonnie's overtly (and overly) nostalgic opening vision, which in the haze of memory recalls the "green . . . early oat fields" and lends a hue of rebirth to the landscape (McMurtry 1985, 3). Another tableau recalls a dream of his in which he imagines looking down from a cliff on "Texas, green and brown and graying in the sun, spread wide under the clear spread of sky like the opening scene in a big Western movie" (70). Together, these vistas set the scene for a rural Texas that no longer exists. In both scenes Lonnie must invoke the past—either through narrative "looking back" or dreaming—to access a rich and detailed image of rural Texas. Yet even Lonnie's visions acknowledge industrial change; his opening subsequently recalls how "a train would go by and blow its whistle," an event that "always took the spirit out of the cowboys' talk; made them [more] lonesome than they could say" (5). Lonnie's Texas may hold the memory of the idyllic, empty space of the nostalgic Wild West, but at the same time it cannot evade the present and its new working order.

Moreover, *Horseman, Pass By*'s landscapes only expose a Texas pulled between older and newer kinds of labor, showcased in a particularly haunting light when the government sends in contractors to dig the execution pits for the diseased cattle: "When I mounted, I noticed the bulldozers. There were eight or ten of them, sitting out in the old grown-over field we never used. By the time I was a mile from the barn they had cranked up, and you could hear them all over the prairie. Huge clouds of dust began to roll out of the fields, and I knew they must be scraping out pits" (121). The sad parallel here between Lonnie riding his horse and the contractors riding in their bulldozers interweaves the forms of labor on display even as it tries to distinguish between them. On the one hand, Lonnie represents the cowboy gearing up for a day of labor on the ranch, as he would have in an earlier time; on the other hand, he recognizes that his labor on this particular day is necessitated by the very presence of the bulldozers. He must spend the day rounding up cattle for slaughter—a familiar task for the cowboy, yet this time with an ending that will halt the work he traditionally does with the cattle on the ranch. He is literally acting as the agent of his own destruction. The bulldozers not only broadly represent this new phase of capitalism—ultimately the space they clear by killing the cattle makes room for the oil rigs Hud will eventually plant across the ranch. It is as if they claim the space of the Texas ranch itself when noise is heard "all over the prairie." They inhabit and repurpose "the old grown-over field we never used."

But *where* these cowboys subsequently go after finishing their work also throws light on the complex interplay of transformation and nostalgia. Pushed off their ranches by the need for the industrially graded and sized products of mechanization, cowboys and ranchers now gather at the rodeo—some for distracting entertainment, some to ride in the rodeo itself and thus participate in the reduction of a cowboy's working identity to a disposable spectacle. Indeed, in *Horseman, Pass By* the urban rodeo scenes occur almost immediately after scenes of preparing to slaughter and the slaughter itself at the ranch. Here the timing seems to suggest the depressing fact that for the cowboys this is the only place they have left to go. Of course for each of these novels' protagonists, employment in the rodeo is not an option because it mocks actual labor and produces nothing. Nevertheless, *The Time It Never Rained* and *Horseman, Pass By* put both the postindustrial cowboy and his new urban working space on display. On the first day the rodeo is in town, for instance, Lonnie takes advantage of the show to distract himself from the awful work he began the day before. While there, he watches "half of Thalia waking up": "I saw a woman stagger out to her clothesline in a bathrobe, to hang out an early washing. In the arena below me a cowgirl was loping her paint horse around and around in circles—she acted like it was the only thing she knew how to do" (101). The scene juxtaposes domestic imagery alongside the rodeo cowgirl's mechanical warm-up, even suggesting that a practice rooted in tending animals, a biologically based job, now merely signals the leaking of the exterior, urban routines into one's "home." Indeed, we learn that "[t]he whole town had a rodeo look already, paper cups and beer cans everywhere, and piles of horseshit drying in the street" (107).

In *The Time It Never Rained*, Charlie Flagg's son, Tom, chooses to embrace the postindustrial cowboy identity and ride the rodeo circuit to make fast and easy money. His decision hinges on the structure of a new western space, organized along the lines of modernization and spectacle. After a successful rodeo ride, Jason Ellender, president of the Ellender Trailer Company, approaches Tom to "'talk some business'" (Kelton 1973, 182). Ellender proposes that Tom relinquish his father's old trailer, one that "Charlie had bought from a tin-barn welder, its running gear made from an old car chassis" and was "hell for stout," and instead haul one of his sleeker, more modern, models (183). When Tom refuses because he assumes the price is too high, Ellender explains why "'[i]t wouldn't have to cost nearly as much as you think'":

"I spend a lot of money on advertising, Tom. And one of the best advertisements I can have is for good rodeo hands like you to be seen pulling my trailers to hell and gone.... We'd paint your name on the trailer in big letters where everybody could see them: TOM FLAGG. And below, much smaller, would be the company insignia. People would say to themselves, 'If an Ellender trailer is good enough for Tom Flagg, it's good enough for me.' And wherever you went, people would know Tom Flagg was in town." (183–84)

Here Tom's prior class status is converted to consumer advertising, and space is organized along the lines of capital's needs. In accepting his new role as a mobile salesperson for the company, Tom (as rodeo cowboy) literally embodies capitalism's growth within space ("to hell and gone"), as well as its power to reorganize that space.

Nowhere is this transformation more evident than in the contrast between the first and final scenes of McCarthy's *All the Pretty Horses*. As the novel opens, John Grady has returned home for his grandfather's funeral (thus beginning where *Horseman, Pass By* ends). To escape from the confines of the coffin and the corpse, he steps into the night for fresh air:

As he turned to go he heard the train. He stopped and waited for it. He could feel it under his feet. It came boring out of the east like some ribald satellite of the coming sun howling and bellowing in the distance and the long light of the headlamp running through the tangled mesquite brakes and creating out of the night the endless fenceline down the dead straight right of way and sucking it back again wire and post mile on mile into the darkness after where the boilersmoke disbanded slowly along the faint new horizon and the sound came lagging and he stood still holding his hat in his hands in the passing groundshudder watching it till it was gone. Then he turned and went back to the house. (McCarthy 1992, 3–4)

While the machine tears apart the garden in the classic manner described by Leo Marx (1964), John Grady's reaction is what interests me. He has not crossed the train tracks, yet he waits for the train to pass as if he had. Moreover, he stands "holding his hat in his hands" and "watching [the train] till it was gone," only moving back toward the house when the ground no longer shudders. In other words, the train arrests John Grady's attention and movement entirely; he loses himself in what McCarthy describes as the train's disruptive yet oddly controlled path through the rural landscape. Here the industrial organization of space undoes John Grady's identity as a cowboy of the rural West; while the train passes, he even goes so far as to remove his hat, as if doffing it to a colonel or a king.

But after spending the entire novel searching for—and failing to find—what he considers authentic cowboy labor, John Grady finds himself again, at the end, at a funeral and again without a job. In a sad attempt to do something cowboylike when he has nothing else to do, he rides through the desert and comes upon a lone bull who eerily evokes his own experience: "There were few cattle in that country because it was barren country indeed yet he came at evening upon a solitary bull rolling in the dust against the bloodred sunset like an animal in sacrificial torment" (McCarthy 1992, 302). Both John Grady and the bull are out of place: their purpose and their identities, tied to the work from which they have been separated, constitute the sacrifice that the bull enacts and the "sacrificial torment" John Grady endures. Lost in a hellish vision without work to save him, John Grady can do nothing but silently walk on: "and horse and rider and horse passed on and their long shadows passed in tandem like the shadow of a single being. Passed and paled into the darkening land, the world to come" (302). Here it is as if he and his horse—emblems of the cowboy's life on the ranch—themselves fade to nothing but shadow. And this moment is reinforced by the other final image of the novel, when John Grady watches a group of Indians—the last, ruined descendants of the Comanche—who pay him no attention: "They had no curiosity about him at all. As if they knew all that they needed to know. They stood and watched him pass and watched him vanish upon that landscape solely because he was passing. Solely because he would vanish" (301).

Here we go again, we might say: the cowboy rides into the sunset. McCarthy's parting shot now describes the West, in Grady's meditations, as a space that "was rushing away and seemed to care nothing for the old or the young or the rich or poor or dark or pale or he or she. Nothing for their struggles, nothing for their names. Nothing for the living or the dead" (301). But although this familiar ending is the one that often crops up in McCarthy's works—the lonely cowboy, dislodged from his place in the old West, staring into a dark future in which he has no place—it is not the only ending these novels imagine. McMurtry's Lonnie, for instance, finishes *Horseman, Pass By* in a similar way—he leaves the ranch, after its purpose leaves him—but he heads to the city.

And Kelton's Charlie Flagg does something entirely different again. Toward the end of *The Time It Never Rained*, West Texas has betrayed Charlie. The drought has stretched on for more years than his ranch can accommodate, and he is forced to turn to raising goats to keep the ranch afloat. But when the rains finally come, they wash most of his protective measures away, drowning most of the newly sheared goats and overwhelming the landscape. As he realizes his efforts to save the goats are in vain, Charlie turns to his wife, Mary, and cries, "'[T]hey saved *me*, but I can't save *them*'" (Kelton 1973, 393). Those haunting words encompass not only this particular scene but the complicated tensions within a rancher's labor, his ranch's economic health, and the environment that he depends on for both. Despite his deep familiarity with the challenges of eking out a living in West Texas—as he confides to Manuel, "'I've lived through other drouths, son. They usually break hard'" (394)—the severity of this environmental crisis represents a challenge beyond his abilities. Even his goats cease responding to Charlie's attempts to save them: "He could sense the fear that was taking hold of the animals. The goat was more sensitive, more perceptive than the sheep, more responsive to weather changes" (389). Charlie tries to drive the goats forward with his pickup and, as a last resort, to build a fire to keep them warm, as if believing that more technology makes for better ranching. Yet even Charlie realizes that "[i]t would have been better, he thought, to have brought two horses" rather than the pickup (388). Encased in his truck, even the natural sensitivity the goats have toward the environment is gone in Charlie himself, as he reacts to them with a useless machine and an ultimately deadly gasoline fire.

These final moments therefore reprise the uneven and messy relationship the ranchers and cowboys of these novels have with the spaces that provide and support their work. Despite advances in industrial ranching techniques, ranching remains a grueling, on-the-ground job that in turn encourages cowboys and ranchers to cast their minds back to when that job wasn't mediated by machines. And at times those machines only cause more harm than good. In that way, the final scene of Kelton's novel recalls McMurtry's harrowing depiction of Homer Bannon's cattle being shot in a pit, execution style, from the safety of bulldozers. Understandably such deadly scenes cause those who witness them to turn to better memories. And yet, as these characters and others stand dumbfounded at the impossible task of rebuilding, Charlie manages an encouraging insight: "'There's still the land,'" he tells them. "'A man can always start again. A man always *has* to'" (394). At the core, the land itself offers the last salvation—it is after all the primary, necessary ingredient to ranch work. And as difficult as that rebuilding is, Kelton's novel ends with the promise that it will come. In the novel's final scene, with dawn breaking over their shoulders, Charlie and Mary "walk back together through the cold rain" (395) as the younger generation loads the still-living goats into the trailer, half armed and half burdened with the knowledge that there is still work to be done. This ending is not the cowboy galloping into the sunset of *All the Pretty Horses*; it's not even the cowboy turning to the urban landscape for redemption, as in *Horseman, Pass By*. It is the cowboy-rancher refusing to vanish—instead staying firmly put, in the coming light of dawn, on the land he owns.

# 5 Tradition and Modernization Battle It Out on Rocky Soil

Sherman Alexie's *The Lone Ranger and Tonto Fistfight in Heaven*, Stephen Graham Jones's *The Bird Is Gone*, and Linda Hogan's *Mean Spirit*

[T]he blood/land/memory complex articulates acts of indigenous minority recuperation that attempt to seize control of the symbolic and metaphorical meanings of indigenous "blood," "land," and "memory" and that seek to liberate indigenous minority identities from definitions of authenticity imposed by dominant settler cultures.

—Chadwick Allen, *Blood Narrative*

The character of survivance creates a sense of native presence over absence, nihility, and victimry.

Native survivance is an active sense of presence over absence, deracination, and oblivion; survivance is the continuing of stories, not a mere reaction, however pertinent. . . . Survivance stories are renunciations of dominance, detractions, obtrusions, the unbearable sentiments of tragedy, and the legacy of victimry. Survivance is the heritable right of succession or reversion of an estate and, in the course of international declarations of human rights, is a narrative estate of native survivance.

—Gerald Vizenor, *Literary Chance*

In the two passages above, one gets a glimpse of two scholarly approaches to the project of reclaiming an American Indian literary history, one that seeks to recuperate ethnic identity after mass historical deterritorialization and massacres suffered at the hands of Anglo-Americans. In different ways Chadwick Allen and Gerald Vizenor both argue that American Indian narratives recover ethnic and cultural stories, traditions, and memories to reclaim indigenous identity in the face of the hostile conditions and consequences of Anglo-American colonialism. Allen's "blood/land/memory complex" (adapted from N. Scott Momaday's trope "blood memory") and Vizenor's "survivance" see narrative as a tool that enables both recovery from the horrors of the past and proactive, productive engagement with the circumstances of the present and future.[1] Recuperating that identity ultimately aids indigenous cultures in establishing their own contemporary agency and presence. This work, and other work like it, has fueled a continuing project that aims to define and continually refine American Indian identity in American and American Indian indigenous literature, especially in American Indian literature from the West, where conflicts between the two groups were especially violent.

What happens to that identitarian project and the related questions of sovereignty it raises when it encounters the nexus of class, labor, and space in western American novels (among which Native American texts should be included)? As I offer some answers in this chapter, I will also maintain that the two dominant approaches I list above do not fully equip us to explore the origins of the communal and individual damage sustained by American Indians in the literature that depicts their cultures encountering American modernization. We must recognize the limitations of both modernization *and* tradition in using the past to understand and represent the present. Indeed, both Allen and Vizenor warn against what Vizenor (1993, 144) terms "terminal creeds" that lock individuals in the past to the detriment of their futures. In this chapter focused on literary depictions of Indian interactions with aspects of modern American class, labor, and space, I consider how uncritical uses of narrative to recall the past can encourage a dangerous stagnation that falsely pits Indian cultural tradition and Anglo-American modernization against each other. Moreover, those uncritical uses of narrative depict cultural traditions as too static to embrace adaptation. Disengagement from the American modernization of class, labor, and space also distracts Indians from the way these structures' inner workings depend on the exploitation of Indians through the feedback loop of modern capital.[2] The stasis thus generated by the false binary between tradition versus modernization traps characters in the destructive relationships they have with newer forms of labor, new uses of capital, and new class demarcations, all unfolding in spaces that were once tranquil and familiar but are now damaged and dangerous.

My approach may initially seem counterintuitive: many of the spaces on display in modern Native American narratives, particularly those set on reservations, seem to make possible only a small number of lived experiences. The historian Philip Deloria (2004, 6) has made this case in *Indians in Unexpected Places*, in which he argues that Indians are most often represented as traditional "Indian people, corralled on isolated and impoverished reservations."[3] Deloria argues that this representation is largely inaccurate, and he supports that view by examining a series of exemplary cases in which American Indians adapted to early twentieth-century modernization and productively interwove its practices into their own cultural traditions.[4] Taking Deloria's argument as my starting point, I have chosen to examine three novels—Linda Hogan's *Mean Spirit* (1990), Sherman Alexie's *The Lone Ranger and Tonto Fistfight in Heaven* (1993), and Stephen Graham Jones's *The Bird Is Gone* (2003)—in which labor *seems* barely present but is actually fundamental in shaping the story. However, departing from Deloria, I argue that these novels explore not only the dangers of uncritically embracing either tradition or modernization but also the need to engage with both. In these novels, as modernization advances and Indians turn to static traditions, memories, and stories that evoke the past, those narratives inhibit relationships and production across multiple platforms—limits that in turn challenge cultural security in a number of ways. Specifically, class mobility is nullified by legal practices and land claims, unfamiliar to Indians, that place money and valuable land in the hands of those for whose benefit such political and economic maneuvers are enacted. And in a similar vein, labor for the self recedes and is replaced by labor that manipulates land as capital or that is work contracted for others, shifting individuals' relationship to labor from rewarding and productive to spectacular or disembodied. Space thus enables forms of labor that bring profit to the few who hold power and disables other forms that once benefited those who performed that labor. And all these negative relationships to space, class, and labor—which recourse to past narratives cannot ameliorate—reinforce and widen the falsified gap between Indians and modernization, a trap into which these novels fall. We can read their paucity of depictions of labor and adaptation as an imaginative consequence of falling into this trap. Given the historical record and the activist tone of these novels, one might expect to read about Indians melding traditional cultural practices with modern circumstances. Instead, the traditional and the modern are typically kept at extreme distance from each other. Unable to productively deploy traditional labor in the capitalist marketplace and purchasing essentially useless consumer goods while bemoaning their lack of income for necessities such as food, Indian characters in these novels share an overcommitment to static traditional practices that bars them from a more proactive and adaptive engagement with modernization.

The depiction of political and legal relationships between Indians and Americans in these novels provides a kind of laboratory for testing how the narrative strategies of the blood/land/memory complex and survivance represent and respond to the circumstances of Indians' relationship to American life. None of the Indians in the works I survey fully meet Deloria's description; instead, they showcase the challenges Indians must but cannot overcome to integrate themselves into and live productively in American culture. On the one hand, these authors deliberately anchor their Indian characters in the past in order to critique the limitations of static tradition, examine the impact of modernization, and refine the narrative elements of the blood/land/memory complex and survivance. On the other hand, reading these novels together allows us to see that they build a case for the importance of adaptation to and a more informed awareness of American modernization. Although the past can offer sanctuary from exploitation in these stories, it ultimately does not lend American Indians the resources they need to shape their own relationships to modernization. In my view, the greater narrative potential of survivance and of the blood/land/memory complex actually lies in their ability to not only reflect the past but also—and more importantly—to participate productively and visibly in the present and future.

Other critics have studied the significance of space and the presence of class boundaries in these three texts, yet labor, which is an integral component of both, often goes unremarked upon, while class is commonly subordinated to ethnicity and race. Reading these narratives that engage survivance and the blood/land/memory complex, we have an opportunity to interrogate the power of labor and class *alongside* space. Moreover, my focus, following Deloria, on how American Indians faced new patterns of class, labor, and space at the turn of the twentieth century also raises the issue of the perceived gulf between tradition and modernization that still influences the way many people view American Indian populations. History scholars have moved to right that perception with work informed by a recognition, as Colleen O'Neill (2004, 2) puts it, that a "rigid modern/traditional dichotomy . . . too often marks historical writing" about American Indians.[5] Literary texts imagine the harmful effects of that dichotomy on Indian identity, balancing the case for why Indians must integrate modernization with tradition against the dangerous, exploitative consequences of that engagement.

Ultimately, because literature does not need to be true to history, these texts can converse with historical events in ways that both depict the past and depart from it. Moreover, because these texts depict minority cultures, it's important that we recognize the constraints such cultures have been put under and the progress they have made in spite of those constraints. Because literature offers an imaginative record of lived experience, in this case figuring social, cultural, and political contexts that have real-life counterparts in the history of abuse and displacement of American Indians, these texts represent historical patterns of survival and resistance and propose the shape of future ones. Beginning with a brief discussion of scenes of labor in Sarah Winnemucca Hopkins's autobiographical *Life among the Piutes* and D'Arcy McNickle's autobiographical *The Surrounded*, I examine the depiction of older forms of labor that emerged before the days of reservation living to offer a comparison to the newer labor "opportunities" oil represents in Linda Hogan's *Mean Spirit* and other works. My first section looks at representations of space that prove disharmonious to more traditional forms of labor. I next explore how those fraught spatial relationships trouble class mobility and class status, in part because new forms of labor funnel capital goods and profits into the hands of those who acquire them immorally or through immoral laws. That financial benefit both draws from and reinforces the overall decline of Indian labor that I examine in my final section. These troubled new relationships to space, class, and labor also cause characters to suffer a continuing loss of identity. In these ways, the works I examine in this chapter imaginatively explore the consequences of instability, frustration, vulnerability, and danger for individuals and their larger communities when faced with a hostile modernization that presumes there will be no place for them. But, as I argue in closing, there are costs to this particular positing of cultural erasure in these novels: *modern* labor is made to disappear with it, and thus our fictional representations render absent a resource that, in modern history, American Indians have in fact drawn upon. I end with some reflections on why that "double erasure" has taken place.

Prelude: Older Forms of Labor and the Mythic Past

*Life among the Piutes*, Hopkins's depiction of life on the Reservation of Pyramid and Muddy Lakes in the mid-1860s (first published in the 1880s), provides a good introduction to the changing patterns of labor, space, and class that frame many Native American narratives:

> No white people lived there at the time it was given to us. We Piutes have always lived on the river, because out of those two lakes we caught beautiful mountain trout, weighing from two to twenty-five pounds each, which would give us good income if we had it all, as at first. Since the railroad ran through in 1867, the white people have taken all the best part of the reservation from us, and one of the lakes also.
>
> The first work my people did on the reservation was to dig a ditch, to put up a grist-mill and saw-mill. Commencing where the railroad now crosses at Wadsmouth, they dug about a mile; but the saw-mill and grist-mill were never seen or heard of by my people, though the printed report in the United States statutes . . . says twenty-five thousand dollars was appropriated to build them. Where did it go? The report says these mills were sold for the benefit of the Indians who were to be paid in lumber for hours, but no stick of lumber have they ever received. My people do not own their land anymore. The white people are using the ditch which my people made to irrigate their land. This is the way are treated by our white brothers. (Hopkins 1994, 76–77)

Hopkins distinguishes between prior and reservation life to draw sharp lines between the ways in which labor done on reservation land both disenfranchised indigenous populations from native lands and shook the foundations of indigenous ethnic identity. Catching fish as labor to sustain a communal ethnic living is superseded by irrigation done for the benefit of unknown others. The railroad, too, interrupts the landscape and brings a new population, with a new ethnic identity, to formerly protected lands. Moreover, the modernization of these industries—railroad, grain milling, and sawmill work—stands in direct contrast to the earlier, more embodied labor of maintaining life via natural resources. And these ventures' false promise of financial payoff for Indians doubles that marginalization and foreshadows a more lasting and more psychological removal from the land. "My people do not own their land anymore," Hopkins remarks, a phrase that ties together emotional and physical distance from familiar space. She uses both kinds of distance to indicate that the limited forms of early reservation labor demanded new systems of class and belonging that left indigenous populations vulnerable to the legal clout of American settlers.

McNickle's *The Surrounded* registers a similar early disconnection between ethnically coded labors when it compares the labor required by Archilde's father, the Spaniard Max Leon, to that of his two young Indian sons, Mike and Narcisse, who identify more with the older ways of their Indian mother, Agnes:

> The grain was being cut on Max Leon's ranch. In the morning he put on his riding boots and followed the men with their two binders into the field. . . . After an oiling and a last tightening up the first binder was set to work. As the white arms revolved they tossed the tall grain stalks against the flying sickle and on to the moving aprons. A bundle collected at the side, was tied with twine and kicked into the carriage. A second bundle followed, then a third. The wheat was heavy and the bundles came through quickly. The second binder started into action. . . .

"Send [Mike and Narcisse] to the field with a jug of water. Tell 'em to stay till the water's drunk up, then fetch more. They got to tend to that while the men are working or I'll give them my whip."

Agnes looked around the yard. "They're not here," she said.

"Then where are they?"

"Fishing, maybe. I don't know."

"Well, damn it all! Find 'em! They got to bring water to the men!" . . .

It was some time before he found the boys. They were lying quietly in a pile of driftwood in the center of the stream, waiting for a shy trout to get into position to be speared. They had already brought up several this way. . . . They were too engrossed in this occupation to see or hear anything. (McNickle 1978, 76–77)

Again, the author creates drastically different associations around two forms of labor taking place on the same land. And because these two forms of labor rely on different patterns that measure labor's success and value by the attitude of those who practice them, labor is linked to how ethnic identity is fashioned. Max's manual work is methodical, detailed, and routine—it evokes the atmosphere of hard labor that must be done on a large, industrial scale to make capital. In this scene McNickle uses a mechanical, almost robotic diction to delineate that atmosphere, and Max must conform to its tempo to extract more labor from his workers. In addition, reaping grain stalks—far more than enough to satisfy one community's needs—positions this labor as one done for profit rather than familial or community survival. In contrast, Mike and Narcisse's older form of self-directed labor (fishing) is patient and contemplative: it does not demand the same anxiety or speed that threshing wheat does. Because their older work is for their own familial benefit, its success reinforces their ethnic identity. Instead of being attached to machines, the boys rely on their own focused yet tranquil perception of their rhythmic connection to nature.

In addition, in both these cases rival forms of labor done on reservation land generate vastly different relationships to the production of resources that in turn dictate characters' interactions with space and one another. More traditional labor connects the self to the land directly, whereas modernized labor divorces bodies and selves from their environments or disenfranchises those who perform it—a black-and-white picture that again suggests an irreconcilable divide between tradition and modernity. And, as reservation politics became intertwined with assimilation and as reservation space itself deteriorated, remnants of earlier labor forms became less and less viable. The poor land on which the reservations were situated often stymied efforts to sustain older ways, as did overcrowding and diminishing or absent government support. Overall these novels suggest that their characters' toxic relationships to class, labor, and space—indeed even their own narrative strategies to capture the past—preclude their reconciling themselves to the emerging practices of modernization. These damaged relationships thus raise the question of whether or not narratives linked to the past, as the three discussed here are, can do much more than carve out imaginative spaces wherein ethnicity can be remembered, while lived experiences remain largely unchanged. The reservation in these depictions becomes a space where *neither* modernization *nor* tradition thrive and where storytelling itself seems trapped in the same dilemma. Ultimately, what Allen and Vizenor call the blood/land/memory complex and survivance are superseded by simple matters of survival.

## On Space

As Linda Lizut Helstern (2008, 164) argues in her chapter in Vizenor's *Survivance*, "Native history is traditionally encoded in landscape." In the years prior to reservation life, this tradition was manifested as an American Indian eco-consciousness that bound inhabitants to the land. But life under reservation regulations shifted

Indian relationships to space, in large part because American Indians' and white settlers' views of land were so different. As Janet A. McDonnell () 1991) explains, the Anglo policy makers who enacted relocation saw moving Indians onto reservation land in the late nineteenth century as a civilizing project:

> Tribal organization was recognized as a defining feature of Native identity, and private ownership of land was seen as a means of civilizing the Indians. By allotting reservation land in severalty, policymakers hoped to replace tribal civilization with a white one, protect the Indians from unscrupulous whites, promote progress, and save the federal government money. Native Americans, however, did not view land in the same way as their white neighbors. They did not regard land as real estate to be bought, sold, and developed. Rather, they valued it for the things it produced that sustained life. To Native Americans the land represented existence, identity, and a place of belonging. (1)

This primary opposition—between land as capital resource and land as a source of survival and belonging—tainted the new relationship to often unfamiliar lands. Abrupt dispossession and these rival views of space have made it easy to draw a strict line between tradition and modernity. In the case above, and in many like it, no longer did American Indians work for sustenance in places they knew well; instead, these unfamiliar spaces were unproductive and often barren in comparison to spaces they had formerly inhabited. Even when Indians remained on land they knew well, those spaces often offered new labor "opportunities" that effaced older patterns of living with the land, as is the case in Hopkins's recollections. The same happens in Linda Hogan's *Mean Spirit*, when oil found on Indian allotments upends the traditional relationships those who live in the area have with their home space. As Alix Casteel (1994) argues, the discovery of that oil rhetorically conflated Indians with their homeland through the word "Osage" in ways that actually hastened their cultural dispossession. Both land and the Indians, in Casteel's argument, are figured as "dark wealth" that needs to be unearthed, a process that further tears Indians from the modernization the oil business represents. The Osage are disenfranchised to the point where they can no longer use their sensitivity to the earth or knowledge of it.

In *Mean Spirit*, which takes place in the early 1920s in the town of Watona and on the Osage Reservation in Oklahoma Indian Territory, oil is discovered on what new settlers regard as otherwise largely unproductive land, a discovery that prompts a number of Anglo settlers—many of whom are guardians of Indians who own oil-rich land—to wield political and legal power in immoral ways and even murder wealthy Indians in order to benefit financially from that oil. At the center of the novel's corruption is an oilman named John Hale, who mediates most Indians' relationships to their land, the money it can make, and what labor is "needed" to make that space profitable. Thus the very structures of modernization that make Indians rich also bar them from productively using that capital to achieve any kind of power. Although stories and depictions of older traditions occur throughout, by and large those traditions do not help Indians forge unmediated relationships to their land and wealth. Instead, the novel falls into the binary trap by representing these older traditions as being at odds with new uses of space, new class systems, and new labor patterns to enunciate the danger such opposition can cause. This dichotomy distances Indians from structures of modernization, reinforces feedback loops that strengthen Anglo control over Indian lives, and locks those Indians' identities in the past.

Here the false gulf between tradition and modernity comes to light—stories and recoveries of older cultural traditions in these novels become ineffective barricades against new structures of class, labor, and space. When Hogan describes the traditional dress of two of her female protagonists, for instance, that description homes in on not only the nostalgia it evokes in the white population but also the divide between tradition and modernity that such dress encourages; the two women's appearances "pleased the spectators.... They liked to romanticize the earlier days when they believed the Indians lived in a simpler way. . . . They believed the Indians used to have power. In the older, better times, that is, before the people had lost their land and their sacred place on earth to the very people who wished the Indians were as they had been in the past" (Hogan 1990, 79–80).

Early in the novel Hogan foregrounds its central conflict as one between Anglo settlers and both the Indians of the area and the place itself, a common war waged in western American Indian novels—and a war that Hogan uses to again draw that tradition/modernization line: "The Indian world is on a collision course with the white world. . . . It's more than a race war. They are waging a war with the earth. Our forests and cornfields are being burned by them" (13). For instance, Lila, a river prophet in *Mean Spirit*, tells the Hill Indians that "the white world was going to infringe on the peaceful Hill People" and that "[s]ome of our children have to learn about the white world if we're going to ward off our downfall" (5). However, no one wants to "give their children up to that limbo between worlds, that town named Watona, and finally Lila . . . selected her own beautiful daughter, Grace, for the task" (6). Lila later sends her two younger daughters, Sara and Molene, to Watona—Molene dies from an illness spread by railroad workers and Sara is paralyzed by it—but Grace's daughter Nola remains in Watona with her. However, even though Lila insists, "We've got too far away from the Americans to know how their laws are cutting into our life" (6), no other Indians come to live in Watona. And of those who remain, Grace is killed for her oil-rich land, Sara dies when those who want her money blow up her house, and Nola's life is constantly in danger because she has inherited Grace's land. Lila's predictions recognize the need for Indians to integrate themselves and their traditions into modern ways, but the events that occur thereafter suggest that that integration is fraught with the life-threatening political and legal ramifications of Anglo capitalism that relies on Indian exploitation. Those ramifications thus reveal the limitations of tradition and modernization and the danger those limitations can present when a relationship develops between the two.

Throughout Hogan's novel, space is vulnerable to a destructive outside influence that aims to make profitable—by burning flora to clear the way for oil rigging, for instance. This influence, which stretches well beyond ethnic identity, undermines traditional indigenous practices that had attended more sensitively to the resources a place can naturally offer. For instance, when Michael Horse, "the small boned diviner," surveys Grace Blanket's land and predicts, "Drill here. I feel water," his foretelling turns out to be wrong: "The men put down an auger, bored deep into the earth, and struck oil on Grace Blanket's land. . . . There was no water on Grace Blanket's land, just the thick black fluid that had no use at all for growing corn or tomatoes. Not even zucchini squash would grow there" (8). This disconnect between the usual success of Michael Horse's predictions and the fact that Grace's property holds oil that cannot grow vegetables and so cannot provide sustenance gestures toward a growing divide between older traditions of reading and using space and what new spatial ventures allow. That divide in turn indicates instability in sense of place; no longer can the Indians of the novel rely on older practices to guide their decisions or reinforce belonging.

Moreover, the climate in the novel portends the same instability that effaces spatial belonging and thus cultural identity. The novel begins with a heat wave, which Michael Horse predicts will last for several weeks, and it encourages the Indians to move their beds out of their houses at night and sleep outside—a traditional custom. But a storm comes up suddenly and upends these preparations: "The wind had whipped up the sheets. One billowed like a sail against the metal bedframe. Another was flat and wet, spread over several rosebushes nearby" (19). Here the traditional practice of sleeping outside—something that Horse himself desires to do when he wants to "live closer to the land [and] escape the bad feeling in Watona"—is usurped by the storm, which foretells both the coming fissures between traditional spatial belonging and new interpretations of space, as well as the growing murkiness of the Indians' identity (110). Although Horse's predictions have rarely been wrong, this misreading of space—especially the activity in space encompassed by weather events—suggests that space is growing antithetical to cultural traditions that had once supported survival. In addition, coupled with an early reference to the nearby oil fields, where "the pumps rose and fell, pulling black oil up through layers of rock," the movement of the unexpected storm and the oil represent a lack of clarity that transcends space and becomes personal (4). In other words, Horse's inability to predict the storm is mirrored by the "black oil" that clouds his vision and so indicates a growing loss of culture. By contrast, when the Watchers arrive to keep an eye on Nola (who inherits Grace's oil-rich land when she is murdered), they are silent, and their reticence implies a closeness to the landscape that others are unable to maintain. When watching one Watcher, Lettie notices that "his legs looked rooted to earth, and he stood like one of the Hill Indians, as if he'd never lived among white people or their dry goods, or the cursed blessing of oil" (29). Here, specifying that the Watcher remains unblemished by the capital goods associated with the Anglo settlers' expansion project imputes to him a kind of clarity that the other Indians, caught up in the capital system of goods and oil, do not enjoy. Yet at the same time the nearly spectral Watchers are almost mystical—they appear never to sleep or eat—and in light of their removal from modern culture and practices, it seems they cannot exist.

In Hogan's novel, exploiting land for capital gain thus becomes a primary deterrent to more traditional relationships with space.

The same occurs in Alexie's short stories, which likewise suggest that traditional cultural relationships to land in postreservation life suffer under new capital practices. In *The Lone Ranger and Tonto Fistfight in Heaven*, for instance, Victor, one of Alexie's (2005, 39) protagonists, poignantly says of a once widely fished river on the Spokane Reservation, "Ain't no salmon left in our river. Just a school bus and a few hundred basketballs." The immediate juxtaposition is obvious here: as opposed to the river in which Mike and Narcisse fish in *The Surrounded*, this river holds no sustenance, only human-made waste. That such waste was once purchased with capital and is located at the bottom of the river mocks the river's potential to sustain the reservation. The position of the bus at the bottom of the river also points to the novel's commitment to the modern/traditional binary, here manifested in the reservation Indians' inability to make modernization align with their older cultural traditions. Furthermore, the importance Alexie places on basketball as a pathway out of the reservation compounds the significance of such "waste." Throughout his collection Alexie makes it clear that being talented at basketball could launch an Indian to a life off the reservation: "We sat there in silence and remembered all of our heroes, ballplayers from seven generations. . . . It hurts to lose any of them because Indians kind of see ballplayers as saviors," Victor muses as he watches a particularly promising young player (52). "God, I hope she makes it all the way," he says (53). Filling the river with a school bus once bound for a basketball game and the basketballs themselves mocks the social capital of the game and reinforces the reservation's quicksand quality: it is not a space that supports survival but rather a space that swallows the very means of that survival. Ironically, even narratives *about* the past, like Victor's own recollections, give way to the ethos of mere survival.

Stagnancy emerges as one of the primary conditions these reservations and territories have in common. When Victor and Thomas return to the reservation one morning after staying out in the city all night, Alexie observes, "It was the beginning of a new day on earth, but the same old shit on the reservation" (73). The circular time on the reservation accentuates how stuck in the past the space and its residents are. Indeed, Alexie's characters rarely do anything other than remember earlier events and watch time pass; for instance, the morning Victor and Adrian express hope that the young basketball player will use her talent to make it off the reservation, the conversation ends when Adrian throws his coffee cup onto the front lawn: "And we both watched with all of our eyes, while the sun rose straight up above us and settled down below the house, watched that cup revolve, revolve, until it came down to the ground" (53). The young men watch "with all of our eyes"—a vague yet satirical reference to a hazy spirituality that positions Indian belief systems against the physical trash of the cup, which itself revolves like the sun behind the house. Conjoining these images in one sentence highlights the uselessness of older Indian stories in the context of present-day life on the reservation. The scene is as bland and motionless as the sun, and the cup settles back to the ground from which it came. That movement acutely demonstrates the stasis of tradition in the face of modernity, which again accentuates the divide between the two.

This stagnancy is not without precedent. Alexie suggests as much later in his text when he describes an older tribe of Indians who have disappeared from their homes: "Those Indians disappeared with food still cooking in the pot and air waiting to be breathed and they turned into birds or dust or the blue of the sky or the yellow of the sun" (119). The wasted food is another lack pointing toward a broader loss of livelihood. And here again Alexie conflates tragedy with self-defeating references to nature and mythmaking, suggesting how impractically wishful storytelling cannot really right the losses of the past. That pattern repeats often in the text: vague references to mythmaking or older spiritual stories are paired with descriptions of emptiness, waste, and useless commodities. For instance, when faced with hunger on the reservation, Victor remembers "eating potatoes every day of my life[:] I imagined the potatoes grew larger, filled my stomach, reversed the emptiness. My sisters saved up a few quarters and bought food coloring. For weeks we ate red potatoes, green potatoes, blue potatoes" (151). Although this moment seems to carry the hope that imagination can grow in narrative space and contradict the poor space of the reservation, Alexie questions its feasibility a few lines later: "How do we imagine a new life when a pocketful of quarters weighs our possibilities down?" He offers a biting answer: "There are so many possibilities in the reservation 7-11," referring to the local convenience store (152). While these stories remember older traditions, they also indicate how modernization impedes "imagin[ing] a new life" because the modern *narrative* tools to which Indians have access tend to oppose cultural tradition and so cannot be wielded successfully. Those modern tools are also tainted; while the quarters represent a tool for survival on the reservation, that tool is only useful at the 7-Eleven (a vexed space of repetitive, endless work in the narrative), and its utility is doubtful at best, which challenges how much imagination and stories can alleviate the trapping mechanism of the reservation, a space where *neither* modernization nor tradition can thrive. Thus, without progress beyond imaging "an escape," these memories and narratives only emphasize how the unproductive space of the reservation traps those who inhabit it.

A similar sterility reflects a cultural difference in expectations of production in *Mean Spirit*, in which individuals cultivate and relate to land in vastly different ways. For instance, the rich Indians of *Mean Spirit* often use their income from oil allocations, which are controlled by the American legal system, to buy American-made, American-sold items, including decorative baubles, clothes, and furniture, which indicates the way modern capitalism exploits and swallows their earnings. The juxtaposition of what Anglo settlers want from oil-rich land and what Indians want in terms of their traditional relationships to land uncovers not only a telling vulnerability of tradition but also the deep legal apparatus created to efface those land-based traditions. Even without the promise of oil, legislatures dominated by whites gauge land by their own standards of production; Belle's land "was 'without improvement,' as they called it when a person left trees standing and didn't burn off the brush or put in a fence to contain their property" (Hogan 1990, 78). That legal distinction values land for capital production and points to an even more insidious fact that Lettie uncovers: the sheriff's wall is lined with "the geologist's yellowed maps of Oklahoma Indian Territory where estimates of oil might exist. Like prophecies, they were, like divining where one black stench of oil might flow into another" (143). If we recall Horse's position as the Indian diviner, this moment mocks tradition's lack of power in the face of the capital value of oil-ridden land, a moment in which Hogan *again* reinforces the binary. The maps that hang in the sheriff's office also reinforce the divide between modernity and tradition—his geologist's maps stand in direct opposition to the geological and spiritual knowledge that Indians like Horse and Lila have of the land. Meanwhile, Horse's recent failure to predict where water is and the geologists' success in finding oil register larger losses of individual and community belonging because modernity and tradition oppose one another.

The novel's depiction of landscape also connects the destruction of specific spaces to losses in community identity and cohesion. When the region is routinely described as worthless, barren, and damaged, it carries connotations of vulnerability and danger that suggest not only the losses of individuals in the face of modernity but of community stability and affiliations as well. The twinned losses of identity and land unveil a larger loss of community solidarity that further troubles the preservation of tradition through narrative as such. Without a stable community to remember past traditions and so craft nurturant spaces in which culture can persevere, blood memory can't fulfill its potential to maintain tradition.

When Nola surveys her land, she realizes the toll even traditional practices now have on land that has been diminished by allotments and subsequent fencing:

> The land was bare. In only a few days, the buffalo had pulled the tall grass up by its roots and eaten the land down to nothing, and now they were standing on the desolate-looking earth and their own manure with their vacant eyes, eyes that had seen too much. They were on their way down in the world, were themselves fallen people, and they knew it and so did all the others who looked sadly on. . . . [T]he fields were becoming [barren], the burned forests, the overgrazed land, the core drillings, as empty as the dark, tragic eyes of the buffalo. (223–24)

Here Hogan fashions the buffalo, representations of an older tradition that cannot find purchase in newer relationships with land, as the harbingers of a decay that modernization brings. The earth is desolate, marked with the curse of age rather than bolstered by the sustaining value of cultural practices or rituals. Moreover, casting the "dark, tragic eyes of the buffalo" on the succession of crises plaguing the landscape—barren fields, burned forests, overgrazed land, core drillings—figures the land as vulnerable to *both* older traditions and newer labor practices. The community that once advocated for these traditions is falling apart under pressure from relocation, murder, and the effects of both modern and older practices that fragment the land.

The novel's murders underscore the vulnerable community's loss of history. Older citizens of the tribe are the ones killed, because they hold the most oil-rich land. The murders therefore indicate not just the broad loss of tradition but also the manner in which individuals play a role in preserving that tradition through cultural memory and personal recollection. In other words, when the modern practice of capital gain through oil threatens individuals, it reveals not only that individual recollection is surely a necessary component to survivance and blood memory but also that it must persist *alongside* modernity to survive. In Hogan's telling, even the connections to landscape that individuals form are not able to provide sanctuary from the greed of oil barons, nor do they promote adapting to these circumstances and taking control of them. Hogan's first depiction of Grace's position in the tribe focuses on the need for tradition in order to pursue survival: "The Hill Indians were a peaceful group who had gone away from the changing world some sixty years earlier, in the 1860s. Their survival depended on returning to a simpler way of life. . . . Grace Blanket had been born of these, and she was the first to go down out of the hills and enter into the quick and wobbly world of mixed-blood Indians, white loggers, cattle ranchers, and most recently, the oil barons" (5). Grace's decision is prompted by a message the Blue River gives her mother, who speaks with the river, which "never lied": "One day the Blue River told Lila that the white world was going to infringe on the peaceful Hill People" (5). Yet Grace's murder for her oil-rich land is only the first such killing in the novel, negating the protection her mother's bond with the narrative of the river should have provided her. This early moment foreshadows the destructive force oil has on the landscape, both physically and in terms of the cultural powers (including memory and narrative) it displaces. Here Hogan early on sets up the division between modernization and tradition, outside of which the novel is unable to move.

Grace's vulnerability parallels that of the space she inhabits. Not only is her ownership of the land and literal belonging to it threatened, but her cultural practices are endangered as well. Owning oil-rich land puts individuals in peril and replaces survivance with mere survival, shifting the focus from the preservation of cultural and narrative traditions to the more basic, if more pressing, preservation of life itself. In this context, survival means surviving on land and maintaining landownership and control. But surviving on land also means keeping the land itself healthy and out of the hands of those who would harm it, and the oil fields make it impossible to preserve the land's health:

> Up the road from Grace's sunburnt roses, was an enormous crater a gas well blowout had made in the earth. It was fifty feet deep and five hundred feet across. This gouge in the earth, just a year earlier, had swallowed five workmen and ten mules. The water was gone from the land forever, the trees dead, and the grass, once long and rich, was burned black. The cars passed by this ugly sight, and not far from there, they passed another oilfield where pumps, fueled by diesel, worked day and night. These bruised fields were noisy and dark. The earth had turned oily black. Blue flames rose up and roared like torches of burning grass. The earth bled oil. (52)

The space of the crater is barren. No longer land that can produce anything of sustenance, it represents a darker reality that literally swallows the possibility of not only community survivance but also sheer survival. Drilling for oil has permanently compromised the land, the vulnerability of which mirrors the vulnerability of characters to personal violence. The blown-out oil field, a static space where nothing grows, figures the situation of the Indians in the novel, stuck in stasis and unable to adapt. Moreover, this "ugly space" is associated with another oil field nearby, which renders the first a foretelling of what will happen to the second. That second site is also already damaged, with "bruised fields" that are "noisy and dark" and "earth [that] turned oily black." That damage is spurred by "pumps, fueled by diesel," which turns the cause and effect of oil extraction into a perpetual, unbreakable cycle. Survival itself thus becomes an impossibility.

The consequences of this decay of the landscape only increase as the novel continues: "Across the land, oil derricks numbered as many and as far as the eye could see" (319). This growth has seeped into the surrounding land and begins to destroy living space as well:

structures of modernization act as a plague that destroys traditional space. Both exterior, natural spaces and interior, domestic ones are threatened by the oil derricks and their waste. In addition to the riverbanks that are "black from oil seepages" and the "rusted oil drums stuck in stagnant pools," the town itself is dirty and decaying: "The camp was an extension of the black and destroyed land, a scramble of structures stretched out a long distance behind the mesquite hills. The shacks and shelters had been put together in any way possible in order to provide cover from the rain, and most of them were covered with black tar paper" (271). These homes covered with black tar paper cannot escape oil's destructive influence. Oil not only renders the homes inhospitable but also brings illness and decay to the population. The inhabitants of the town "[live] there in poverty and misery . . . broken men and destroyed women who had once been singers and kind mothers. The scrawny brown children did not look full of a future" (275). Here the destructive force of oil has robbed individuals of their identities and their futures. Oil has the power to shape time as well as space. If future generations lose selfhood early because of oil's negative influence, then the chances of rescuing older cultural traditions from that influence correspondingly erode.

Even members of the younger generation of Indians who have not experienced the same poverty reflect a loss of respect for and knowledge of tradition. When auction day comes to the town, for instance, the younger Indians represent a new perspective on relationships to land: "The younger Indian men thought it was a wondrously funny thing that Indians who wound up living on the dry, untillable, scorched plots of land turned out to be rich with oil and gas. They sat on chairs in the front row, waiting for the auctioneer to begin. They were wrapped up in coats and blankets. They nudged each other, laughing about the large sums of money being spent on black oil that trickled beneath this worthless earth. This time, at last, they were coming out ahead. They thought it was about time"

(145). By this point in the novel several Indians who own these oil-rich plots have died under mysterious circumstances, yet the younger men here only find amusement in the fact that these dry lands hold oil. The flippancy of this younger generation exposes a deeper loss of community connection. The land is "dry, untillable, scorched," yet their attention is on the auction starting up, not the state of their landscape, with which the older Indians of the novel are concerned. Moreover, their focus on the "large sums of money being spent on black oil that trickled beneath worthless earth" recalls what Stacey Red Hawk, the Indian investigator sent from Washington, observes of this region when he first begins his investigation: "He'd heard about what Indians still called Indian Territory. It was where every outlaw and crook used to hole up and be safe from the law. Now there were new thieves, those who bought and sold Indian lands" (50). To the extent that there is a new tradition taking hold among the young, it is using illegal or dubiously legal means for capital gain—something to which the younger generation ironically contributes when they attend and participate in the auction. The younger Indian men, mocking the older ways, thus seem little different from the Anglo settlers who used shady laws to obtain profitable lands in the first place. Hogan's divide between older traditions and the younger generation thus foretells a divide in perspective that runs very deep.

Alexie also registers that divisive loss in his depictions of landscape and of the relationships different generations have with the landscapes they inherit. Much of the younger generation in his text has left the reservation for the city. At first this is seemingly a smart move, but it actually results in the loss of both personal and community health: "Urbans are city Indians who survived and made their way out of the reservation after it all fell apart. There must have been over a hundred when they first arrived, but most of them have died since. Now there are only a dozen Urbans left, and they're all sick. The really sick ones look like they are five hundred years old. They look like they have lived forever; they look like they'll die soon" (Alexie 2005, 105). Leaving the reservation "after it all fell apart" seems like a survival technique, but the consequences prove dire. Alexie's reservation may be inhospitable, but his city is also toxic and brings a mysterious illness that prematurely ages younger Indians, literally erasing their futures. Alexie will only call this mysterious illness "a white man's disease in their blood" (107).

One might also think that coupling this illness with ethnic markers is meant to suggest that, while the reservation is not a place of survival, the cultural tradition it represents might offer some kind of protection. It might seem that Alexie suggests that memories held by community members could be tools of survivance, which would suggest that survival through narrative is possible. But examined more closely, the protections provided by narrative resemble a static preservation—like the reservation, storytelling may keep ethnic illness at bay, but its stagnancy freezes progress and similarly halts the future. Alexie's description of the reservation, of those who remain, and their survival rate suggests this: "At night it is cold, so cold that fingers can freeze into a face that is touched. During the day, our sun holds us tight against the ground. All the old people die, choosing to drown in their own water rather than die of thirst. All their bodies are evil" (106–7). The cold conditions that cause "fingers [to] freeze into a face" represent a kind of numbness of identity that erases individuality and locks cultural history in time. Without the ability for forward progress, those on the reservation die a stagnant cultural death. And "our sun [which] holds us tight against the ground" indicates the binding, constricting force of the reservation. When read in tandem, these two passages suggest that no space is safe: both urban and reservation spaces exude toxicities that freeze and erase cultural traditions and future potential.

In these novels, therefore, space exerts a constricting and damaging force that more often than not ends in the destruction of individuals, communities, and cultural inheritances. The losses of community, culture, belonging, and identity take a backseat to the actual loss of life—in other words, the narrative of survival usurps the narratives of blood memory and survivance. Escaping these binds seems impossible. That outcome signifies an even larger gap between tradition and modernization that these authors routinely reinforce: when Indians own land under white laws, they still do not possess the capital to use those structures of modernization to their benefit. They have neither the cultural capital that would enable them to navigate those structures more effectively nor the financial capital that would give them more control.[6]

## On Class

Social class—particularly the failed promises of monetary gain and class mobility—also emerges as a factor that damages the individuals of these novels in ways that are both personal and communal. As Donald L. Fixico (2004, viii) recognizes in his foreword to the edited volume *Native Pathways*, "Whereas before [native people] had depended on their natural environments for their livelihoods, the shift of dependency to a paternalistic federal government and an opportunistic mainstream re-educated American Indians in white ways and capitalism." In other words, contact in space with Americans and their structures of order changed Indians' understanding of exchange from one largely based on systems of barter to one now based on capital accumulation, monetary gain, and consumption. Fixico in fact argues that American Indians understood and took an active part in this re-education. But in these fictional representations, class mobility as an element of modernization turns out to operate in much the same way as transformations in space: it only reflects and demonstrates the difficulty Indians have in adapting to modern structures. Moreover, examining the frustrations of class mobility demonstrates again the ways that the preservation of tradition enables neither productive adaptation nor resistance and survival. In Hogan's novel, for example, capital gain that should result in rises in value instead brings losses in value in multiple ways. Specifically, oil-rich lands owned by Indians not only put their lives in danger but are also associated with unfair real estate auctions, suspect legal rulings and life insurance policies, poor government payouts, and questionable land purchases initiated by Americans and unquestioned by Indians until it is too late. Ultimately, if land itself becomes valuable as capital, it ends up serving mainly as a tool of cultural, class, and legal dispossession. As Hogan (1990, 261) puts it, "It doesn't matter anymore if there's oil under it; if it's land, someone wants it." By controlling the laws of capital in ways that subtly edge out Indians, white settlers can maintain control over land in ways that assure class mobility and control for themselves. Money and the legal and political issues that come with it render individuals and the larger ethnic community vulnerable to a systematic erasure of identity on multiple fronts. Scenes that foreground class issues project the same stasis, frustration, vulnerability, and danger found in other parts of the novel, its white system of capital taking the place of the land as the condition that traps Indians in stasis and immobility. The Indians of each novel slowly lose cultural identity even as they attempt to recover it through traditional practices, stories, and references. Class mobility and capital acquisition only propel them toward a variety of losses that sap the resources of community, familial, and individual stability, safety, and livelihood.

Early in her novel, Hogan contextualizes these losses with her description of how the Dawes Act affects its protagonists. She accentuates both the individual and the communal costs of capital gain:

[I]n the early 1900s each Indian had been given their choice of any parcel of land not already claimed by the white Americans. Those pieces of land were called allotments. They consisted of 160 acres a person to farm, sell, or use in any way they desired. The act that offered allotments to the Indians, the Dawes Act, seemed generous at first glance so only a very few people realized how much they were being tricked, since numerous tracts of unclaimed land became open property for white settlers, homesteaders, and ranchers. Grace and Sara, in total ignorance, selected dried up acreages that no one else wanted. No one guessed that black undercurrents of oil moved beneath that earth's surface.

When Belle Graycloud saw the land Grace selected, and that it was stony and dry, she shook her head in dismay and said to Grace, "It's barren land. What barren, useless land." But Grace wasn't discouraged. With good humor, she named her property "The Barren Land." Later, after oil was found there, she called it "The Baron Land," for the oil moguls. (7–8)

Much like the failed Homestead Act, the Dawes Act promised to lend the Indians who benefited from it a degree of agency and power, but those who truly benefit from the act are the "white settlers, homesteaders, and ranchers" who later become the oil moguls after whom Grace names her land following the discovery of oil. Moreover, those barren stretches of land Grace and Sara buy "in total ignorance," coupled with naming the plot "The Baron Land" and rhetorically giving it to those who ultimately murder her, gesture toward a loss of knowledge of place that class mobility entails. That loss is only deepened by Grace's new purchasing habits: she buys "crystal champagne glasses that rang like bells . . . a tiny typewriter that tapped out all the English words she learned in school, and a white fur cape" and "enjoy[s] the pleasures money could buy" (8–9). Grace's purchases are Euro-American and effectively replace her Indian culture with the white culture that values land for the capital it can produce, rather than the traditions it carries. In addition, her purchases are decorative and luxurious; they are unnecessary objects that do not provide sustenance. This exchange of tradition for modernity does not confer power, however, because it does not interweave the two but instead suggests that the two cannot coexist. Grace is thus not productively using the structures of modernity but—as these two actions demonstrate—is doing quite the opposite: just "buying" into them without enlarging her power or autonomy.

At the same time, Grace's ignorance about her own land and her renaming it after the oil moguls signifies the larger loss of class power and mobility that owning such profitable land entails for the Indians of the novel. While she uses capital to buy luxuries that she enjoys, these luxuries only decorate her house but do not secure her place in it: modernity for show is not productive—instead, it foretells danger. When Grace is murdered, Belle muses "it was a plot since Grace's land was worth so much in oil. All along the smell of the blue-black oil that seeped out of the earth smelled like death to her" (28). Here the new "place" provided by her upward mobility is not only dangerous, but the oil itself, which enabled her to buy such luxuries in the past, effectively also bought her death. Grace's purchases and renaming of her land thus hand over its power to those who then kill her for it. Other Indians who own oil-rich land suffer the same fate: "It was hard for the newly rich Indians to take their wealth seriously and most were more than happy to buy any and all of the gadgets the scalpers sold from their rickety tables and stands, no matter how much the prices had been marked up. The women bought red and pink satin ribbons, black patent leather shoes, and expensive jeweled watches they pinned on their dresses. The men bought bow ties and Gillette razor blades, and carried bags full of trinkets to the children back up at the camp" (55–56). Again, class power initially becomes ineffectually decorative buying power, which only superficially demonstrates wealth. And again, these purchases are Euro-American goods, a fact that divorces those Indians who purchase them from the more traditional goods they once valued.

By contrast, Moses aims for new stability for his family. We learn that he, "who received his money from grazing leases, not from oil," gets a "minimal" payment of only "two thousand dollars, but it was a decent income. It kept his family in food and supplies" (57). Moses's source of income, he hopes, will not only separate him from the class politics of oil but also save him from the loss of cultural tradition and knowledge that besets the Indians earning money from oil land. Moses's conscious decision to participate productively in capitalism without losing his traditions indicates the folly of seeing the two in absolute opposition to each other. His income might be "minimal," he thinks, but his land practices and that income reflect a productive interweaving of modern capital and traditional practices. Although he does not enjoy outward signs of the upper class, he also does not suffer the false delusions of class status and mobility that ultimately do not offer the security such power should provide. Nor do his cultural traditions become too static to adapt to modernization.

Yet the vulnerability of those who flaunt their purchasing power affects all those who benefit from government payouts for land, a situation that ties the supposed "legal system" to the changing shape of class domination that in turn makes corruption possible. During payment day, that vulnerability comes into particularly clear focus when Moses discovers that neither he nor any other full-blooded Indians will actually receive full payment. As the pay clerk tells him, "They changed the regulations. . . . Full-bloods only get part of their money. You're getting ten per today. . . . We don't have any say in the matter. . . . The Indian Commission changed the rules. . . . There's nothing we can do here. I'm sorry" (59). Subject to the decisions of a distant government, the Indians are actually punished for their ethnic identity, and that punishment registers as cultural, legal, and monetary dispossession. That even Moses, who seemed to balance modernity and tradition, has his payout cut exemplifies the novel's skepticism that ethnically "othered" Indians can receive fair treatment at the hands of those with capital and power. By accentuating this doubt, Hogan passes over historical examples of Indians' influence on modernization to suggest that there is no way to productively intertwine Anglo modernity and Indian tradition. Ultimately, in Hogan's novel these governmental financial decisions, made manifest at the pay office, have a profound impact on the collective mood of Indians, whose surrender positions survival as the most important pursuit: "They might be cheated, but they still had life, and until only recently, even that was guaranteed under the American laws, so they remained trapped, silent, and wary" (61). Tying together ethnicity, capital, and legality and linking these elements to corruption and the survival that must ensue despite that corruption, Hogan thus uses this scene to suggest that class mobility is not only an unstable lure but is possible only for those who possess the ethnic capital of whiteness as well as economic capital. But that divide further dispossesses many Indians from their own position in modernity and renders tradition vulnerable to its practices: as Ruth, Moses's sister, reflects in frustration at another auction day, "We gave up our better ways for this oil business" (146).

Losing those old traditions to superficial capital gains has an impact on individual lives in ways that point to deep rifts in family relationships and intimacy. Those rifts indicate that the loss of culture is not only a communal experience but also a personal one that superficial displays of class mobility only exacerbate. As Nola and Will's marriage fractures, for instance, that fracture is reflected in their differing capital priorities. Nola "continued to furnish the house with glass and crystal. It was her desire to put everything in its place. She wanted things in order and permanence, yet she felt desolate; every glass-filled room looked fragile and breakable no matter what she added, no matter how solid and dark the furniture" (192). By contrast, Will buys "arrowheads . . . and small pots painted with spirals and birds . . . [and] a trumpet made of human thighbone from Tibet" (195). This is certainly a curious reversal, given that Hogan identifies Nola as one of the most spiritually and culturally connected Indians of the novel and

Will is a white lawyer's son; Nola even worries that to Will, "as an Indian woman [she] represented something old and gone to him, something from another time" (195). But the point may be that Nola's obsession with fragility merely mirrors the vulnerability of not only her marriage and family (and also recalls the early familial vulnerability captured in the death of her mother, Grace) but her own identity as well. She sees herself disappearing in her husband's romanticized view of cultural history—his purchases not only accentuate her own ethnic ties but also indicate a fetishizing of Indian culture, of which his wife is a part. In deliberately cutting her ties to her heritage, Nola is thus encouraging Will's unhealthy relationship to it; he even buys his artifacts from "looters" who raid traditional grounds and graves for goods from which they turn a profit. Their individual obsessions with each other's cultures only widen the gap between them, again indicating that Anglo modernity and Indian tradition do not mix. Cultural loss again indicates not only other losses that are more poignantly felt on individual levels but also a number of declines in multiple value systems—here, the system of family.

But vulnerability is not the only force of loss at work in the novel, especially with regard to issues of capital. Stagnancy emerges as another predictor of loss, and to foreground this element I turn again to Sherman Alexie's text. Alexie links loss of purchasing power to stagnancy in his first vignette in *The Lone Ranger and Tonto Fistfight in Heaven*, in a passage that homes in on the destructive power of capital loss and acts as a telling counterpoint to Hogan's representations of capital gain and purchasing power:

> Just the week before, Victor had stood in the shadows of his father's doorway and watched as the man opened his wallet and shook his head. Empty. Victor watched his father put the empty wallet back in his pocket for a moment, then pull it out and open it again. Still empty. Victor watched his father repeat this cere-

mony again and again, as if the repetition itself could guarantee change. But it was always empty. . . .

Victor and his parents would be sitting in Mother's Kitchen in Spokane, waiting out a storm. Rain and lightning. Unemployment and poverty. Commodity food. Flash floods. (Alexie 2005, 5)

Waiting out the storm with "commodity food" becomes a kind of class *im*mobility that traps Victor and his family in the pattern of unemployment on the reservation. Moreover, the "commodity food" evokes the multicolored potatoes and purchases from 7-Eleven that indicate the limits of purchasing power in reservation space. The term "commodity food" also highlights a contrast to the more traditional foods the reservation could have provided, suggesting that tradition provides sustenance that modernization cannot. Alexie's characters are thus doubly bound by failed class mobility and the landscape itself, as both exert insurmountable challenges that threaten survival. When we read this scene alongside Hogan's vignettes of money's purchasing power and the unwise and meaningless decisions "newly rich" Indians make with that power, ironically both the lack *and* the possession of capital become sources of stagnancy: one encourages empty repetition and empty stomachs, while the other encourages useless purchases that superficially represent but actually efface the power wealth should bring.

In Hogan's novel, when Benoit is wrongly arrested for the murder of his wife, Sara, and then jailed, his difficulty in finding a lawyer and managing his affairs arises from capital restrictions that Anglo laws have placed on Indians, leading not only to personal stagnation but to the lack of legal recourse. Here modernization is deliberately used to usurp ethnicity and tradition, preventing Indians in the novel from making modernity work for them. Broadly, Indians are legally barred from filing claims or accessing their money because of ethnic status—they are not considered full citizens by Anglo-run courts. Lettie finds out that "someone put in a claim for Sara's money," which she earned from oil found on their land (Hogan 1990, 82). When Lettie tries to discover who filed the claim by filing one of her own, she's told, "You're an Indian. You can't file a claim. Indians are not citizens and this claim would go through a United States court of law" (84). And when Benoit wants to hire his own lawyer, Lettie tells him, "You can't. Your money's tied up until you are acquitted. . . . A husband suspected of murdering his wife can't lay a finger on their property. Besides, we're not legal, Benoit. The law doesn't apply to us" (84). Sara's money is thus a source of immobility rather than mobility; it is not only kept from Benoit but is the primary motive the sheriff imagines he has for murdering his wife. Moreover, capital flexibility depends on national belonging and civic identity, which here serve as another set of tools for ethnic dispossession. Benoit's life is thus frozen both financially and personally, as he faces restrictions that ultimately lead him to suicide when these legal, capital, and personal issues dovetail and overcome his individual identity. The opportunity for a wider, fuller citizenship and "personhood" in this instance is overwhelmed by capital access; the intersection of finance and legality thus renders civic identity—justified by capital—more relevant than cultural or ethnic identity. The same thing happens during the Fourth of July picnic, when those in attendance feel that "[t]hey were in a trap, a circle of fear, and they could not leave. Money held them. It became a living force" (289). But Hogan's decision to represent this history in this way questions how effectively the Indians in *Mean Spirit* can forge their own identities in an ever-changing landscape. In other words, what does it mean that Hogan focuses on ethnic dispossession here to such an extent that Indians seem to have no ability to defend their identities, and therefore their lives, against the intrusion money represents?

Casting money as "a living force" thus signifies the growing challenge characters in the novel face when attempting to find productive identities. Money lends particular people power and divests others of it; this dichotomy creates deep rifts in both their "routes" upward and their "roots" to tradition. But the answer to my question above thus becomes twofold: Indians are faced with wholly unfair and wholly controlling circumstances, *but* at the same time those circumstances very often result in large part from their own reluctance to make modernization work for them until it is too late. For instance, one afternoon Rena and Nola take a trip down to the creek and discover oil on Belle's land:

> Rena smiled with pleasure and excitement. "Oh my God," she said, "It's oil." She was, they were, going to be rich. Her grandmother would have a new stove. They would buy back their cattle and horses. They would no longer talk of selling the Buick. But [the Watchers] began immediately moving stones over the place, trying to cover up the source of the oil seep. Rena didn't understand. They did not want such good fortune. . . . They didn't want to be around the earth's black blood and its pain.
>
> Rena cried herself to sleep that night, her small body wracked with sobs. Her happiness over the oil turned to fear. Floyd and Moses had spent the day at the water covering the seeping oil as best they could, their faces grim and set against everything. (226)

When Grace's land and creek break open to reveal oil, Rena's initial happiness reflects the potential money has in the novel to enable class mobility. But the things she imagines they can do with the money—buy "a new stove . . . buy back their cattle and horses" and keep the Buick—are all presented as superficial desires that indicate how money can distort cultural values and traditions. Indeed, when Watchers immediately recoil from the oil and start moving stones to cover the spot where it emerges, Rena's perspective changes, indicating this novel's overwhelming insistence that modernity is harmful to the stability found in traditional ways of life.

On the other hand, the desire—first the Watchers' and then Moses and Floyd's—to hide the oil and its source is also a desire to hide the rift in the earth that revealed the oil, which symbolizes the rift in Indian culture that the oil has caused. "The earth's black blood and its pain" is on the one hand the result of the literal and metaphorical cracks in the earth that drilling for oil causes, but it also represents a loss of these routes and roots to identity; when the security of the earth is cracked, so is security of the self. The oil's presence in the river thus becomes doubly important. Throughout the novel water is associated with both retelling the foundational mythic past and predicting the future. Hogan claims early that "[a] river never lied"; Michael Horse reads water to predict the weather and the future; Grace's mother, Lila, was a river prophet; and Nola is described as "the river's godchild" (5, 9). That the river is now the source of oil shakes the ground upon which the tradition of trusting water stood, rendering its link to identity unstable as well. The river's rootedness in both the earth and Osage culture renders its rift and staining by oil especially dangerous, as that damage represents and produces similar damages in the place-based roots of Osage culture and identity. Hiding that break is thus a tactical move in the pursuit of survival; however, this is not survivance or blood memory rooted in narrative space but rather basic survival rooted in sealing or closing space to head off financial and thus personal danger.

Much as money comes to indicate and cause stagnancy, it also leads to the closure of ethnic identity. Money and the desire for it causes many of the deaths in the novel; beyond that, however, money also closes off the roots of cultural and traditional identity and opens other routes, which rest on American ideals of capital gain and socioeconomic success. These routes are figured as threats to individual survival, which again suggests that modern capital cannot exist alongside cultural and traditional Indian identities. Hale, a white American oilman who used to be a rancher in Osage territory and was once a friend to the Indians, begins taking out life insurance policies on Indians who own plots of land rich with oil—

Indians who later mysteriously die. Benjamin Black, the region's doctor, muses one night when Hale comes in for a checkup:

> He looked at Hale, then looked out the window at the crowds of people on the busy street, the fast business of oil money changing hands, hawkers selling Indian people useless baubles, and white men collecting on their debts. He didn't like any of it. He'd written a letter to Washington. The last two Indians who died had insurance policies. One of them named Hale as beneficiary. And Hale had a lien on the property of the other one. But in D.C. they told him there wasn't enough evidence. And it was outside their jurisdiction. (64)

Dr. Black's distaste is for the interaction of Indians and money—interactions that take them far from their culture and traditions and instead fill their time with consumerist quests for money or goods that will define their identities. But he does not disparage the Indians for their wealth and misguided use of it. He instead mourns the losses they experience as a result; "the fast business of money changing hands, hawkers selling Indian people useless baubles, and white men collecting on their debts" accentuates how every action on the "busy street" concerns economic exchange, indicating that the citizens of Watona—Osage land—have shortchanged their region's and thus their own identity. Crafting a new identity thus would not link them to cultural tradition but rather to capital itself, and again it is as if one cannot exist alongside the other. Moreover, naming Hale early as the sole individual linked to the murders of wealthy Indians (though we learn later that others are involved as well, under Hale's direction) grants him enormous capital power in the novel. From this moment on, he becomes the force of corruption driven by capital gain and desire itself; moreover, the power he derives from the allure of money gives him control over cultural belonging. That control uses individual wealth to define what people are worth and so effaces cultural traditions and belonging.

We see this control over identity in sharp focus in Hale's dealings with John Stink, an older Indian who dies from a heart attack that some believe is the result of poisoning. In this case it comes to light that Hale's power is not limited to those who are living—he interacts with and controls a dead John Stink in ways that benefit him financially. This action not only colors him with an overwhelming, otherworldly power but also hands him the cultural power the Osage associate with the dead. He uses that cultural power to reinforce his capital power, thereby displacing the Indians' sources of both cultural and financial agency. Ironically, Hale is thus the only character to interweave cultural and traditional knowledge and modernity to his benefit, but he does so in horribly manipulative and unethical ways. When Stink dies in the novel but resurrects himself (or becomes a ghost—the novel intentionally accentuates the mythic side of the occurrence) and wanders around town, the Indians of the town will not acknowledge him. But Hale sees his potential as an investment and convinces his girlfriend, China, to marry him:

> Stink was one of the richest Indians in the territory, but few people knew it. And, if any of the crooked white people had thought he was dead and a ghost, they would have laid claim right-off to his money and his land, but the news had somehow managed to escape them. But Hale's plan was clever. He thought John Stink was crazy. Years before, Stink had given his father's Arabian thoroughbreds away, and now he refused to accept oil payments or live in a regular house. . . . Hale thought it was a cinch that John Stink would marry [China], and he was sure Stink wouldn't be any trouble after the wedding, since the old man had no use for money, no concept of it even. (165–66)

Hale is the only "crooked white person" who recognizes that Stink is no longer alive, and that recognition separates him, by way of cultural insight, from other American oilmen who might have taken similar advantage of the situation. Such cultural insight marks him as insidiously in touch with the Indian community, which suggests that the Osage cultural tradition is a weakness of the tribe that others can exploit once they learn about it. Stink is "one of the richest Indians in the territory," but his refusal "to accept oil payments or live in a regular house" gestures toward the uneven relationship Osage Indians have with their own money. Moreover, Stink's unwillingness to use his money in any way that might benefit him could be read as an empowering move that removes him from Anglo-American structures of class: for instance, we learn that he "liked nothing more than to pick up the golf balls white golfers lost and resell them" (165). Here he engages with Anglo culture and, instead of subverting its systems, participates in both its class and cultural systems by collecting and then reselling golf balls at bargain prices to wealthy Anglo-Americans. Hale's plan thus exploits Stink's engagement with Anglo culture and disengagement from class, which again points toward the vulnerability and stagnancy the entire tribe faces. Moreover, reading Stink's financial situation alongside Hale's manipulation of culture and modernity suggests that tradition and modernization cannot exist in tandem without poisoning each other and leading to ruin.

Hale abuses the legal system for capital gain at the expense of other Indians as well, a fact that comes to light during his trial at the end of the novel and accentuates his manipulations throughout. His legal maneuvering often draws on cultural knowledge. For instance, when Belle finds a man who works for Hale erecting a buffalo fence on her property, she questions him and learns that "Hale leased this land from the Indian agent" because Belle "didn't improve it" in accord with Anglo expectations of land use (210). Unlike Osage traditions of living with the land as benignly as possible—for instance, Michael Horse writes, "Honor mother sky and father earth. Look after everything. . . . Live gently with the land"—those who enforce and those who benefit from the American legal system expect land to be used aggressively for production (337). Hale's awareness of that dichotomy enables him to essentially steal land—he leases Belle's land "for a payment of only twenty-five cents a year"—and use it for his own capital gain and also to exert legal power over the Indians (210). Later, when Belle discovers that Hale has leased even more of her land and she goes to make a complaint to the Indian agent, the agent apologizes and reveals his own inability to intervene: "So sorry, Belle, Moses. It's not me doing it. It's not even the leasers. It's what's legal" (302). Effectively absolving Hale, the man who leased her property, of responsibility and deeming his actions legal, the Indian agent somewhat reluctantly perpetuates a cycle of exploitation and endangerment and reinforces its basis in legalized action. As Belle says, "Why is it that so many crimes are backed up by your laws?" (302).

The events at the end of the novel, especially Hale's trial, tie crime and legality to money in ways that further dispossess the Osage and highlight the danger that capital gain holds for some and the power it gives others. Even though he is eventually found guilty (but only after a second trial) and the evidence against him is more than significant, Hale's demeanor at the outset of the trial is jovial:

> He was all friendly business. He smiled and shook hands with several of his friends and business associates before he sat down . . . he looked calm and collected. . . . He looked, in an odd way, handsome and untouched by the weight of events. . . . Hale sat tall, almost self-righteous, his circle of stolen money and power had built him far beyond human feeling and, it seemed, far above the law. He leaned over to whisper to his attorney. His every movement and expression seemed calculated to his advantage, as if he were playing a game of chess, thinking of which pieces and plays supported his holdings. (321–22)

Hale's expression of security and lightheartedness, reflecting his own quest for class mobility and status, is in direct contrast to the demeanor of the Indians—which again indicates the distance between tradition and modernity—who come to the trial and "stand in the back of the room, against the wall, their arms folded across their chests. They were dressed in traditional clothing. . . . They stood ready to listen. They eyed the neat stacks of paper on the tables" (321). Hale's entrance seems not only contrived but excessive, not just an expression of confidence but also a reminder that his financial connections give him a certain degree of power over those who do not enter in the same humor. "His circle of stolen money and power" thus not only boosts his mood in this scene and allows him to act with calculation, "as if he were playing a game of chess," but also reflects the outcome of the trial and how much it depends on capital power. Whereas Hale remains in charge and dominates the first trial through capital—he gives his lawyer money to make witnesses disappear and to bribe government agents to coerce others into confessing to crimes that Hale committed—the Indians standing in the back leave in disgust or hopelessness and speak of "danger and giving up" (327). Hale's manner emphasizes the powerful role of capital and the legal leverage it buys in not only shaping cultural identity but in depriving the Osage of their civic and cultural identities. Monetary gain and upward mobility are thus turned into a collective liability that causes class damage and stagnation.

The trial, especially the testimony of Mardy Green, discloses the extent of Hale's careful orchestration of the entire plot and by extension the Indians' vulnerability to the capital maneuvers Hale plans. The references throughout to the Indians' awkward and often ill-defined relationship to money, in light of Mardy's testimony, take on a particularly dark hue:

> His long testimony unraveled much of the complicated plot involving Hale and the sheriff: Hale could not kill both Benoit and Sara because the money had to go through Benoit. They were certain that the sheriff would later find a way to marry Lettie. Then they

would claim money through her. . . . Palmer had kept the store records and was always a witness when a lien was filed against an Indian's property, so he too was implicated, but he'd been another citizen the Indians knew well and liked. . . . It seemed as if everyone was involved, Palmer and his books, the banker, the dead cowboy and roper Fraser who knew too much, and a large number of the attorneys who were guardians for oil-rich Indians. (347)

Mardy's testimony mimics a narrative of survival because it recalls the wrongs of the past in an attempt to right them. However, Mardy's revelations of Hale's corrupt but well-calculated manipulations of the Indians only further assert that Indians and modernity do not mix. Likewise, when the trial ends, Hale is acquitted despite the mountain of evidence against him; as a narrative that should encourage survival, the trial does the opposite and lets Hale loose to pursue his plans and commit more murders. Mardy's testimony reveals how Hale *and his associates* have wielded capital as a powerful tool of corruption and community erasure through control over individuals. Thus, Hale's "group" survives as a community while the Osage community fractures. And those involved in the plot are very often those whom the Indians liked and trusted in their community—Hale, Palmer, Jess (the sheriff), and others—and that admiration and trust render their community unsafe because of the presence of money. All those involved in the plot had ties to places of capital gain, as is the case with Palmer and his store; political power, like the sheriff; or a powerful mix of both, like Hale, whose money controls political decisions and those who make them. That the Indians initially trust these men gestures toward a deceit in relationships among members of the same community. That deceit in turn indicates an ethnic divide based on modern capital—a divide particularly evident when Nola, fearful of her white husband, Will, kills him in a panic.

But Will's death is unlike the others in *Mean Spirit*. Whereas the Indian murders are for capital, Will dies because Nola believes she is protecting herself, her unborn child, *and* her wealth—though Will is not involved in the scheme to kill Indians for their oil money. When Michael Horse comes to watch over Nola following the murder, he notes that "everything had turned around, had swirled into an ever-tightening circle of danger. Fire, which had meant warmth and light, had come to mean death. Wealth meant poverty. And for Nola, love had turned to loss" (355). Will's death thus reflects not only the various losses in the novel but how those losses are specifically tied to capital. Nola, in her act of killing Will, has become no better than Hale and his constituents, and while she suffers because of his murder, she remains financially intact and ultimately finds cultural and individual wholeness. Nola seems able to interweave Indian cultural tradition and modernization to her benefit, but the losses of security, community trust, family, and individuality that Will's murder represents go largely unremarked upon and unexplored. Why doesn't Will's death matter to this novel? Is it because, though he is a protagonist, he is white? Or does it have more to do with his associations with modernization?

More likely the latter. Will's father, we discover halfway through the novel, is a lawyer involved with Hale and his purchases of oil-rich Indian land, and he has invested Nola's family money in Hale's business. When Will protests that his father should not use Nola's money without asking him first, because she is his wife, his father's response reveals one area where tradition and modernity do intersect, though dubiously:

"She's your paycheck. Now she is the one who pays for your good suits and hats." . . .

Will himself had thought it an embarrassment to have no livelihood of his own, which was why he had taken an interest in helping to manage Nola's royalties and holdings. But now, dismissed by his father, he felt ashamed of his own lack of legitimate work. (189)

After this moment, Will is haunted the rest of the night by comments that focus on the "business" of his marriage. Throughout the novel Hogan has portrayed marrying an Indian woman as a get-rich-quick scheme because, once married, the woman's husband controls her finances: "The women were business investments. Another white man, when asked what he did for a living, said by way of an answer that he'd married an Osage woman, and everyone who listened understood what that meant, that he didn't work; he lived off her money" (33). While this is an ethically unsound practice that turns Indian women into financial objects, Will's reaction to his father pointing out his role in this system and his similar reactions the rest of the evening reveal a more complicated issue. If, as Colleen O'Neill (2004, 8) suggests, "privileging 'culture' . . . conflates class with ethnic and racial identity," then the novel's reliance on culture and tradition for character identification ultimately identifies Will as a white man who participates in the "business" of marrying a wealthy Indian woman. Despite his discomfort with not having a business of his own and despite his final plea after Nola shoots him—"I loved you. I loved you. . . . Why? Why did you do this?" (Hogan 1990, 358)—Will's racially based class identity and attachment to the modern business of profiting off an Indian wife effectively erase him from the novel. After Horse's final sentiment about Nola's love turning to loss, Will's name is never mentioned again.

## On the Absence of Modern Labor in the American Indian Novel

Despite his removal from the narrative, Will's shame about not having "legitimate work" raises the question of labor in the novel. Namely, and to put it bluntly, where is it? While Hogan mentions labor a few times, these instances can be easily sorted into two descriptive and analytic categories: modern, capital-driven white labor, like work in Watona's stores or in the oil fields, or traditional Indian labor, like Belle's work in her garden or Lettie's labor digging holes on Belle's property. In all three of the novels discussed here, these two types of labor are clearly contrasted largely by their cultural, ethnic, and class associations. The oilmen work "in their steel-toe boots as they pulled the great chains back and forth and, inch by inch, drove the pipes down into the earth. The sound of metal grated against metal out there. Gas rumbled under the ground like earth complaining through an open mouth, moaning sometimes and sometimes roaring with rage" (Hogan 1990, 145). Belle, on the other hand, tells her family, "The earth is my marketplace . . . and they understood what she meant, for they ate the fruits of her labor" and "worked in the fields daily and without fatigue. When she was not with the corn, she was cutting wild asparagus from along the roadways and taking watercress home for dinner" (16, 207). The difference between the two depictions is palpable: the oilmen are ruining the earth to pull profit from it, whereas Belle gently engages with the earth to maintain her and her family's sustenance, much like the differences in labor in McNickle's *The Surrounded* and Hopkins's *Life among the Piutes* with which I opened this chapter. The distinction between these labors rests on the divide between tradition and modernity: neither Belle nor the oilmen would be caught doing the labor of the other, nor would either find the others' labor productive.

But like *Mean Spirit*, neither of the works I discussed at the beginning of this chapter offers more sustained, or even more numerous, depictions of labor. *The Lone Ranger and Tonto Fistfight in Heaven* and *The Bird Is Gone* have similar blind spots that on the one hand point to ways in which reservation and postreservation life changed patterns of labor for Indians. In *The Lone Ranger and Tonto Fistfight in Heaven*, Alexie's Indians either work in low-wage service jobs—like at the 7-Eleven or in the cleaning service—or don't have jobs at all and instead spend their time drinking. And *The Bird Is Gone* takes place largely in a bowling alley—seemingly the only place of work in the novel's imagined

Dakota Indian Territory—yet the novel is almost entirely devoid of representations of work in that setting; instead Stephen Graham Jones for the most part depicts his employed Indians as sitting around chatting, drinking, and sometimes discussing the tourists who have gone missing. One character, LP Deal, keeps a meticulous set of notebooks wherein he records his manifesto, but that work is never depicted as "work" in the novel. On the other hand, these apparent blind spots suggest that modern Indians cannot forge productive relationships to the structures of modernity because they literally have nothing to forge with—they have no labor and thus no product to offer as a cultural olive branch to modernity. Even Belle's declaration that "[t]he earth is my marketplace" (16) reinforces the lack of connection between traditional Indian labor and the labor and structures of modernity: Belle does not sell the produce she gathers for profit.

What might it mean that Indian labor doesn't exist in these novels? I doubt that making such a move—delineating modern forms of productive labor in detail—would erase the reader's sense of the horrors of acculturation or assimilation or in some way make them appear ultimately beneficial. For example, historians I referenced earlier in this chapter prove this by careful critical work that downplays neither the benefits nor the costs of modernization for Indian populations, culture, traditions, and ways of living. On the contrary, by acknowledging both, these historical narratives recover a more pluralistic view of contacts between Indian life and Anglo culture. These narratives are not Pocahontas-type tales of seamless cultural amalgamation but rather complicated narratives of how Indians took both the damaging and advantageous elements of modernization and manipulated them in order to preserve cultural identity. So why doesn't literature imagine such a situation? What does this omission say about literature's relationship to history or Indians' historical connections with modernity? To what extent is it a reflection of what happens when literary texts position modernization and tradition as antithetical to each other, as all of the novels here have done?

One way to suggest answers to these questions is to ask another, which I previewed in my introduction: What *takes the place of labor* in these novels and why? Ethnicity is their dominant focal point; preserving it and the cultural history that accompanies it consumes these novels' energy. In *The Lone Ranger and Tonto Fistfight in Heaven*, Alexie pairs scenes of characters' stasis (or lack of work) with stories of cultural remembrance—moments of blood memory and survivance. Hogan's and Jones' texts make similar moves—when Indians cannot do anything, they recall the past, either through dialogue or narration. For instance, Horse writes about the loss of Osage tradition the evening after Hale's first trial in *Mean Spirit*, and sections of LP's memoirs that cover cultural recovery are reprinted in *The Bird Is Gone* at points when the plot encounters particularly slow or unproductive nights at the bowling alley. In these cases ethnic remembrance takes the place of profitable labor, which again showcases the gap between tradition and modernity. And I argue that such replacement occurs because the overwhelmingly negative force of modernization in these novels forces their stories toward rescuing and preserving an "authentic" Indian identity that modernization tries to efface.

As a result, there is simply no space for labor—which tells us something about these novels' relationships to history and the messages they carry about Indians and modernity. In these novels modernized labor does not help Indians to preserve their ethnic identity in the way that Deloria and others argue it does. Instead, these novels present the modernization of labor, like modernization in general, as a challenge to cultural and traditional ways of living. These authors use modernity as a counterpoint to ethnicity, which replaces physical labor with the labor of maintaining ethnic identity. When successful, this "work" is a source of pride; when unsuccessful, it often portends danger and loss. Either way, however, this positioning of tradition and modernity against each other effaces the complicated middle ground on which Indians have negotiated the meeting of the two. Focusing on class, labor, and space in these novels reveals the devastating effects of maintaining a fissure between the old and the new that makes Indian identity, agency, and culture seem to have no place in modern society, thus displacing whatever influence these elements historically had. Literature is under no obligation to align with the historical record—though Hogan's novel is explicitly based on the events of the Osage oil crisis—but ethnic minority literature often suffers the burden of also acting as historical memory. American Indian literature has not kept up with the work of historians, which details the damaging effects of American expansion but also explores the ingenious ways American Indian populations navigated the consequences of that expansion and created opportunities for their own communal, individual, and ethnic salvation.

In retrospect, that has been a principal theme of the texts analyzed throughout this work—how individuals adjust the labor practices that craft their identities to new conceptions of space, new class lines, and new uses of capital in the American West. If class is a function of labor in a particular space, then losing traditional or older forms of labor is a challenge in nearly every novel I have examined. And each particular novel's way of handling this challenge speaks to the literal and figurative "investment" of capital in specific historical moments—including when it is *dis*invested. The money to be made from the loss of working traditions also had a strong impact on how those labor patterns evolved or were memorialized as time passed. For instance, as Nancy Cook (2007) has pointed out, cowboy labor has been memorialized as nostalgia about the American West to the point where a version of it still thrives in popular culture even as the labor itself has nearly vanished. And American Indian labor has suffered from a similar nostalgic trap that contains traditional labor within county and craft fairs. In both cases a mythic history sells—cowboy hats, old-style riding whips, carefully woven straw baskets, and hand-beaded dream catchers find their way into American houses and hands by the thousands every year—but it is largely a history of dispossession. This is not only exploitative—you lost your way of life, let's profit on that!—but it is also a way that we, as consumers, impose an aesthetic judgment on history. We like these things, so we're not willing to let them go—well, not *quite*.

And although we think we know the story about how history commonly becomes memorialized, the particular story I've tried to tell in this work is a little different. This time we aren't memorializing the winners but the losers. The workers of the Dust Bowl laid the foundation for union labor parties out West but often didn't profit much from those campaigns. And María Amparo Ruiz de Burton's Californios lost their ranch empires in ways that damaged an emergent Chicano identity for years to come. And even the small cross section of skilled workers who became unskilled manual laborers like Frank Norris's McTeague offers a reflection on the labor laws that supposedly protected national interest—in *McTeague*, health associated with dentistry—but damaged many individual lives. In retrospective acts of often insincere generosity, we prefer to rescue Dorothea Lange photographs and early glass medicine bottles and medical instruments in order to display the roots of America's national identity we would like to believe in: identities rooted in labor. These nostalgic purchases serve to reaffirm our already nationalistic faith in the image of hard-working Americans pulling themselves up by their bootstraps. Our national reaction to those who lost their identities and histories, therefore, is to seamlessly slide them into ours, smoothing over any cracks that mar the new portrait of American achievement.

The importance of reading the novels analyzed in this work, and of reading American Indian novels as part of this larger body of literature, is thus threefold. We must not only recognize but also be in no rush to reconcile the dark stains these stories leave on American history. We must also work to integrate stories of those who lost ways of working, ways of believing, ways of life, into the broader portrait of American culture. Finally, if these stories all represent moments of American history as a whole and not just the history of the American West, then we must seize those stories and retell them alongside easier-to-digest ones. Only then can we represent how we made the West and its identities, as well as how those labors helped make the America of our present.

# 6  From Prairie to Oil

Hybridization and Belonging via Class, Labor,
and Space in Philipp Meyer's *The Son*

On the first page of Philipp Meyer's (2013, 1) *The Son*, Colonel Eli McCullough, one of the novel's three protagonists, remarks, "Should my son appear, I would prefer not to suffer his smile of victory. Seed of my destruction. I know what he did." A curious beginning—one reviewer even claims that here "Eli rambles only half intelligently" (Pickard 2014, 60)—but in light of the book as a whole, these words say far more than one might initially register. In one sense Eli rejects his son Peter's empathy for the Garcia family, wealthy Hispanic neighbors of the McCulloughs for many years whom the McCulloughs, except for Peter, gun down one night in a vicious massacre. But in a wider sense Eli is bemoaning the loss of a West to which he ties and ascribes himself and, more broadly, his family.

*The Son* uses the McCullough family history to narrate the uneven growth of Texas's capital, space, and labor from 1849 to 2012, and, vice versa, it uses the developmental history of Texas to tell the McCulloughs' story. The novel's broad historical scope allows it to cover a variety of Texan versions of characters we have encountered in previous chapters—Mexicans, Indians, and American settlers, farmers, and working cowboys, to name a few—and their participation in this growth. It also surveys the various claims to belonging in Texas—or belonging *to* Texas—put forward by the families of these different characters in their various contexts. My primary objective in using *The Son* to wrap up this book's argument is to show how the two elements enhance each other—specifically, how the socioeconomic development of Texas over time changes what "belonging" means for these individuals and their families. As such, themes like genealogy, family legacy, civic identity and legitimacy, inheritance, and nation-building feature prominently and combine to offer a rich and diverse account of Texas during some of its most significant moments of expansion.

*The Son*'s primary characters all seek to establish their belonging by successfully manipulating class, labor, and space to claim a legitimate Texan identity. They purchase or otherwise annex land, develop that land with laborers they hire, trade for provisions and supplies, and amass capital to establish and sustain their wealth in order to protect the family's right to remain safely in place. Behind these socioeconomic concerns is an ethnic component that infuses belonging with the danger of bigotry. When belonging demands it, characters in *The Son* turn to enslaving or killing ethnic others to sustain capital growth. Belonging is thus a process of acquisition—a procedure that manipulates the fruits of capital from ethnic exploitation—to construct a secure region wherein individuals build their homes in a previously "empty" space and claim it as their own.

For the McCulloughs, "to belong" is to derive regional, civic, and political security and identity from a continuous, often violent dynastic presence. As Texas develops, the McCulloughs make sociopolitical moves to direct that growth in their favor. For instance, Eli illegally manipulates his investments in cattle to claim ownership of larger tracts of land than are normally permitted by law and so extends his and his family's assets. That belonging, which grants the McCulloughs great power over the socioeconomic landscape of Texas, also enhances their civic, capital, and regional control. Texas "belongs" to them to the extent that its land and resources fall—and stay—under their control. The ranch they construct on the land is their dynastic home, the central place of a belonging achieved and protected not only through control of class, labor, and space but through the McCulloughs' historical legacy. Their family's history of living in the region grants them formal civic identity as Texans and Americans, categories that solidify along with the family's claim as the novel's historical narrative rolls forward. In other words, at the start of the novel the McCulloughs' command of southwestern Texas derives from their successful participation in nation-building. That familial and civic identity also contributes to a sense of security rooted in genealogical belonging—a long-term presence that benefits the McCulloughs politically and personally. *The Son* braids together the quests for genealogical and national belonging, suggesting that the two not only draw from each other but also pursue similar legitimacies to authenticate civic and personal identity. That's the context in which I consider how *The Son* frames and responds to the question of who *belongs* in or to Texas, why, and by what means.

The multiple intersecting dimensions here—of history, family, morality, space, and loss, to name a few—only begin to gesture toward the ways that Texan, western, and American histories are braided together with the story of the McCulloughs in the novel. Eli, Peter, and Jeanne Anne's experiences track how the family's structure changes in response to broader historical circumstances as Texas moves from being a frontier territory to a state dominated by ranching and then oil. Almost archival in nature, this tactic recalls Hayden White's (1978, 2) literary or poetic claim that history is primarily "a verbal structure in the form of a narrative prose discourse." While White focuses primarily on texts of the nineteenth century, his attention to the uncertainty of what it means to think historically, develop historical consciousness, or settle on historical knowledge helps frame *The Son* as a novel that interrogates the justification of historical legitimacy. Its dual focus on genealogical and regional-national history identifies it as a postwestern generational novel—a hybrid text that draws on literary characteristics common to postmodernism in general and the postmodern western in particular—that aspires to dismantle western regional gen-erational metanarratives. Generational novels are typically about politically powerful families, like the McCulloughs, who craft and determine national belonging. But *The Son* manifests an urge to interrogate and disassemble the metafiction of the McCulloughs' monolithic regional and political power through its intersecting, kaleidoscopic representation of the McCulloughs' relationships with one another, with other families, and with shifting arrange-ments of class, labor, and space. *The Son*'s multigenerational sweep uses family heritage and legacy to showcase Texas as a dynamic regional process and not a static place. In the novel Texas is a space with its own set of characteristics (both inherited and cyclical, like the environment—cycles of violence, conquest, density, loss) that change over time as different groups seize, inherit, and change the land to suit their purposes and as new socioeconomic and socio-political orders are imposed on the region. These changes, all with bearing on the problem of belonging, shape political, social, cultural, and regional identities, which in turn shape evolving interpretations of American nationalism and national identity.[1]

*The Son*'s illustration of Texas history through the McCulloughs' family history—and vice versa—also gestures toward the postmodern interpretation of that rhetorical construction. Critics have suggested that postmodern literature is generally marked by a dismantling of master narratives that claim primacy and thereby displace others. *The Son* is in many ways a compelling piece of postmodern literature that recalls what Hayden White (1978) terms the poetic potential of history to productively reorient and reinterpret master histories. The master narrative here is about how the McCulloughs' politi-cal control over Texas shapes the region. *The Son* deploys famil-iar postmodern markers of positionality, irony, obscurity, chaos, and heterogeneity to help dismantle that master narrative and the claims underlying it. Additionally, the novel employs those same postmodern techniques to unravel the long development of capitalism in Texas and the West. In these ways *The Son* might seem to be a postmodern western, which critics have defined as a genre that refuses and disrupts notions of authenticity and clearly defined centers of power specifically in the West.[2] As Krista Comer (1999, 5) argues, postmodernism's "ultimate expression might be found in the figure of the hybrid and in notions of hybridity and hybridized subjectivity. It is this last proposition that, at bottom, is so often at issue in western contexts." In other words, the postmodern western seeks to challenge claims to an authentic West that offers particular cultural objects or icons as wholly representational of the "true West."[3]

Fredric Jameson's canonical view of postmodernism and late capitalism as working hand in hand to support each other doesn't fit *The Son* very well.[4] Rather than accepting this claim of complicity, my argument here pushes against the conception of postmodernism as chained to uncontrolled capital growth and empty cultural reproduction; instead, I read *The Son*'s postmodernity as rich and pluralizing. In this sense *The Son* is closer to what critics have called the postwestern novel, a form that uses elements of hybridization—rhizomatic zones, borderlands, pluralized and hybrid identities, and little-known or ignored narratives—to undo the cowboy-obsessed master narrative that embraces rugged individualism, exploitation, and violence as necessary components to nation-building in the Old West.[5] Broadly, my analysis of the kaleidoscopic experiences of *The Son*'s complicated family, whose members claim vastly different belongings and identities during Texas's equally complicated development, emphasizes the way nation-building is as deconstructive as it is constructive. Animated by this analysis, my question of who really belongs in Texas and by what means challenges not only national terms of belonging but social and cultural terms as well, calling attention to the way belonging rests on a number of factors that may or may not be granted legitimacy in given civic, political, or economic arenas.

*The Son* devotes much of its energy to tracing the network of fractures that threaten to bring down this edifice of the McCulloughs' historical legitimacy, political sovereignty, and civic belonging. For instance, when Eli identifies as Comanche, it strains his interactions with the Texas Rangers, the army, and settlers who believe that their national and civic identities grant them the right to claim whatever land they want and defend it by whatever means necessary.[6] And when Eli signs up with the Texas Rangers, his new state identity pushes aside (but cannot totally dismiss) his discomfort with the rangers' violence toward the remaining Indians with whom he personally sympathizes. In both cases persisting family ties (here, tribal and military) complicate the process of claiming new spaces, a tension that suggests that the family's yoking of its lineage to histories of political belonging exposes the painful frictions among groups still at odds in the West. And like many other elite families in the West, when the McCulloughs experience slippages in their political monopolies of class, labor, and space, the anxieties of these losses shake their faith in a stable, salutary process of nation-building.

Meyer's narrative of kaleidoscopic families told through kaleidoscopic histories offers crucial insight into how the West developed multidirectionally as new forces and identities emerged. It is from *this* vantage point that I suggest turning to another set of stories within the novel that dismantle the McCulloughs' metafictions of generational belonging and bring other narratives forward: those of the Garcias and the Comanche. Reading these narratives alongside William Cronon's argument that the West is a space always in flux calls attention to and mirrors the rhizomatic growth of Texas's space—specifically, the ways in which these more ethnically diverse families contributed to regional and national hybridization. In this context that flux reconstructs recognizable regional spaces with more dynamic cultural identities that ultimately disorient families like the McCulloughs, who rely on uniform definitions of national identity. The novel is what I would call a *generational* postwestern. In the process of shuttling among the private and public lives of the McCulloughs, the Garcias, and the Comanche—their emotions, as well as their political ambitions—the novel reveals the frictions, anxieties, fractures, and losses that ultimately weakened the elites' hold on Texas and the West and thus carved a space for hybridized belonging.

On Class, Labor, and Space

One of the novel's most revealing narratives is that of Jeanne Anne, who learns what constitutes success and national identity in the context of specific regional histories of capital, space, and work. Her sense of this social and historical development is informed by a theory of legacy that she inherits from previous generations of her family. Drawn to the family's two most prominent businessmen, Eli and his son Phineas, she feels that if she can protect the legacy of political power the McCulloughs have amassed, she can also protect and maintain their belonging. As the youngest McCullough with her own narrative in the novel (though most of it takes place at the end of her life), Jeanne Anne filters the other McCulloughs' experiences through her memories, witnessing the growth of Texas through the prism of the McCullough ranch. Jeanne Anne's need to fiercely protect the work of her family follows a long literary tradition of western women doing just that in hostile environments. For example, in two western classics, O. E. Rølvaag's *Giants in the Earth* (originally published 1924–25) and Wallace Stegner's *Angle of Repose* (1971), women's work is foregrounded as a necessary component of both domestic and national growth and stability. In Rølvaag's novel (1999, 29), when the Hansa family first arrives in the Dakota Territory, Beret, the mother, feels lost in the open space: "Why, there isn't even a thing one can hide behind," she reflects. That perspective initially overwhelms her—"This formless prairie had no heart that beat, no waves that sang, no soul that could be touched . . . or cared" (37)—but over time she learns to contend with the prairie on its own terms: "What she cannot get easily she wrests by subtle force" (443). At the same time that she makes this shift from a more passive to a more assertive and productive relationship with the environment, her housework assumes a more forceful and organized tone as well. She cooks more, cleans more, and begins pushing her sons to become more thoughtful. As a microcosm of an early American domestic scene, Beret's work—and especially the legacy she hands down to her children through that work—reflects the way women figured as stalwart guardians of national and domestic identities on sparsely settled territories. But Beret's work is undercut by her husband's death at the end of the novel, which does not shy from the failures that can undo the master narrative of successful western expansion.

In the same vein, Stegner's Susan Burling Ward follows her husband, Oliver, a geological engineer, around the West and etches out her own working identity based on her knowledge of his work and her need to maintain a stable domestic life on the road. Susan's primary goal is to create a home for her family that recalls her home back East—"Like some shaped stone, the fully formed architecture, the household with its routines as fixed as holy offices" (Stegner 1971, 330)—and her image of this home rests on conventional American notions of housekeeping and its role in nation-building. Alongside her domestic work, Oliver's geological work takes on a similar character: he too is charting a West that can then be cataloged as part of America. Yet the success of Oliver's work relies on a constant uprooting that undermines Susan's constructions of home, because the pressure it puts on their financial stability distracts Oliver from attending to his family's happiness. Much like Rogier's blindness to all but the mine in Frank Waters's *Below Grass Roots*, Oliver's tunnel vision prevents him from registering the literal cost both of his work and of Susan's need to continually construct a new home. Thus, both families leverage their land's development—

environmental *and* domestic—for nation-building, but they always do so under the threat of failure.

These canonical renditions of American nation-building in western literature provide a context in *The Son* for not only Eli McCullough's career but Jeanne Anne's as well. She, like Beret Hansa and Susan Burling Ward, takes whatever measures necessary to secure her family's belonging in uncertain space. But her personal understanding of this tradition is marked by an ethnic discrimination that is deeply threaded into her need to maintain the metafiction of the McCulloughs. In many ways Eli's own class relationship to the Garcias is reflected in Jeanne Anne's inheritance of the McCullough mind-set, which is unforgiving in its genealogical control of class, labor, and space. When Eli tries to reconcile and explain the massacre of the Garcias to Peter in financial terms, he focuses on the money the McCulloughs have lost through the Garcias' alleged thefts. He frames Peter's inheritance in terms of financial loss:

> In the west pasture alone, we lost forty thousand dollars. In other pastures, maybe eighty thousand. And I would judge they have been robbing us for quite a while, at least since the first of the sons-in-law showed up. Now there has been a drought these four years, but does a drought reduce your calves fifty percent? Not if you've been feeding them like we did. Do you suddenly lose thirty percent of your momma cows? No, you do not. That is the hand of man. You figure the increase, they have stolen close to two million dollars from us. (Meyer 2013, 165)

Those questions, however, extend beyond simple interrogations of how and why ethnic "othering" breeds unreasonable fear and corresponding xenophobia. Instead, Eli's responses—always measured, always precise—indicate a more nuanced consideration that allows for shifts in his sociopolitical affiliations that actually *resist* firm national and cultural identities. We might recall some of the major themes of not only *Mean Spirit* and *The Lone Ranger and Tonto Fistfight in Heaven* but also *The Squatter and the Don*: if marginalized groups often fight for civic and cultural legitimacy simultaneously, should civic belonging be resituated elsewhere to preserve identity? In other words, do ethnic and/or regional affiliations—American Indian or Mexican or white—falter in the face of cultural decay or do such challenges point to new national identities that can also be financially exploited? When the last of Eli's tribe begins to die from cholera, the remaining Comanche take desperate measures to save themselves: they kill their blind children to reduce the number of mouths to feed. And Mountain Rocks, one of the tribe's chiefs, has a similar conversation with Eli that reads ethnic identity by its civic viability: "'There is a way for you to help.' I knew what he was getting at. The government was still paying high prices for returned captives" (319). The crossing of these two economies—Indian and Anglo—poses no threat to Anglo settlers, especially those who, like Eli and the West writ large, have flexible civic, political, and cultural identities. Here the intersection of those two economic identities is benign because in this context the biological weakness of one protects and reinforces the capital security of the other: to the McCulloughs, captives only count as currency. Initially reluctant to leave and, until his death, always respectful of Comanche ways, Eli has made a transition into Anglo identity and political life that both preserves the cultural and historical legacy of one group and makes possible the genealogical and political heritage of another. But at what cost?

Earlier, when Eli's influence might have encouraged Jeanne Anne to tolerate Texas's growing ethnic hybridization, she instead resists it and the capital erosion she assumes will accompany it. For instance, when older Indians come by the family house, Jeanne Anne is uncomfortable with the colonel's behavior: he "did not hold court as he did around the whites but rather sat and nodded and listened. She did not like to see it. The Indians did not dress the way they should have—they might as well have been grangers or Mexicans—and they smelled strong and did not pay her any attention" (111). In addition, she links the colonel's reluctance to treat the Indians as lesser individuals to their "misuse" of the house, which she sees as indicating Eli's loosening control: "many mornings she came into the guest room to discover a dozen old men asleep among their former enemies, spilled beer and whiskey, a beef quarter half-eaten in the fire" (112). In each of these complaints Jeanne Anne sees spatial and financial chaos as being the result of an ethnic intrusion that has the potential to undo the family's power. The colonel's encouragement of such behavior reinforces her fear of hybridized belonging because she fears that his acceptance of it means he has lost any sense of wholesale discrimination against ethnic others, something that he has never in fact had. Thus, although Eli reflects the hybridization of Texas's cultural heritage over time, Jeanne Anne's perspective betrays how, in her eyes, maintaining the socioeconomic elements of ethnic discrimination is central to protecting genealogical nation-building.

Jeanne Anne's inheritance of this economic history and its outcomes, alongside her own genealogy, grants her a great degree of political flexibility, yet that latitude is one for which she must nonetheless fight. In comparison to earlier settler women like Rølvaag's Beret and Stegner's Susan, whose nation-building projects could only grow from period expectations of women's domestic responsibilities, Jeanne Anne can participate directly in the protection of her family's political legacy, a job usually reserved for (McCullough) men. But although Jeanne Anne's maneuvers—figured as mastery of specialized spatial skills like riding bareback and climbing fences and pitching in to help with an oil rig—fit into the broader women's rights movement, her focus on genealogical belonging and legitimacy disengages her from the pursuit of more traditional, more national women's rights like suffrage, body rights and autonomy, or the right to serve in the military. In other words, her awareness of the movement in the novel is meager at best. Instead, her working relationships with the men in the McCullough family business constitute her biggest challenge: those men block her from influencing the politics of her family, but she resolves to leverage what little socioeconomic power she can to subvert their control over her. For instance, when she discovers that her father's lack of interest in the ranch would eventually leave it "bankrupt and all they had ever done would be forgotten," she decides, "*It is up to me. . . . I will have to do something*" (219). Here Jeanne Anne sees herself as the inheritor of the McCullough ranch and its wealth, and she invests her time and energy in learning the basics of the oil business of southwest Texas: "which wells were producing more than she'd hoped (less, she thought, it was always less), what new fields might be in play and what plays the majors were giving up on. Which drillers might be hired, who was out of credit, what could be bought on the cheap" (53). And soon after, "when she was old enough to look at the books" and meticulously study the family's cattle and oil holdings, the expertise she gains reveals that her father belongs to "a dying breed . . . of . . . old time ranching families who had gone bankrupt," whose capital investments relied on unprofitable ranching ventures that were increasingly outmoded, like Old West shows and felt cowboy hats (217).

Her great uncle Phineas similarly recognizes this and discloses to Jeanne Anne that they need to begin drilling for oil on their own ranch. As she understands her great uncle's thinking, "he wanted her to betray her father. Her father, for all his rough-and-tumble image, was a dandy. She had always known this, perhaps because the Colonel was always pointing it out. Earning money was the furthest thing from her father's mind[;] he wanted to be on magazine covers, like the Colonel had been. She had always known that the Colonel did not respect him and now she saw that Phineas—the other famous member of the family—did not respect him, either" (215). But beyond not respecting Jeanne Anne's father, Phineas and Eli don't trust Charles because his economic decisions are dubious at best. Whereas Phineas understands the class patterns of the oil business, right down to the finer details of the depletion allowance—"if you drill for oil, you can write twenty-seven point five percent of your proceeds off as a loss"—Charles stubbornly hangs onto cattle. "How your father can still be thinking about cows is a mystery," Phineas observes (216). Charles's inability to make sound financial decisions and his need for fame paint him as an unworthy successor to his McCullough ranching forebears, as does his desire to live in a past he imagines grants him the McCullough legacy without his working for it. And Clint and Paul (Charles's sons and Jeanne Anne's brothers) have gone to fight in Germany, drawn by the thrill of battle, and so while their choice engages nation-building and civic belonging, being "dragged . . . into the modern age" in a war zone thousands of miles away hardly promises a safe return to the ranch (217). The McCulloughs lack a young, healthy male heir, which threatens the family's socioeconomic genealogy and stability. Phineas recognizes the weight of this threat and that Jeanne Anne is the only member of the immediate family who is prepared to assume the mantle of socioeconomic power for the McCullough dynasty.

Jeanne Anne's business acumen grows along with the genealogical belonging she understands to be linked to it. Successfully demonstrating to Phineas that she is concerned enough with the domestic home front and the family's socioeconomic legacy to maintain and pursue both, she sees the McCulloughs as an inelastic family and an unyielding civic business. These two images of the family thus bind tightly together to form a genealogical metanarrative that Jeanne Anne knows Phineas will note well.

Jeanne Anne understands what it takes to maintain the construct of the McCulloughs' belonging, but the novel continually asks—as I do—who belongs in Texas and by what means that belonging is established and maintained. In Jeanne Anne's final memories, the consequences of her family's autocratic control of Texas's class, labor, and space force her to confront the terms of her own belonging. The final series of scenes, when Ulises—son of Peter McCullough and Maria Garcia—shows up at Jeanne Anne's door to prove *his* heritage, mark the crucial role these forms of legitimacy can play in securing—or dismantling—metafictions of belonging and nation-building:

> From his leather bag, which he had also cleaned and oiled before coming over, he removed all the letters and papers. . . .
>
> She read the first few pages, but then she was going through the papers faster than she could read them.
>
> "We are family," he repeated.
>
> Her eyes showed nothing, but he could see that her hands had begun to shake.
>
> "I'm afraid I'll have to ask you to leave," she said.
>
> He pointed again to the papers.
>
> "You will leave this house right now," she said. "Mr. Colms will have your check." (550)

After her initial reaction, Jeanne Anne grows more anxious, and when she misreads Ulises's step toward his briefcase (he had hoped that the care with which he cleaned it would communicate his financial and individual stability), she backs away too suddenly and falls, hitting her head on the marble fireplace. Once Ulises realizes that as "a Mexican in the house of a rich lady" (551) he will inevitably be held responsible for her injury, he engineers the gas explosion that will destroy the McCulloughs' house. As he escapes on one of the McCulloughs' horses, he thinks, "All around the land spread out in the dusk, there was nothing in sight that did not belong to the McCulloughs" (552). In her last conscious moments Jeanne Anne admits to the truth of Ulises's claim—"She had known from the moment he spoke he was telling the truth" (554)—and her subsequent fear of what his existence signifies with regard to the continued success of her family. If Ulises can claim genealogical belonging, he can infiltrate their delicate family structure and undo the metafiction of their ethnically exclusive dominion, symbolized by the house itself. Jeanne Anne's fear of the ramifications of their relationship is not only unfounded but also exposes her to the biological danger of crafting a narrowly defined nationalism. In essence her reluctance to make room for Texas's hybridization has prevented her from developing a wider perspective that would have diversified her sense of belonging and preserved her from harm.

Much like the early scene of the novel with which I opened this chapter, this later episode gestures toward the intersections among a number of the novel's central topics: history, ethnicity, genealogy, loss, region, belonging, legitimacy. Yet until now both Ulises's and Jeanne Anne's memoir-style narratives have been filtered through the burning of the house—the facts of which remain hazy. In Meyer's hands the postwestern genre generates a kind of uncertainty that undermines the standard metafictional account of the McCulloughs' power. As Ulises remarks,

> The Americans . . . he still allowed his mind to roam. They thought that simply because they had stolen something, no one should be allowed to steal it from them. But of course that was what all people thought: that whatever they had taken, they should be allowed to keep forever.
>
> He was no better. His people had stolen the land from the Indians, and yet he did not think of it for an instant—he thought only of the Texans who had stolen it from his people. And the Indians from whom his people had stolen the land had themselves stolen it from other Indians. (553)

Not only does Ulises begin to disentangle how those issues intersect with his own familial history, but he can do so in a way that widens his historical purview to include the particular spaces the McCulloughs and others have expropriated. Yet that broadened perspective only muddies the waters more, proving that the road to western conquest was a compromised and unforgiving one. He once assumed western conquest rested on a legitimate geographic belonging. However, examining this dynamic more closely reveals that "[h]is people had stolen the land from the Indians," which more closely interrogates the McCulloughs' familial legitimacy. If, as he reflects, he feels he belongs *to* the land because he is part of the family, and if, as Jeanne Anne reflects, she feels she belongs *on* the land because of her financial control, then who actually poses a greater threat to the McCullough estate? Ulises represents the Garcias' culture, which Jeanne Anne worries will dilute the McCulloughs' genealogical power, but the McCullough dynasty rests on uncertain ground because Jeanne Anne has so stridently resisted that hybridity and the less monolithic, more diversified socioeconomic order associated with it. Ulises's arrival thus only reinforces the truth of that ethnic hybridity: Mexicans, American Indian tribes, Asian ethnicities, eastern European ethnicities, and others would continue to populate and change the region in Jeanne Anne's eyes, ultimately encouraging her growing xenophobia and unreasonable reactions. Jeanne Anne and Ulises's interaction thereby unmasks the truth: that the base of the McCulloughs' monolithic ethnic façade is cracking.

In fact in the early twentieth-century portion of the novel, these conditions come to a head and lead to the massacre of the Garcias, which the McCulloughs hope will reassert their ethnic and regional dominance. They counterattack the Garcias for stealing over time a large number of cattle and for attempting to kill Glenn McCullough. As the "bloody summer" of 1915 progresses and ethnic tensions continue to mount, the McCulloughs become more adamant that the Garcias abandon their national power and identity (9–10). However, the cattle thefts and the attempt on Glenn's life are unverified, and Peter's revelation that the Garcias "have been in this country far longer than any of the white families [and] were once proper hidalgos, having been granted this land by the king of Spain himself," calls attention to the extensive socioeconomic, territorial, and historical belonging the Garcias enjoyed in the past, as well their current respectability (68). Hidalgos were traditionally second-rank Spanish nobility that the king of Spain favored with elevated social class and land grants; however, their national ties to Spain faded over time as their civic identity grew hazy on American soil. In other words, as time passes and it becomes less clear what protection the Garcias' social and class status grant them, the McCulloughs take advantage of that lack of clarity and consider it their right to eliminate the Garcias and their socioeconomic legacy from the larger community.

The McCulloughs' attack on the Garcias bears the marks of a style of violence that reinforces the metafiction of the "Old West." Even the McCulloughs' vaqueros are willing to fight to maintain the thrill of violence and discrimination, because that thrill creates a certain degree of dangerous allure: playing Old West cowboy means acting out a role of power, however fleeting or fabricated. In other words, even the ethnic mix of their rough-and-ready army stands behind Eli and defends the principles for which he stands. On the other hand, the Garcias also signify ethnic difference—their historical ties to Spanish nobility represent an important segment of the hybridized West. That segment is dismantled in this massacre of almost all of the Garcia family, which only brings to light more unevenness in belonging and national identity. Eli commands the vaqueros, ranchers, and the Texas Rangers with ease because all see themselves as heroes valiantly protecting the Old West by destroying the Garcias. To this end, Eli's wearing his Apache vest to command his attacking force is an act of cultural appropriation that convinces the makeshift army of his imagined authority: it undermines the authenticity of the Comanche historical legacy and reaffirms Eli's position as a makeshift colonel. His dressing and acting the part blinds his followers to the fallacy of his overwhelming power. While both the vaqueros and the Garcias represent ethnic hybridization, the roles they play in the massacre and how Eli responds to those roles indicate how dangerous Eli considers their ethnic hybridization to be. More significantly, the Garcias' attack on the McCulloughs threatens the latter's sociopolitical leverage. As Peter recognizes, "Glenn and our cattle no longer had anything to do with this" (65). In other words, the McCulloughs know that the fiction of protecting their West only masks the political truth behind the destruction: that their family dynasty is in great danger. In the end the extreme violence undertaken and the extreme satisfaction felt by all those who participate in the massacre reveal their underlying dedication to the myth of the Old West that protects the McCulloughs' capital security.

Eliminating the Garcias does just that; when Peter follows Maria through the *casa mayor* after the massacre and listens to her reflect on the event, he comes to realize the true extent of the damage. He recognizes that the McCulloughs had meant to eliminate more than just the Garcias. After murdering the family, Eli "pulled all the papers from their cabinets, old letters, stock records, deeds, certificates of birth and death for ten generations, the original land grant, back when this place was all a Spanish province" (167). When Peter and Maria return to survey the damage, Maria confirms that "[t]he papers were gone. Every single document and letter, every record had been removed. And then I knew it had been intentional. It was not enough to exterminate my family, it was also necessary to remove every record of our existence" (317). These documents confirm the Garcias' civic belonging and legal existence; without them the Garcias have no history. Such a maneuver showcases the terrible power the McCulloughs exercise when it comes to rewriting the past. Not only do Eli and his ilk eradicate the Garcias' genealogy, which the novel posits as a crucial component of nation-building, but they also eliminate the record of the Garcias' sociopolitical legitimacy in Texas, which thus questions their belonging.

The attack on the Garcias by a motley force composed of the McCulloughs and their allies and employees is one of the novel's most dramatic illustrations of how class, labor, and space, when bound together, produce physical places in which genealogical dynasties are protected. That's why it is so important to destroy the Garcias' home in addition to their family; the casa mayor "had come to be something else: the guardian of an old, less civilized order, standing against progress and all that was good on the earth" (62). Eli understands the casa mayor to *represent* and so *protect* a backward-looking socioeconomic political system. He knows that gesturing toward that understanding will rally those around him to dismantle the genealogical protection that the Garcias' house provides this "old, less civilized order." By a similar logic, the McCulloughs' ranch needs extra, *legalized* protection: "After the Garcia troubles, the ranch had been declared a state game preserve, which meant that, in addition to the vaqueros, the McCulloughs had game wardens—technically employees of the state—as additional security" (143). The McCulloughs' now mandated security draws a parallel between Eli's ranch and the state of Texas, which he reinforces in his WPA recorded interview at the end of his life: "Most will be familiar with the day of my birth," he says. "I was the first male child of this new republic," he adds, after which he proceeds to describe the legal steps his father took to claim their land (2–3). This legality, which confirms the McCulloughs' civic identity, when read alongside the details of Eli's birth, which confirms their heritage, establishes the genealogical and legal terms of the family's Texan belonging, which underwrites the command of class, labor, and space necessary to the project of nation-building.

A Western Education

Eli's understanding of Texas and his place in it is rooted in but also presented in contrast to his youthful insights in the period following his kidnapping by a group of Comanche. During his captivity, he witnesses the unique circumstances that have radically altered the Comanche nation's status. He comes to empathetically recognize how the remaining Comanche people struggle to survive under new national conditions that fundamentally challenge their inherited processes of belonging and community-building. Specifically, when the Comanche tribe's interactions with class, labor, and space occur in nations and not geographies, those interactions undermine belonging and community-building.

Here I need to refine "region" to differentiate between geography and nation in terms germane to the novel's account of community-building and belonging. Regions are areas that possess definable characteristics, which can be enclosed by fixed official boundaries yet are often not, thus leaving open multiple possibilities about what those characteristics can be. In *The Son* the Comanche broadly define region as geography or nation, where geography signifies unconstructed space—a map with no lines—and nation signifies politically constructed space, a map with lines. Geographies are typically open to many kinds of inhabitants, whereas nations are already divided and suited to specific populations and thus less accepting of the living patterns of othered populations. Although both nation and geography have kaleidoscopic potential—ethnic, cultural, and natural, to name a few—geographies remain flexible enough to support many more kinds of inhabitants. Many of the kaleidoscopic elements needed by the Comanche to establish community or belonging—like familiar natural spaces or forms of wildlife and plant life—are threatened and then destroyed by nation. Thus, the limits of nation, when compared to the kaleidoscopic potential of geography, help to explain how Anglo nation-building undermines geography's contributions to Comanche community-building and belonging. Specifically, building the structures and systems that produce the lines of nation turns the pursuit of capital, the act of labor, and the design of space into isolating acts that eliminate the potential for the Comanche to form new bonds and pursue multidirectional living patterns.

For instance, when Eli regrets the loss of Texas's open land, his words also betray broader losses of belonging: "and now the whole of Texas was open to the white man. I told Madeline I needed some time alone, saddled my horse, and went up the Colorado. I was riding and riding but no matter how far I got there were hogcallers and boatmen. I rode into the night until finally it was quiet. I climbed a ledge and built a fire and howled out into the wolves. But nothing howled back" (533). Although he once found belonging in open, unclaimed spaces, Eli can no longer locate that sort of place. Those spaces are now owned and controlled by American men and laws and are managed in such a way that "ruined [them] forever" (165). Alongside Eli's earlier remark that nothing is "worth a shit until you put your name on it," these comments reflect how the civic landmarks of white settlers dismantle the geographies needed to support the belonging practices of the Comanche, "who, civilized or not, lived closer to the natural ways than most whites" (114, 461). In other words, because the Comanche rely on nature to belong in space, the loss of nature results in a corresponding loss of belonging that unveils the consequences of Anglo settler boundaries and spatial control. These legalized boundaries and their mandates directly and indirectly govern what populations can inhabit those spaces. Under the pressure of American metanarratives and the damaging changes to the land they enable and justify, these spaces became unfriendly and poorly equipped to support their original populations. Thus, the populations once common to these areas are largely gone, further emptying the geographic space. For instance, the lack of wolves historically indicates that particular kinds of wildlife do not belong in civilized, national space and are more suited as decorative pieces in homes; they have therefore been hunted out of existence. And the presence of hog callers and boatmen calls attention to who *can* live in these spaces and for what purpose—here, those allowed are white men who further sabotage natural patterns. Both the hog callers and the boatmen drive away nature—the hog callers hunt and kill a population, while the boatmen disturb water flow and indigenous populations while capturing them as well. Both are part of a new population that, under the umbrella of national space, dedicates itself to fixing that space by eliminating elements of geography. The resulting spaces with static boundaries do not support the full, kaleidoscopic range of living patterns and belonging.

While the Comanche secure belonging via geography, labor defines the terms of their community and indeed plays a key role in constituting it. Every member of the Comanche nation has a particular role that is crucial to the literal construction and upkeep of their dwellings and the necessities they need to survive. These roles are important because they organize and maintain not just the physical structures of the Comanche but their social order as well. In other words, Comanche labor practices build community in two ways: they both reflect individual identity and indicate an individual's working role. For instance, when the Comanche first capture Eli, he is tasked with what is typically women's work, which communicates and reinforces his role in the group:

> Unless I wanted a hiding, I was up before the sun, walking through the wet grass, filling the water jugs in the cold stream and getting the fire going. The rest of the day I did whatever the women didn't feel like doing. Pounding corn for Toshaway's wife, cleaning and flaying game the men brought in, getting more water or firewood. . . .
>
> But that was all women's work. If Toshaway [the chief] called me over everything else stopped. (97)

The same situation emerges as Eli grows and is allowed free time during which he is encouraged to interact with other adolescent boys to learn Comanche hunting methods. Despite the obvious gender divide, that scene, alongside learning the components of bow making, indicates to Eli that the Comanche must closely interact with one another from a young age to learn work that braids the tightly interwoven community necessary to the group's survival (107).

The close attention Eli pays to weapon making and to the self-constitutive labor the Comanche perform is a trait he carries with him throughout his time with them. His portions of *The Son* are richly detailed and indicate a growing curiosity about the pragmatic actions the Comanche take to sustain and protect their own people. That Eli learns these lessons firsthand lends him access to a form of sovereignty he otherwise would not have witnessed; as he recalls, "the Indians had their rules same as we had ours" (81). Overall the Comanche rely on strict, cyclical customs that develop the strength and insight of the group over time. For instance, they utilize the environment's patterns to benefit their sustenance over generations; they plant dogwood in such a way that "[t]he next spring each trunk would send out dozens of thin new shoots. . . . The location of these arrow groves was kept track of, and they were harvested carefully, making sure that the trees would survive," as they could provide both food and weaponry (107). Additionally, the Comanche maintain a violent hold on the regions they own—"many years ago [this] was Tonkawa land, but we liked it, so we killed the Tonkawa and took it from them" (95) and "[t]he Comanche *owned* all the territory between Mexico and the Dakotas"—to protect the supremacy of their people, especially over potential enemies (169; emphasis added). And most important, the Comanche cultivate a leadership that is not only consistent, firm, and farseeing but also responsive to the broader needs of the group. For instance, when Toshaway returns with Eli, the chief allows the tribe to express its excitement over the return of the raiders but keeps their violence in check to remind them of his consistent and resolute authority: "They beat my legs and tried to pull me off my horse. Toshaway let this go on until one of the old women came at me with a knife. . . . There was a long negotiation over my future [but] Toshaway was defending his property" (75). Allowing this violence to become excessive would endanger the Comanche's viability and Toshaway's legitimacy. Instead, Toshaway models the kind of behavior he expects of the tribe; his command thus forces the tribe to consider the long-term effects their actions will have on their communal health. Together these sociopolitical components of tribal organization and territorial control fashion a unique form of nation that roots itself in geographic community and belonging.

But while Eli acquires most of this pragmatic knowledge directly from close observation, he indirectly absorbs the most significant elements of Comanche nationalism, because living with the tribe takes him out of history. *The Son* presents Comanche nationalism as unblemished by the history of western expansionism, so that the lessons Eli learns are contextualized by a tribal sovereignty that roots its nation in geography. Spatially, the earth still seems in an early process of growth—"as if this place were His forge and the Creator himself were still fashioning the earth" (72)—and time operates on a grander scale: "Upriver were big cypresses with knock-kneed roots. Five hundred years was nothing for them" (33). Correspondingly, the Comanche regard long-term procreation and hybridity through their captives as a means of eternal tribal existence, as it "kept our blood strong all these years" (250)—an achievement the Comanche people celebrate with the scalp dance: "this was the point of the scalp dance, we were eternal, the Chosen People, and our names would ring on in the night, long after we'd vanished from the earth" (133). As the novel would have it, not only does the landscape thus engulf Eli in an ahistorical space but the Comanche people's tribal immortality removes him from the linear time of the white race and deposits him into cyclical, ahistorical Comanche time. In that broader context the pragmatic lessons Eli learns assume a wider purview that highlights their cyclical, inherited, ahistorical nature: all draw from the principle that the essential customs of the group should be performed in such a way that they sustain themselves by their own repetition. And that matrix of ahistorical space and time is maintained by cyclic, pragmatic practices that are repeated over hundreds or thousands of years.

This state of cyclical timelessness cannot last forever. Eli remarks that in the summer of 1850 "the Penateka, the largest and wealthiest of all the Comanche bands, had been mostly wiped out" (199). He recalls being in a "dry, unfamiliar country" where their "sense of order continued to slowly break down" (206). Indeed, "[i]n June, they captured eight hundred horses but there had been an ambush—the army and the Mexicans were working together now, instead of killing each other as they had always done—and nearly half the Kotsoteka warriors were killed or scattered. The army, along with several ranger companies, had chased the remaining warriors deep into Mexico" (208). And Toshaway mutters, "Strange," upon seeing the heavy marks of a howitzer on a hill, pointed directly at a hidden Indian camp; despite Eli's reassurance that "[t]hey put the guns in place in the dark," Toshaway realizes that "[s]omeone was leading them. . . . They knew the Indians were here" (237). These events unveil a new kind of warfare that is particularly dangerous to the Comanche. Working together, the army, the Texas Rangers, and Mexicans not only outnumber the Comanche but also have more deadly and unfamiliar weaponry, like artillery. These uncommon features of warfare denote that the terms, needs, and stakes of war have changed significantly and that the ahistorical existence of the Comanche, as well as their nationalism and geography, is not immune to the history that has always been moving toward them. Now that the doors to the West have been thrown open by western expansion and Manifest Destiny, new partnerships emerge as past enemies form alliances to seek spatial control—land acquisition, along with the bonuses of profit and slave labor. Perhaps most depressingly, Toshaway realizes who is behind the series of attacks: "Those were fucking Indians leading them . . . Lipans. And there were white men as well . . . [t]he Apaches sucking the cocks of the Mexicans who are sucking the cocks of the whites. The world is against us" (247). When these new forms of warfare bear down violently on weakened Comanche nationalism and geography, they erode the stability of the tribe to such a degree that Eli finds it necessary to sell himself back into Anglo society for provisions in order to give the remaining Comanche a fighting chance at survival.

But the novel imagines the forces of Anglo expansion to be disorganized and vulnerable in their own right. When Eli joins the Texas Rangers upon his return, he finds that, unlike the Comanche raiders under Toshaway's firm and long-sighted leadership, the rangers and the army are disordered and unfocused. As a captive, Eli was carefully assimilated into Comanche culture, whereas neither the army nor the rangers even have a cohesive culture of which to speak: they are "an assortment of bankrupt soldiers and adventure seekers, convicts and God's abandons" (402). They are poorly supplied and unprepared for battle: "All we did was shoot" without supervised direction or lessons, and with unreliable weapons (402). The men themselves are regarded as tools for warfare, like the guns and bullets with which they are paid: "[V]ouchers were always traded for equipment. . . . Our only other remuneration was ammunition, which we got in unlimited supply. Everything else—from corn bread to side meat—we were expected to forage or otherwise annex" (402). These more immediate, physical shortages indicate a larger governmental disregard: "As for the legislature, lice-ridden clodhoppers did not vote or donate to political campaigns, so their problems, quietly viewed to be of their own causation—though necessary for the state—were ignored. No new taxes. Rangers cost money" (425).

Unable to supply leadership, discipline, training, equipment, good horses, or provisions, the nation itself appears so inchoate as to be a space not worth fighting for. In other words, the fact that these nation-building tools are missing from the beginning indicates the shakiness of a nation constructed on appropriated space. The West Eli signs up to defend is still a wild frontier waiting to be tamed and not a viable portion of America. Performing military labor, unpaid, in this uncertain space leaves those who muster for such service with hazy nationalistic incentives that are simply not worth fighting for.

That contrast between Comanche and Anglo community and belonging practices, specifically framed in the requirements for successful warfare, implies that Eli's hybridized, ahistorical, cyclical upbringing has taught him the necessary tactics to manipulate class, labor, and space to build the developing West. The lessons he has learned from the Comanche about community, belonging, and highly effective leadership, when read alongside the gaps in those key elements he witnesses on the part of the army and the rangers, reveals that, by entering ahistorical space and time, Eli has emerged much better prepared for his role as a successful businessman. The Comanche people's community and belonging remained powerful and cohesive because they relied on time-tested ways to harness the power of class, labor, and space as equipment for fashioning dynastic continuity.

Eli will eventually emulate this model. After the Civil War ends and Texas is clear of Indians, a series of events leads to the murder of his father-in-law. Eli is "not content to see the great house fall." Taking control of the family, he changes the direction of its ambitions. He claims that "the Comanche in me held grubbing in the dirt to be lower than slops. And I wanted to make my money work" (500). But his discomfort with these unproductive uses of class, labor, and space does not end with mere complaints:

> For twenty-eight cents an acre I picked up sections in La Salle and Dimmit Counties. I considered parcels on the coast but the Kings and Kenedys had already driven up the prices, and the Nueces Strip was rich, well watered, and so cheap I could acquire a proper acreocracy. There were bandits and renegades but I had never minded packing my gun loose, and in that part of the state a man with a rope could still catch as many wild cattle as he wanted, which sold for forty dollars a head if you could get them north. It was not panning for gold, but it was close, and I rode out to save the family's good name. . . . For room, board, and a sliver of the

future profits, I hired two former confederates, John Sullivan and Milton Emory, along with Todd Myrick and Eben Hunter, who had spent the war dodging the Home Guard in Maverick and Kinney Counties. They all knew the land better than I did and were not allergic to sweat or blood. (501, 518)

Here Eli recognizes that to turn his "family's good name" into a genealogical legacy he must first establish the kind of socioeconomic powerhouse now possible in post–Civil War Texas, an ambition rooted in the Comanche understanding of the power of belonging and community, coupled with what Anglo structures of class, labor, and space allow for. Weaving the two precedents together, he mates the Comanche people's cyclical command of ahistorically rooted geography to the Anglo-style genealogical control of nationally defined land and the labor that develops it.

Taken out of a highly individualistic society in which there is no larger communal history or responsibility or deep-seated sense of belonging, immersed in an ahistorical culture that balances more effectively the individual and communal, Eli ultimately manages to fuse both strands of his personal history into an effective manipulation of class, labor, and space. While it lasts, his family dynasty rolls with the changes—from plenty to drought, from cattle to oil, from frontier to urbanization—and sustains its belonging. Unlike most of the other characters in the texts I've taken up in this book, the McCulloughs are unequivocal winners. Even so, Jeanne Anne's demise in the burning house after her confrontation with Ulises suggests that in the end the internal contradictions of the ideology of genealogical belonging and the ceaselessly dynamic action of class, labor, and space in the West will undo even the seemingly invincible edifice of Eli's dynasty.

# Notes

## 1. Naturalism's Handiwork

1. For a discussion of the novel's historical context, see the essay by Robert Lundy (1997). William Issel and Robert Cherney (1986, 66) also affirm *McTeague*'s characterization of Polk Street.
2. See works by Krista Comer (1999), Susan Kollin (2007), and Neil Campbell (2008) for more detailed discussions of "the gridded West."
3. Scholars like Brent Rogers (2011, 269–71) have likewise emphasized mining industries as the "trigger" of the so-called "instant cities" of the American West. See also the monograph by William Issel and Robert Cherney (1986, 23ff).
4. See works by Mark Feldman (2006), Charles Child Walcutt (1956), and Donald Pizer (2000). Of late, critical responses to Norris's work have reflected the ongoing reimagining of American literary naturalism, sounding novels like *McTeague* for their antecedents in Romantic, gothic, and sentimental literatures. It is thus unsurprising that two prominent books on Norris and naturalism cite Norris's (1997c) essay "Zola as a Romantic Writer" in their titles: Eric Carl Link's (2004) *The Vast and Terrible Drama* and Mary Papke's (2003) edited collection *Twisted from the Ordinary*.
5. June Howard's (1985) discussion of Gilded Age fears of proletarianization is helpful here.
6. On this rhetoric in San Francisco's labor conflict during this era, see the article by John Elrick (2011); on the class make-up of the electorate in this era, see the monograph by Philip Ethington (1994, esp. 230ff).
7. The labor question, as Martin Burke (1995, 133) argues, "included the issues of strikes and labor radicalism, the social effects of economic development and depression, and the growth of an apparently permanent laboring or working class" in the latter half of the nineteenth century. Norris was undoubtedly aware of this conversation.

8. Donald Pizer (1984, 14), for instance, says such scenes invoke "the source of [the novel's] violence beneath the surface placidity of life is the presence in all men of animal qualities that have played a major role in man's evolutionary development but which are now frequently atavistic and destructive."

9. Likewise, when McTeague, Trina, and her family attend the Orpheum, McTeague watches the acrobats with admiration; they "left him breathless. They were dazzling young men . . . continually making graceful gestures to the audience" (Norris 1997a, 60). Here McTeague recognizes that the acrobats embody an agility McTeague associates with his own skilled work.

10. Or, as Walter Benn Michaels (1987, 140–54) has suggested, she doesn't use it as money but hoards it as an object.

11. See works by Karl Marx (1990) and David Montgomery (1987). Sara Quay (2001) likewise argues that McTeague and Trina's Marxian alienation from their identities manifests in the repetition with which Norris describes their manual work. David McGlynn (2008) argues that McTeague's class imprisonment is due to his simultaneous desire for material objects and his fear of the loss of those objects.

12. Even minor characters, like Old Grannis and Uncle Oelbermann, who find financial success but do not let greed drive them to grotesque actions, nonetheless suffer similar losses. Old Grannis sells his binding machine and receives only a check: "It was large enough, to be sure, but when all was over, he returned to his room and sat there sad and unoccupied" (Norris 1997a, 178). Until he realizes his love for Miss Baker, Old Grannis out of work is like McTeague out of work: without identity, without motivation, without purpose. And Uncle Oelbermann is more bank than human, acting with a "machine-like regularity" in his financial dealings and without "much to say"; as Marcus observes, he "never opens his face" (97).

13. Common but not always consistent: Old Grannis and his binding machine represent profitable, enjoyable labor that does not degrade him—though whether or not that work qualifies as manual is open for debate. Nonetheless, Old Grannis gives up his work: without the machine between them, he must speak to Miss Baker when she enters. Selling the machine also gives the Old Folks their first topic of conversation, which eases them into each other's company (Norris 1997a, 180).

14. Interesting to note here is the rhetorical similarity of Norris's passage to Marx and Engels's (1888, 24) description of the lower middle class in an early English-language edition of their *Manifesto of the Communist Party*: "The lower strata of the middle class" includes "the small tradespeople, shopkeepers, and retired tradesmen generally, the handicraftsmen and peasants."
15. Pizer notes that this avenue is "Van Ness Avenue, one of the fashionable residence streets of San Francisco during the 1880s and 1890s" (Norris 1997a, 8n8).
16. For this familiar reading that sees Death Valley as a representation of untamed, brutal nature, see the works by Feldman (2006), Walcutt (1956), and Pizer (2000).
17. See the book by Michaels (1987), specifically his introduction and chapter 5, about greed in naturalism.
18. While Marcus is involved in this representation, he acts more as a vehicle for McTeague's violence. He is not as firmly connected to the lower class during the course of the novel and does not directly commit murder, as McTeague is capable of doing. Recall that he loses the fight in the park and is only capable of "vociferating" political ideals. Physical violence, in other words, is not Marcus's modus operandi.

## 2. Civic Identity and the Ethos of Belonging

1. The Chicano movement's ethos is historically tied to working-class ethics and the financial and national rights of migrant workers, especially in terms of their children's rights to national belonging and education.
2. Here I will use the term "squatters" to refer to those who fence and thus claim land already owned by Californios and the term "settlers" for those who buy their land from the owners.
3. Crucial to this argument is the novel's distinction between nationality and ethnicity, which comes into focus through laws that use definitions of nationality to, as the novel articulates, "favor one class of citizens against another class" (Ruiz de Burton 1992, 66). While ethnicity can be shaped by personal decorum, nationality can also be a political affiliation concretized by law. For instance, Don Mariano Alamar differentiates himself from the novel's Indians (who work on ranchos and are characterized as "wild"), while singling out American settlers as gentlemen (176). These laws govern how to

locate land claims and, through a legal feedback loop, reward those who stake those claims with citizenship.

4. Although space and class have inflected discussions of the novel's ethos, labor is an issue that critics mention but leave undeveloped. For instance, while Sánchez and Pita (1992, 21, 33) note that Don Mariano Alamar is a "practical cattleman" and that Gabriel Alamar must "learn a trade and become a mason," their discussions about labor only identify the kind of work done. Labor as such disappears.

5. For instance, Priscilla Ybarra (2012, 135, 142) has argued that the Alamars' aristocratic class success is a reward of ethnic ecological awareness: "Ruiz de Burton's writings comprise an early Mexican American environmentalism" that financially "demonstrates *Californio* authority regarding the land." Similarly, Sánchez and Pita (1992, 34–35) argue that in the aftermath of Californio dispossession, "ethnically . . . a new construct is suggested in the intermarriage of *Californios* and Anglos to produce new 'mestizos.' . . . These children thus also embody a resolution, which can be read ethnically or culturally, that is, as constructs of acculturation." And Marcial González (2009) and others argue that Ruiz de Burton's racial stereotyping of "Indians"—a catch-all term the author used for working-class mestizos and indigenous peoples residing in the United States—as unreliable, lazy, and largely invisible is a form of combined ethnic-class posturing that portrays the Californios as the opposite—hardworking, dignified, and elite.

6. Indeed, in their breakdown of the novel's ideological rubrics, Sánchez and Pita (1992, 26) subsume "Spanish/Mexican land grants" under "*Californio* Ranchers" and so bypass the powerful but subtle role government plays in the Californios' class status.

7. Lee Edelman (2005) makes his argument in the context of queer studies, but his primary argument holds true outside that context: that literature often uses children to represent the future.

8. It is of course important to note that Clarence's first business venture—in mining—fails.

9. Compare Stephen Tatum's (2007, 16) comments on a "spectral" West, produced when "distinctive geographical realities, finanscapes, and emergent types of divisions of labor" follow upon deterritorialization.

10. Critical work on the novel's environmental dimensions has largely ignored these complications. For instance, even though Ybarra (2012, 144, 145) does acknowledge that "the colonization of the Ameri-

cas by the Spanish initiated an ecological revolution from lower-impact American Indian horticulture . . . to European-style ranching," that revolution is not examined for its ecological impact. The ecological harm of Californio settlement, resulting from the ways inhabitants treat land as a tool for citizenry, is thereby neglected.

11. This outcome suggests the socioeconomic and national rationale behind Don Mariano's warning about one of the earlier scenes as well. When he initially warns the squatters of the dangers of making ecologically unwise agricultural decisions, Don Mariano cautions, "The foolishness of letting all the rainfall go to waste, is an old time folly with [the Californios]. . . . But we were not then, as now, guilty of the folly of making the land useless. . . . But now . . . no money [will be] made out of land, for the grazing will be useless, when there will be no stock left to eat it" (Ruiz de Burton 1992, 93). What earlier seemed environmental consciousness now looks like environmental exploitation: without agricultural use—grazing—land is valueless. Clarence likewise voices an apparently eco-conscious plea in business terms when he affirms Don Mariano's view on planting wheat: "'Now it kills the cattle, afterward it will kill the county. . . . Plant wheat, if you can do so without killing cattle. But do not destroy the larger industry with the smaller'" (96). This aim is reaffirmed later, when in financial and civic terms Clarence reveals to Doña Josefa his motives for buying the Alamar ranch: "Don't forget I am a money-making Yankee. I think four—or even three—dollars per acre is a high price for land in this county now. . . . I am trying to make money out of you" (360).

## 3. Watching the West Erode in the 1930s

1. The publication of Babb's novel did not occur until 2004, despite having been originally slated for publication in 1939. Because the popular *Grapes of Wrath* so authoritatively occupied the cultural space for the migrant worker novel, publishers thought Babb's novel redundant and unnecessary.

2. For a historical analysis and track of this failure, see, for instance, Donald Worster's (1979) introduction to his book *Dust Bowl* and Michael Bordo, Claudia Goldin, and Eugene White's (1998) analysis of economic and ecological disaster in their edited volume *The Defining Moment*.

3. In this and all my chapters, I consider the West to be the wide expanse of land west of the ninety-ninth meridian, where water density and aridity rates change drastically.

4. For instance, see the reference acts and reforms associated with the First New Deal, including the Emergency Banking Act, the Agricultural Adjustment Act, the National Recovery Administration, and those associated with the Second New Deal, including the Social Security Act, Works Progress Administration, growth in organized labor through the National Labor Relations Board, and so on.

5. What little critical work exists on these novels is largely limited to introductions to Babb's and Waters's texts, a handful of analyses of Fante and ethnicity, and unpublished dissertations on Babb.

6. Bandini is Italian American, yet he and his family often sideline their heritage to prove themselves true American citizens. See the essay by Rocco Marinaccio (2009).

7. See the essay by Charles Scruggs (2003) for an analysis of nationality and racism in Fante's (1980) *Ask the Dust*.

## 4. He Was a Good Cowboy

1. Critical studies have also tracked the increasing significance of work to both western *and* American identity. Liza J. Nicholas (2008, 67), for instance, argues that the dude ranch in particular "provided significant status for both working-class icons like cowboys and the work they performed. In a Depression era that saluted the cultural importance of working Americans, dude ranches lauded physical work as the key to personal happiness." Similarly, Blake Allmendinger (1992, 1) argues that "cowboy [literature] values historically documented labor routines that cowboys have traditionally acted out in their work culture." Here Allmendinger ties the history of cowboy labor to its artistic expression, suggesting that the way historical and political modes of identity are woven into literature can unveil what qualities individuals value in their cultures and customs.

2. This argument is a common one; indeed, most criticism on *All the Pretty Horses* delivers or relies on some manifestation of it. Phillip Snyder and Delys Snyder (2013, 203), for instance, claim that, while John Grady Cole is faithful to the mythical and vanishing cowboy code, he and Rawlins must ultimately "engage other identities, as well as the binary cowboy codes, on ethical terms, because the cowboy culture in

which they operate is not a unified totality but an infinite heterogeneity." Even critical work on *All the Pretty Horses* that focuses on the novel's ethnic and racial components often extends this argument; Daniel Cooper Alarcón's (2002) "All the Pretty Mexicos: Cormac McCarthy's Mexican Representations" stipulates that McCarthy's reproduction of Mexico as an "Infernal Paradise" calls attention to the multiple dialogic planes on which western racial identities, especially cowboys and vaqueros, are constructed. More broadly, José Limón (1998) names McCarthy the "Mexican from Tennessee" because he successfully integrates authentic gestures toward Mexican culture into the traditional format of the western cowboy novel.

3. The vaquero past McCarthy gestures toward here and elsewhere— and that Grady and Rawlins go to Mexico to rediscover—functions as an ironic indication of how dangerous seeking a cowboy identity can be. Positing Mexico as a space of the past where one can seamlessly assume the role of the "vaquero" suggests that the boys remain ignorant of Mexico as a nation with its own complicated political ranching history. See the works by Limón (1998), Alarcón (2002), John Cant (2008) and Sara Spurgeon (2011) on border crossing, multiethnic identities, and cowboy histories.

4. Texas's "farm population declined from 1,500,000 in 1945 to 215,000 in 1980, the number of farms from 384,977 to 186,000, and farmworkers from 350,000 (including part-time workers in the cotton fields) to 85,000" in this era (*Handbook of Texas Online* 2010).

## 5. Tradition and Modernization Battle It Out

1. Momaday's "blood memory" claims that there are "intrinsic variables in man's perception of his universe, variables that are determined to some real extent on the basis of his genetic constitution" whereby memory derives from "my experience, my deepest, oldest experience, the memory in my blood" (quoted in Krupat 1989, 13). Allen's (2002, 1) "blood/land/memory complex" "indicate[s] a fluid movement between the key terms" and seeks to "evoke the complicated, multiperspectivist, and sometimes controversial maneuvers that are employed by indigenous minority writers when they attempt to render contemporary indigenous minority identities as literary and activist texts." Similarly, Vizenor's survivance focuses on uses of new methods, technologies, and narratives to promote native presence over

absence and so encourage activist maneuvers that put those narratives and experiences in popular view. In this chapter I use the shared importance of narrative in Allen's blood/land/memory complex and Vizenor's survivance to draw the two together, but it is important to recognize that survivance is a method of categorizing native acts and narratives, while the blood/land/memory complex is a theoretical mode. It is also important to read the three theories in a lineage; their similarities come from their influences on and textual conversations with one another. For instance, Allen is critical of how scholars overuse the term "survivance" without etching out a precise definition of it, while Vizenor is skeptical of the applicability and the essentialism of blood memory; as Arnold Krupat (1989, 13) puts it, the concept of blood memory "only places unnecessary obstacles in the way of a fuller understanding and appreciation of Native American literature." However, I think it is important to look at their similarities in order to recognize the way modernization must be a productive component of contemporary native life.

2. By "feedback loop," I mean the self-reinforcing structure of modern capitalism, in which low-income members of society—here, disenfranchised American Indians—are exploited by unfair legal processes that evoke a false sense of economic gain that is unaccompanied by the power such gain should provide. Those who are exploited then spend their money in ways that benefit those doing the exploiting and so provide capital to fuel further exploitative practices.

3. This lack of variety in depictions of spaces occupied by American Indians resonates with Robert Dale Parker's (2003, 5) recognition that, beginning in the 1930s, American Indian literature depicts young American Indian men as "restless . . . with nothing to do," which again suggests that modern forms of labor and uses of land for profit barred Indians from practicing their more traditional, land-based labors.

4. Deloria (2004) emphasizes how American Indians used modern forms of labor as a means of self-representation in the public eye. For instance, Indians joined sports teams, composed and performed popular music, and represented themselves in both film and theater. While the forms of labor I refer to are different than Deloria's, his overall commentary on how Indians productively participated in modernity while maintaining their cultural identities helps me read the ghostly presence of labor in this chapter's texts.

5. As Deloria (2004) has argued, American Indian tribes participated in modernity far more often and with far more vigor than is widely recognized. And, as Donald L. Fixico (2004, ix) states, "the success of American Indian sovereignty" in the face of the intrusion of American white culture demonstrated American Indians' ability to "deal effectively with the white man's linear world" in both business and culture. O'Neill (2004, 3) correspondingly argues that "American Indians crafted resourceful ways to make a living without abandoning their cultural values and traditions." Brian Hosmer (2004), William Bauer (2004), and Paul C. Rosier (2004) have argued similarly about the ingenious ways tribes were able to blend newer and older economic, political, spatial, cultural, and labor systems. Even Vizenor (2008) and the critics in his collection *Survivance* recognize and relate narratives of Indians using modernization to their benefit.

6. For those Indians who do own oil-rich land, most often their money is under the control of legal guardians appointed to oversee and dictate how much money they get, when they get it, and how they use it.

## 6. From Prairie to Oil

1. See works by Thomas Heise (2011), Hsuan Hsu (2010), and Neil Campbell (2008).

2. See also works by Nathaniel Lewis (2003), Neil Campbell (2008), Stephen Tatum (2007), and Susan Kollin (2007).

3. Texts like Gloria Anzaldúa's *Borderlands*, Sam Shepard's *True West*, Ivan Doig's Montana trilogy, Maxine Hong Kingston's *The Woman Warrior*, Douglas Coupland's *Microserfs*, Leslie Marmon Silko's *Ceremony*, and James Welch's poetry have been included in the category of postmodern westerns because they represent characters, spaces, and experiences not normally included in the western canon that add hybridity and pluralism to what constitutes the West and westernness, denying the canonical authenticity of any one experience or narrative.

4. Jameson (1981) argues that the economic and cultural attributes of late capitalism and postmodernism were not only linked but were born of the same social forces of pastiche and replication that emerged in the 1950s. He further argues that other postmodern aesthetic traits came from the same cultural scaffolding. But while his understanding of the negative effects of the overwhelming power of late capitalism and his enumeration of postmodernism's aesthetic

traits are similar to Meyer's inclusion of both in his novel, Meyer uses postmodernism's literary style to dismantle the political power of centralized capital, whereas Jameson laments both as a paired entry.

5. The term "rhizomatic" derives from Gilles Deleuze and Félix Guattari's (1993) theories of the rhizome, which Neil Campbell picks up as the rhizomatic zone that describes a region influenced by multiple cultural, social, and political forces and so is considered a hybridized zone. I extend this zone to include the forces of class, labor, and space as they appear in conversation with one another in *The Son*.

6. The Comanche were a large tribe that historically occupied broad swaths of the Southwest, including most of southwestern Texas. However, they were not a tribe in the traditional sense of the word. Instead, they divided themselves into subnations, then divisions, and then bands. The Indians in *The Son* are referred to as the Comanche tribe but most likely belonged to the Kotsoteka division. To avoid confusion, I will refer to them as the Comanche here.

# References

Alarcón, Daniel Cooper. 2002. "All the Pretty Mexicos: Cormac McCarthy's Mexican Representations." In *Cormac McCarthy: New Directions*, edited by James Lilley, 141-52. Albuquerque: University of New Mexico Press.

Alexie, Sherman. 2005. *The Lone Ranger and Tonto Fistfight in Heaven*. New York: Grove Press. Originally published in 1993.

Allen, Chadwick. 2002. *Blood Narrative: Indigenous Identity in American Indian and Maori Literary and Activist Texts*. Durham NC: Duke University Press.

Allmendinger, Blake. 1992. *The Cowboy: Representations of Labor in an American Work Culture*. New York: Oxford University Press.

Aranda, José. 1998. "Contradictory Impulses: María Amparo Ruiz de Burton, Resistance Theory, and the Politics of Chicano/a Studies." *American Literature* 70 (3): 551-79.

Babb, Sanora. 2004. *Whose Names Are Unknown: A Novel*. Norman: University of Oklahoma Press.

Barrio, Raymond. 1971. *The Plum Plum Pickers*. Binghamton NY: Bilingual Press/Editorial Bilingüe. Originally published in 1969.

Bauer, William. 2004. "Working for Identity: Race, Ethnicity, and the Market Economy in Northern California, 1875-1936." In *Native Pathways: American Indian Culture and Economic Development in the Twentieth Century*, edited by Brian Hosmer and Colleen O'Neill, 238-60. Boulder: University Press of Colorado.

Bold, Christine. 1987. *Selling the Wild West: Popular Western Fiction, 1860 to 1960*. Bloomington: Indiana University Press.

Bordo, Michael D., Claudia Goldin, and Eugene Nelson White, eds. 1998. *The Defining Moment: The Great Depression and the American Economy in the Twentieth Century*. Chicago: University of Chicago Press.

Burke, Martin J. 1995. *The Conundrum of Class: Public Discourse on the Social Order in America*. Chicago: University of Chicago Press.

Campbell, Neil. 2008. *The Rhizomatic West: Representing the American West in a Transnational, Global, Media Age*. Lincoln: University of Nebraska Press.

Campbell, Randolph B. 2003. *Gone to Texas: A History of the Lone Star State*. New York: Oxford University Press.

Cant, John. 2008. *Cormac McCarthy and the Myth of American Exceptionalism*. London: Routledge.

Carlson, Paul H., ed. 2000. *The Cowboy Way: An Exploration of History and Culture*. Lubbock: Texas Tech University Press.

Casteel, Alix. 1994. "Dark Wealth in Linda Hogan's *Mean Spirit*." *Studies in American Indian Literatures* 6 (3): 49–68.

Clayton, Lawrence. 2000. "Today's Cowboy: Coping with a Myth." In *The Cowboy Way: An Exploration of History and Culture*, edited by Paul H. Carlson, 201–8. Lubbock: Texas Tech University Press.

Clayton, Lawrence, and Sonja Irwin Clayton. 1985. *Clear Fork Cowboys: Contemporary Cowboys along the Clear Fork of the Brazos River*. Abilene TX: Cowboy Press of Abilene.

Comer, Krista. 1999. *Landscapes of the New West: Gender and Geography in Contemporary Women's Writing*. Chapel Hill: University of North Carolina Press.

———. 2011. "Exceptionalism, Other Wests, Critical Regionalism." *American Literary History* 23 (1): 159–73.

Cook, Nancy. 2007. "The Romance of Ranching; or, Selling Place-Based Fantasies in and of the West." In *Postwestern Cultures: Literature, Theory, Space*, edited by Susan Kollin, 223–44. Lincoln: University of Nebraska Press.

Cresswell, Tim. 2006. *On the Move: Mobility in the Modern Western World*. New York: Routledge.

Cronon, William, George A. Miles, and Jay Gitlin, eds. 1992. *Under an Open Sky: Rethinking America's Western Past*. New York: Norton.

Deleuze, Gilles, and Félix Guattari. 1983. *Anti-Oedipus: Capitalism and Schizophrenia*. Minneapolis: University of Minnesota Press.

Deloria, Phillip. 2004. *Indians in Unexpected Places*. Lawrence: University Press of Kansas.

Denning, Michael. 1987. *Mechanic Accents: Dime Novels and Working-Class Culture in America*. New York: Verso.

Edelman, Lee. 2005. *No Future: Queer Theory and the Death Drive*. 2nd ed. Durham NC: Duke University Press.

Elrick, John. 2011. "Social Conflict and the Politics of Reform: Mayor James T. Phelan and the San Francisco Waterfront Strike of 1901." *California History* 88 (2): 4–23, 54–56.

Erickson, John R. 1981. *The Modern Cowboy*. Lincoln: University of Nebraska Press.

Ethington, Philip J. 1994. *The Public City: The Political Construction of Urban Life in San Francisco, 1850–1900*. Cambridge: Cambridge University Press.

Fante, John. 1980. *Ask the Dust*. Santa Barbara CA: Black Sparrow Press. Originally published in 1939.

———. 1983. *Wait Until Spring, Bandini*. Santa Barbara CA: Black Sparrow Press. Originally published in 1938.

Fehrenbach, T. R. 2000. *Lone Star: A History of Texas and the Texans*. Boulder CO: Da Capo Press. Originally published in 1968.

Feldman, Mark. 2006. "The Physics and Metaphysics of Caging: The Animal in Late-Nineteenth-Century American Culture." *Mosaic* 39 (4): 161–80.

Fixico, Donald L. 2004. Foreword to *Native Pathways: American Indian Culture and Economic Development in the Twentieth Century*, edited by Brian Hosmer and Colleen O'Neill, vii–x. Boulder: University Press of Colorado.

Foley, Barbara. 1993. *Radical Representations: Politics and Form in U.S. Proletarian Fiction, 1929–1941*. Durham NC: Duke University Press.

González, Marcial. 2009. *Chicano Novels and the Politics of Form: Race, Class, and Reification*. Ann Arbor: University of Michigan Press.

Gordon, Joe. 2002. Foreword to *Below Grass Roots*, by Frank Waters. Athens: Swallow Press/Ohio University Press.

Graham, Don. 1978. *The Fiction of Frank Norris: The Aesthetic Context*. Columbia: University of Missouri Press.

———. 1980. "Art in *McTeague*." In *Critical Essays on Frank Norris*, edited by Don Graham. Boston: G. K. Hall.

———. 2003. *Kings of Texas: The 150-Year Saga of an American Ranching Empire*. Hoboken NJ: John Wiley.

Graulich, Melody. 2007. "I'm Just a Lonesome Korean Cowgirl; or, Adoption and National Identity." In *Postwestern Cultures: Literature, Theory, Space*, edited by Susan Kollin, 186–205. Lincoln: University of Nebraska Press.

Gutman, Herbert G. 1976. *Work, Culture, and Society in Industrializing America: Essays in American Working-Class and Social History*. New York: Knopf.

*Handbook of Texas Online*. 2010. "Texas Post World War II," by Robert A. Calvert. Texas State Historical Association, posted June 15, 2010. http://www.tshaonline.org/handbook/online/articles/npt02.

Handley, William R., and Nathaniel Lewis. 2004. *True West: Authenticity and the American West*. Lincoln: University of Nebraska Press.

Heise, Thomas. 2011. *Urban Underworlds: A Geography of Twentieth-Century American Literature and Culture*. New Brunswick NJ: Rutgers University Press.

Helstern, Linda Lizut. 2008. "Shifting Ground: Theories of Survivance in *From Sand Creek* to *Hiroshima Bugi: Atomu 57*." In *Survivance: Narratives of Native Presence*, edited by Gerald Vizenor, 163–90. Lincoln: University of Nebraska Press.

Hogan, Linda. 1990. *Mean Spirit*. New York: Atheneum.

Hopkins, Sarah Winnemucca. 1994. *Life among the Piutes*. Reno: University of Nevada Press. Originally published in 1883.

Hosmer, Brian. 2004. "'Dollar a Day and Glad to Have It': Work Relief on the Wind River Indian Reservation as Memory." In *Native Pathways: American Indian Culture and Economic Development in the Twentieth Century*, edited by Brian Hosmer and Colleen O'Neill, 283–307. Boulder: University Press of Colorado.

Howard, June. 1985. *Form and History in American Naturalism*. Chapel Hill: University of North Carolina Press.

Hsu, Hsuan L. 2010. *Geography and the Production of Space in Nineteenth-Century American Literature*. New York: Cambridge University Press.

Issel, William, and Robert W. Cherney. 1986. *San Francisco, 1865–1932: Politics, Power, and Urban Development*. Berkeley: University of California Press.

Jameson, Fredric. 1981. *The Political Unconscious: Narrative as a Socially Symbolic Act*. Ithaca NY: Cornell University Press.

Jones, Stephen Graham. 2003. *The Bird Is Gone: A Manifesto*. Normal IL and Tallahassee FL: FC2.

Kelton, Elmer. 1973. *The Time It Never Rained*. Garden City NY: Doubleday.

———. 2007. "Ranching in a Changing Land." In *Texas Almanac, 2006–2007*. Austin: Texas State Historical Association.

Klimasmith, Betsy. 2005. *At Home in the City: Urban Domesticity in American Literature and Culture, 1850–1930*. Hanover: published by the University Press of New England for the University of New Hampshire Press.

Kollin, Susan, ed. 2007. *Postwestern Cultures: Literature, Theory, Space*. Lincoln: University of Nebraska Press.

Krupat, Arnold. 1989. *The Voice in the Margin: Native American Literature and the Canon*. Berkeley: University of California Press.

Lewis, Nathaniel. 2003. *Unsettling the Literary West: Authenticity and Authorship*. Lincoln: University of Nebraska Press.

Lilley, James David. 2002. *Cormac McCarthy: New Directions*. Albuquerque: University of New Mexico Press.

Limerick, Patricia Nelson. 1988. *The Legacy of Conquest: The Unbroken Past of the American West*. New York: Norton.

Limerick, Patricia Nelson, Andrew Cowell, and Sharon K. Collinge, eds. 2009. *Remedies for a New West: Healing Landscapes, Histories, and Cultures*. Tucson: University of Arizona Press.

Limón, José E. 1998. *American Encounters: Greater Mexico, the United States, and the Erotics of Culture*. Boston: Beacon Press.

Link, Eric Carl. 2004. *The Vast and Terrible Drama: American Literary Naturalism in the Late Nineteenth Century*. Tuscaloosa: University of Alabama Press.

Lomelí, Francisco A. 1984. "Depraved New World Revisited: Dreams and Dystopia in *The Plum Plum Pickers*." Introduction to *The Plum Plum Pickers*, by Raymond Barrio, 9–26. 2nd ed. Binghamton NY: Bilingual Press/Editorial Bilingüe.

Lookingbill, Brad D. 2001. *Dust Bowl, USA: Depression America and the Ecological Imagination, 1929–1941*. Athens: Ohio University Press.

Lundy, Robert D. 1997. "The Polk Street Background of *McTeague*." In *McTeague: A Story of San Francisco; Authoritative Text, Contexts, Criticism*, edited by Donald Pizer, 257–62. 2nd ed. New York: Norton.

Lutz, Tom. 2004. *Cosmopolitan Vistas: American Regionalism and Literary Value*. Ithaca NY: Cornell University Press.

Marinaccio, Rocco. 2009. "'Tea and Cookies, *Diavolo!*' Italian American Masculinity in John Fante's *Wait Until Spring, Bandini*." *MELUS: Multi-Ethnic Literature of the U.S.* 34 (3): 43–69.

Marx, Karl. 1990. *Capital: A Critique of Political Economy*. Volume 1. Edited by Ben Fowkes. New York: Penguin Books in Association with *New Left Review*. Originally published in German in 1867.

Marx, Karl, and Friedrich Engels. 1888. *Manifesto of the Communist Party*. London: W. Reeves. Originally published in German in 1848.

Marx, Leo. 1964. *The Machine in the Garden: Technology and the Pastoral Ideal in America*. New York: Oxford University Press.

McCarthy, Cormac. 1992. *All the Pretty Horses*. New York: Knopf.

McDonnell, Janet A. 1991. *The Dispossession of the American Indian*. Bloomington: Indiana University Press.

McGlynn, David. 2008. "McTeague's Gilded Prison." *Rocky Mountain Review* 62 (Spring): 25–44.

McKenna, Teresa. 1997. *Migrant Song: Politics and Process in Contemporary Chicano Literature*. Austin: University of Texas Press.

McMurtry, Larry. 1985. *Horseman, Pass By*. College Station: Texas A&M University Press. Originally published in 1961.

McNickle, D'Arcy. 1978. *The Surrounded*. Albuquerque: University of New Mexico Press. Originally published in 1936.

Meyer, Philipp. 2013. *The Son*. New York: Ecco Press.

Michaels, Walter Benn. 1987. *The Gold Standard and the Logic of Naturalism*. Berkeley: University of California Press.

Miller, Yvette E. 1976. "The Social Message in Chicano Fiction: Tomas Rivera's *And the Earth Did Not Part* and Raymond Barrio's *The Plum Plum Pickers*." In *Essays on Minority Cultures*, edited by George E. Carter and James R. Carter, 159–64. La Crosse: University of Wisconsin–La Crosse.

Montgomery, David. 1987. *The Fall of the House of Labor: The Workplace, the State, and American Labor Activism, 1865–1925*. Cambridge: Cambridge University Press.

Moore, Jacqueline. 2009. *Cow Boys and Cattle Men: Class and Masculinities on the Texas Frontier, 1865–1900*. New York: New York University Press.

Nicholas, Liza J. 2008. *Becoming Western: Stories of Culture and Identity in the Cowboy State*. Lincoln: University of Nebraska Press.

Norris, Frank. 1997a. *McTeague: A Story of San Francisco; Authoritative Text, Contexts, Criticism*. Edited by Donald Pizer. 2nd ed. New York: Norton. *McTeague* was originally published in 1899.

———. 1997b. "A Plea for Romantic Fiction." In *McTeague: A Story of San Francisco; Authoritative Text, Contexts, Criticism*, edited by Donald Pizer, 277–80. 2nd ed. New York: Norton. The essay was originally published in 1901.

———. 1997c. "Zola as a Romantic Writer." In *McTeague: A Story of San Francisco; Authoritative Text, Contexts, Criticism*, edited by Donald

Pizer, 273–74. 2nd ed. New York: Norton. The essay was originally published in 1896.

Nugent, Walter T. K. 1999. *Into the West: The Story of Its People*. New York: Knopf.

O'Neill, Colleen. 2004. "Rethinking Modernity in the Discourse of Development in American Indian History, an Introduction." In *Native Pathways: American Indian Culture and Economic Development in the Twentieth Century*, edited by Brian Hosmer and Colleen O'Neill, 1–24. Boulder: University Press of Colorado.

Papke, Mary, ed. 2003. *Twisted from the Ordinary: Essays on American Literary Naturalism*. Knoxville: University of Tennessee Press.

Parker, Robert Dale. 2003. *The Invention of Native American Literature*. Ithaca NY: Cornell University Press.

Pickard, Kevin. 2014. "*The Son* by Philipp Meyer." *World Literature Today* 88 (1): 60–61.

Pizer, Donald. 1984. *Realism and Naturalism in Nineteenth Century Literature*. Rev. ed. Carbondale: Southern Illinois University Press.

———. 2000. "Frank Norris's *McTeague*: Naturalism as Popular Myth." *ANQ* 13 (4): 21–26.

Quay, Sara E. 2001. "American Imperialism and the Excess of Objects in *McTeague*." *American Literary Realism* 33 (3): 209–34.

Rogers, Brent M. 2011. "The Urbanization of the American West." In *The World of the American West*, edited by Gordon Morris Bakken, 267–307. New York: Routledge.

Rølvaag, O. E. 1999. *Giants in the Earth: A Saga of the Prairie*. New York: Harper Perennial Modern Classics; Perennial Classics edition. Originally published in Norwegian in two volumes, in 1924 and 1925.

Rosier, Paul C. 2004. "Searching for Salvation and Sovereignty: Blackfeet Oil Leasing and the Reconstruction of the Tribe." In *Native Pathways: American Indian Culture and Economic Development in the Twentieth Century*, edited by Brian Hosmer and Colleen O'Neill, 27–51. Boulder: University Press of Colorado.

Rotella, Carlo. 2002. *Good with Their Hands: Boxers, Bluesmen, and Other Characters from the Rust Belt*. Berkeley: University of California Press.

Ruiz de Burton, María Amparo. 1992. *The Squatter and the Don*. Edited by Rosauro Sánchez and Beatrice Pita. Houston TX: Arte Público Press. Originally published in 1885.

Sánchez, Rosaura, and Beatrice Pita. 1992. Introduction to *The Squatter and the Don*, by María Amparo Ruiz de Burton, 5–51. Houston TX: Arte Público Press.

Schocket, Eric. 2006. *Vanishing Moments: Class and American Literature*. Ann Arbor: University of Michigan Press.

Scruggs, Charles. 2003. "'Oh for a Mexican Girl!' The Limits of Literature in John Fante's *Ask the Dust*." *Western American Literature* 38 (3): 228–45.

Seltzer, Mark. 1992. *Bodies and Machines*. New York: Routledge.

Slotkin, Richard. 1998. *The Fatal Environment: The Frontier in the Age of Industrialization, 1800–1890*. Norman: University of Oklahoma Press.

Smith, Neil. 1984. *Uneven Development: Nature, Capital, and the Production of Space*. New York: Blackwell.

———. 2008. *Uneven Development: Nature, Capital, and the Production of Space*. 3rd ed. Athens: University of Georgia Press.

Snyder, Phillip A., and Delys W. Snyder. 2013. "Modernism, Postmodernism, and Language." In *The Cambridge Companion to Cormac McCarthy*, edited by Steven Fry, 27–38. Cambridge: Cambridge University Press.

Spurgeon, Sara L. 1999. "Pledged in Blood: Truth and Redemption in Cormac McCarthy's *All the Pretty Horses*." *Western American Literature* 34 (1): 25–44.

———, ed. 2011. *Cormac McCarthy: All the Pretty Horses, No Country for Old Men, The Road*. London: Continuum.

Stegner, Wallace. 1971. *Angle of Repose*. New York: Penguin.

Steinbeck, John. 2006. *The Grapes of Wrath*. New York: Penguin Books. Originally published in 1939.

Tatum, Stephen. 2007. "Spectrality and the Postregional Interface." In *Postwestern Cultures: Literature, Theory, Space*, edited by Susan Kollin, 3–29. Lincoln: University of Nebraska Press.

Tompkins, Jane P. 1992. *West of Everything: The Inner Life of Westerns*. New York: Oxford University Press.

Turner, Frederick Jackson. 1998. *Rereading Frederick Jackson Turner: "The Significance of the Frontier in American History" and Other Essays*. With commentary by John Mack Faragher. New Haven CT: Yale University Press. Essays originally written between 1891 and 1925.

Veblen, Thorstein. 1934. *The Theory of the Leisure Class: An Economic Study of Institutions*. Edited by Stuart Chase. New York: Modern Library. Originally published in 1899.

Villa, Raúl Homero. 2000. *Barrio-Logos: Space and Place in Chicano Literature and Culture*. Austin: University of Texas Press.

Vizenor, Gerald. 1993. *Narrative Chance: A Postmodern Discourse on Native American Literatures*. Norman: University of Oklahoma Press.

———, ed. 2008. *Survivance: Narratives of Native Presence*. Lincoln: University of Nebraska Press.

Walcutt, Charles Child. 1956. *American Literary Naturalism: A Divided Stream*. Minneapolis: University of Minnesota Press.

Waters, Frank. 2002. *Below Grass Roots*. Athens: Swallow Press/Ohio University Press. Originally published in 1937.

White, Hayden. 1978. *Tropics of Discourse: Essays in Cultural Criticism*. Baltimore: Johns Hopkins University Press.

White, Richard. 2011. *Railroaded: The Transcontinentals and the Making of Modern America*. New York: Norton.

Williams, J. W. 1999. *The Big Ranch Country*. Lubbock: Texas Tech University Press.

Wilson, Christopher P. 1992. *White Collar Fictions: Class and Social Representation in American Literature, 1885–1925*. Athens: University of Georgia Press.

Worster, Donald. 1979. *Dust Bowl: The Southern Plains in the 1930s*. New York: Oxford University Press.

Ybarra, Priscilla Solis. 2012. "Erasure by US Legislation: Ruiz de Burton's Nineteenth Century Novels and the Lost Archive of Mexican American Environmental Knowledge." In *Environmental Criticism for the Twenty-First Century*, edited by Stephanie LeMenager, Teresa Shewry, and Ken Hiltner, 135–47. New York: Routledge.

Zandy, Janet. 2004. *Hands: Physical Labor, Class, and Cultural Work*. New Brunswick NJ: Rutgers University Press.

# Index

# IN THE POSTWESTERN HORIZONS SERIES

To order or obtain more information on these or other University of Nebraska Press titles, visit nebraskapress.unl.edu.